THE

50 GREATEST PLAYERS

IN

DENVER BRONCOS

HISTORY

MIKE KLIS

GUILFORD, CONNECTICUT

An imprint of Globe Pequot

Distributed by NATIONAL BOOK NETWORK

British Library Cataloguing in Publication Information available

Library of Congress Cataloging-in-Publication Data available

ISBN 978-1-4930-2917-4 (hardcover)
ISBN 978-1-4930-2918-1 (e-book)

♾™ The paper used in this publication meets the minimum requirements of American National Standard for Information Sciences—Permanence of Paper for Printed Library Materials, ANSI/NISO Z39.48-1992.

Printed in the United States of America

*To Bouch, who still can't believe I was able to limit
the greatest Broncos players list to 50.*

*And to my 50 greatest family members of the 1960s, '70s,
'80s, '90s, 2000s, and 2010s. You know who you are.*

CONTENTS

ACKNOWLEDGMENTS

Thank you to former Broncos PR maven Jim Saccomano, Denver-area and University of Colorado multisport star Dave Logan, who is also the team's longtime radio announcer, and lifelong fan Richard Hesse, who sent me multiple drafts of his top-50 list. These are the three people I most sought counsel from while organizing this project of *The 50 Greatest Players in Denver Broncos History*. They made recommendations, all of which I considered, although they will notice I failed to execute a few.

To Steve Carter, Tim Dietz, Christy Moreno, and Brian Olson, my bosses at KUSA-TV Channel 9 (Denver), for allowing me to take on this project.

To Broncos assistant PR guy Erich Schubert, for his remarkable work in posting on the team's website every official game book of every preseason, regular-season, and postseason game the Broncos ever played. This is a researcher's dream. To Schubert and Broncos PR boss Patrick Smyth, for helping to arrange interviews with several of the top 50 players.

To my wife, Becky, and my kids, for insisting they did not need me around, thus allowing me to work on this project guilt-free.

To my mom, for giving me a week in semi-seclusion at her Oswego, Illinois, home, where I was able to generate momentum to finish this project.

To executive editor Rick Rinehart, for his patience with the author who missed his first deadline by a lot, and second deadline by a little. And to editors Meredith Dias and Evan Helmlinger, copyeditor Melissa Hayes, layout artist Joanna Beyer, proofreader Susan Barnett, and all the people whom I've never met but did a great deal of the work in putting this book together. To Eric Lars Bakke for digging up the photos in this book.

To "Bronco" Billy Thompson, No. 17 among the greatest players in this book. As head of Broncos alumni, Thompson had access to more phone numbers of the former greats than any other.

To Nickie Gonsoulin and Randy Tripucka, wives of two of the original Broncos stars.

A special mention to Craig Morton, Haven Moses, Riley Odoms, Rick Upchurch, Otis Armstrong, Louis Wright, Tom Jackson, Randy Gradishar, Steve Foley, Barney Chavous, Rubin Carter, the spirits of Lyle Alzado and Paul Smith, and Bronco Billy. That's 14 players from the magical Orange Crush season of '77 who made the top 50. And had it been a top-55 book, Bob Swenson, Jim Turner, and Paul Howard would have made it 17 from that pioneering team.

I didn't realize until I'd researched the full span of the Broncos years and interviewed the subjects just how special that '77 team was to the franchise. History is there so yesterday is not forgotten, and the Broncos' remarkable 45-year run of playoff contention started with the Crush era, folks.

And finally, my appreciation to the top 50 players for their cooperation and participation in this project. Whatever enjoyment Broncos Country and football fans everywhere may get from this book is because of them, the players.

INTRODUCTION

Steve Watson was the genesis of this project.

The former Denver Broncos receiver is now a motivational speaker, and his bureau people told him it would help if he had, as a point of reference, a book about himself. We came up with the working title *From Underdog to Top Dog*, but as it had been nearly thirty years since Watson played his final game with the Broncos, it was suggested by Rick Rinehart, executive editor at Globe Pequot, to fold Steve's story into *The 50 Greatest Players in Denver Broncos History*.

To confess, when I agreed to take on this project, I thought it would be a breeze. One chapter on each player. I could write it in five weeks.

It took me nine months.

I freshly interviewed, specifically for this project, 40 of the 46 living players who made the Broncos' Top 50 List, along with family members, friends, former teammates—or all of the above, in some cases—for the four Broncos greats who are no longer with us.

I became fascinated with each player's story. The special bond that exists among the players from the Orange Crush era was such that star linebacker Randy Gradishar traveled to California to visit backup quarterback Norris Weese, who was on his deathbed with cancer. Weese's nurse would become Gradishar's wife. You had to understand Tom Jackson's unique relationship with his father to fully appreciate T.J.'s best-ever game, played during the Broncos' first-ever playoff match on Christmas Eve, 1977. And to appreciate Terrell Davis's unlikely journey to the Pro Football Hall of Fame, you had to understand T.D.'s own unique relationship with his father. Haven Moses's journey to school each day, and his return during his post-playing days from a debilitating stroke, remain inspirational feats.

Several of these stars knew hard work as children—players like Shannon Sharpe, Louis Wright, Gary Zimmerman, Rubin Carter, and Barney Chavous. Steve Foley and his twelve brothers and sisters lived in a convent, as good a place as any to raise the Broncos future all-time interceptions leader. And in a remarkable example of typecasting, Sammy Winder's childhood dream was not playing running back in the NFL, but operating a bulldozer.

Research can be a wonderful exercise. I was astonished by the careers of safety Austin "Goose" Gonsoulin and receiver Lionel Taylor. Charter members of the Broncos Ring of Fame, the busts of Gonsoulin and Taylor should be placed in Canton. It's too bad legendary NFL writer Paul Zimmerman resigned from the Pro Football Hall of Fame Senior Committee back in 2004. Otherwise, there would be a bronze bust of Rich "Tombstone" Jackson.

Research also led me to the discovery that tight end Riley Odoms is the most underrated player in Broncos history. And if there's one player who made the Orange Crush, members of that vaunted Denver D almost unanimously said it was nose tackle Rubin Carter.

The easiest decision was John Elway as No. 1, but I otherwise agonized over the other forty-nine Broncos greats. And not only in regard to the final 10 membership slots, but the overall order after Elway.

I had well more than a dozen drafts of the Top 50. I sought counsel from several longtime Broncos followers, most notably Jim Saccomano, Dave Logan, and Richard Hesse. They provided encouragement and made the occasional recommendation, but disputes should be directed solely to me. This is my list.

Even my criteria were colored as much in gray as black and white. For the most part, my factors were, in order: greatness of performance, impact on winning Super Bowls, role in leading the Broncos to Super Bowls, election to the Pro Football Hall of Fame, Pro Bowl selections, and length of Broncos service.

Elway was the only one who checked every box. Terrell Davis was No. 2 largely because he was the primary reason the Broncos won their first two Super Bowls. He was ranked No. 2, by the way, well before he was elected into the Pro Football Hall of Fame.

Peyton Manning was No. 3 because he single-handedly carried the Broncos to one Super Bowl game, and he helped guide them to their Super Bowl 50 victory. And his play for two-and-a-half seasons with the Broncos is arguably the best stretch any NFL quarterback has ever put together.

My initial drafts had Champ Bailey ranked No. 4 and Shannon Sharpe No. 5. I confidently hedged that Champ would be a first-ballot Hall of Famer while Sharpe went in on his third ballot.

Bailey, in my estimation, was the all-time best Broncos defensive player at the time of his retirement, while Sharpe is the third- or fourth-best offensive player. Sharpe's two Super Bowl rings, however, caused me to flip-flop his ranking with Champ.

Von Miller, who hopefully is not halfway through his ongoing career, is already No. 6 because he was primarily responsible for the Broncos winning Super Bowl 50. He is also about two Von-like seasons away from replacing Champ as the top defensive Broncos player.

I know you, the reader, will disagree with some of the inclusions and omissions. Floyd Little, "The Franchise," comes in at No. 7? I apologize in advance, but I am also comfortable in the conviction that sports lists were invented for discussion, if not barstool arguments.

Research of each player's story was often tedious and time-consuming, but also compelling and rewarding. Some of the former greats had remarkable recall. Many remembered certain plays and games although they were shaky in their details.

The intention of this project was to celebrate the fine careers of the 50 best Broncos, with perhaps one exception. Lyle Alzado's NFL career demanded critical examination. To his credit, Alzado admitted he was an artificially enhanced player. This admission, coupled with his play that could not be denied, pushed him just inside the top 50.

If I may, the stories of those at the back end of the list were just as compelling, if not more so, as those at the front end.

Watson came in at No. 42. There was never a doubt. During a five-year period in the 1980s he was one of only three NFL receivers who recorded at least 5,000 receiving yards. The other two, James Lofton and Steve Largent, are in the Hall of Fame.

I could have written a book on Watson's climb from underdog to top dog. Instead, here are 50 stories about the 50 Greatest Players in Denver Broncos History in one book.

1

JOHN ELWAY

Quarterback, 1983–98

We all have one moment that sticks in our minds more than the others whenever we think back to John Elway playing quarterback.

"The Drive" was his leap from enormous potential to legitimate championship quarterback. "The Helicopter" epitomized his hypercompetitiveness.

" 'The Drive' put me on the map," Elway said. "That was my coming-out party. That legitimized me in big games. 'The Helicopter' kind of helped win the championship, because of the mentality and the energy it created."

TV flashbacks also often show his Kirk Gibson–like fist pump and dance step following his fourth-quarter, 3-yard touchdown run that iced Super Bowl XXXIII, which turned out to be his career walk-off.

"I was 95 percent there," Elway said, referring to the likelihood he would retire after winning his second Super Bowl in as many years. "If I hadn't got banged up that year—I tore that hamstring and I fell on the ball and hurt my ribs. Missed four games. I might have come back if I hadn't had those deals. But I was getting to the point where after you had won two, three would be great, but you've answered the questions you needed to answer."

I have covered Elway since he became the Denver Broncos general manager in 2011. I was an impartial observer in front of the TV, and an occasional reporter on game days, during his playing career. I have two strong memories of Elway the quarterback.

The first was his monstrous spike in the end zone, followed by two raised fists in a championship-boxer pose, after he scored on a 4-yard touchdown run during his *Monday Night Football* classic showdown with Joe Montana. This memory is indelible because I was standing a few feet away behind that same end zone at Mile High Stadium. I was covering the October 1994 game for the Colorado Springs *Gazette-Telegraph*. My assignment was to come up with a sidebar story on the visiting Kansas City Chiefs.

Elway's touchdown gave the Broncos a 28–24 lead with 1:29 remaining in the back-and-forth game. Montana then completed, with remarkable ease and precision, seven of eight passes to lead a 75-yard drive against Wade Phillips's soft cover 2 defense, a systematic march that ended with a 5-yard touchdown pass to Willie Davis in the right corner of the end zone, with eight seconds remaining. Chiefs win.

The Broncos weren't very good that year—they fell to 1-5 after this loss—but they were keeping score in this game, and therefore Elway badly wanted to win.

That's one. The play I most remember about Elway, though, was during a regular-season game. I don't remember which game or even exactly what season, although I'm certain it was in the late 1980s. I just remember the action of the play as I watched from the Mile High press box. It was a play where Elway started to scramble right to escape what appeared to be a certain sack; then, as the pressure gathered to his right-side rollout, he pivoted in reverse and started scrambling left.

He made one more pass-rusher miss as he got outside the left hash, then stopped and turned his body back so he could see downfield.

Wide open about 25 yards down the right side of the field was Broncos receiver Vance Johnson. Only Elway was way over there on the left side, behind the line of scrimmage. No problem. Elway planted on that strong, muscular trunk of his and rifled—I mean, threw a high-velocity laser—to Johnson, who caught it for a big gain.

To me, the scramble left and fastball thrown clear across to the far-right quadrant of the field was Elway's skill set personified.

"John comes in to throw in this rookie minicamp," said Broncos linebacker Tom Jackson, who was nearing the end of his playing career in 1983. "And a bunch of us [veterans] go to watch. And John Elway starts throwing the ball. And we watched him throw for about ten minutes. Ask Billy what I said to him. Hopefully he'll remember."

"T.J. turns to me and says, 'We're going to be going to some Super Bowls,'" said Broncos safety Billy Thompson, who had been retired as a player by then but was still around.

"I was smart enough to understand what I was looking at," Jackson said.

The Broncos went to five Super Bowls with Elway as their quarterback, a record at the time, although since broken by New England's Tom Brady. But while Brady went to seven Super Bowls, winning five, with one coach, Bill Belichick, Elway went to three Big Games with the conservative-minded, if offensive-sophisticated Dan Reeves, and two more with the offensive "Mastermind," Mike Shanahan.

Elway clashed with Reeves, but the fact is, they won a lot of games together. Three times Elway, Reeves, and the Broncos beat the Cleveland Browns in the AFC Championship Game—to finish the 1986 season because of "The Drive," to finish the 1987 season because of "The Fumble," and to finish the 1989 season because Elway was sensational, throwing for 385 yards with no interceptions and touchdown passes of 70 yards to receiver Michael Young, 5 yards to tight end Orson Mobley, and 39 yards to running back Sammy Winder.

Elway and Reeves just didn't win the final Super Bowl game together. By the time Shanahan became the Broncos head coach in 1995, Elway's body was far more beat-up, his legs had slowed, and his fastball had lost a few mphs. But he was smarter, more experienced, and therefore a better quarterback.

Elway finished his career by winning those elusive Super Bowls in the final two years of his 16-year career.

"I think Mike Shanahan coming to Denver was a blessing for him and blessing for Mike as well, because he was able to put together a balanced offensive attack that took some pressure off him," said Ed McCaffrey, one of Elway's three favorite receivers, along with Rod Smith and Shannon Sharpe, in the late 1990s. "In the past, we needed John to work miracles in order for the team to get to the Super Bowl, but they couldn't quite get over the hump and win one. And that's why it was just a match made in heaven.

"That's why—and you can always play the 'woulda coulda shoulda' game—but you wonder, had Mike been his head coach for his whole career, I think John could have had a Joe Montana–type scenario where he won four Super Bowls, instead of two.

"In the era John played, he was as tough and as good of a quarterback as there was in the NFL. He would have made any team better. He was also unselfish. He wasn't about stats. He was about winning. He was about leading, and it was such a Cinderella storybook ending for him. And one that was very much deserved."

In any sport—whether it's baseball, football, basketball, or hockey—the kid with the most intuitive instincts on the team is always the coach's kid. Elway was Coach Jack Elway's kid, and he seemed to know which way to move before the play developed.

Yes, Elway was the most sacked quarterback in the NFL at the time of his retirement, with 516. (Brett Favre later passed him with 525.) But Elway might have escaped 500 others.

The thing about being the kid of a major college coach, though, is it means the house never quite becomes a home. In his youth, John and his twin sister Jana bounced with their parents, Jack and Jan, between college towns in the states of Washington, Montana, and California before John decided to attend Stanford in Palo Alto, California.

Stanford wasn't very good in Elway's four years as a starter. Under coach Paul Wiggin, the Cardinal went 5-5-1, 6-5, 4-7, and, after losing to Cal on the Band Play, 5-6.

Still, there were enough college highlights shown on ABC every Saturday for the nation to see that Elway was a can't-miss NFL quarterback prospect. Even Bob Irsay, the hard-drinking, boorish owner of the Baltimore Colts, could see that.

Jack Elway, though, had been around college football enough to know Colts coach Frank Kush and his taskmaster methods were not what he wanted for his son. The Colts selected Elway with their No. 1 overall pick in the 1983 draft, even though Elway and his dad let it be known he would not play for their franchise.

Later, Elway said it wasn't Kush so much as the Colts organization that caused him to force a trade.

"Look at the history of the organization at the time," Elway said. "They were terrible. And I had a chance to play baseball. So, I looked at it as, Do you want to take a chance on playing football where chances are you're not going to be successful—or do you go play baseball for a year, see how baseball goes, and then your name goes back in the [1984 NFL] draft?

"I wanted to play football, but I was going to play baseball for a year. But then once I made my bed and I was not going to Baltimore, I was not going to go back on it. Who knew how long Kush was going to be there, but organizationally, it was not one I wanted to step into. I had a chance to do something else."

In 1982, between his junior and senior years at Stanford, Elway had played one minor-league season for the New York Yankees Class A Oneonta team. A right-handed throwing outfielder and left-handed batter, Elway hit .318, with 4 home runs and 13 stolen bases in 42 games.

He would have played a second, minor-league season for the Yankees in 1983 had it not been for Broncos owner Edgar Kaiser. The 1983 NFL Draft was held on April 26. Despite his objections, Elway was drafted No. 1

by the Colts. The Denver Broncos with the No. 4 overall pick took Northwestern offensive lineman Chris Hinton.

Six days later, Kaiser, one of the few people who could get along with Irsay, arranged a trade that sent Elway to the Broncos in exchange for Hinton, Broncos quarterback Mark Hermann, and a first-round pick in the 1984 draft that turned out to be guard Ron Solt.

The Broncos, who were 2-7 in the strike-shortened season of 1982, were forever changed.

"Billy called me from a basketball game where Dan Reeves happened to be in attendance," Jackson said. "And when he called he said, 'We have John Elway.' And I was like, 'Yeah right.' And Billy went, 'No, really. We have John Elway. We're making a trade and we're going to get Elway.'"

The Denver Nuggets beat the San Antonio Spurs in a playoff game on the night of May 2, 1983, at McNichols Sports Arena. It was the Nuggets' only victory in the second-round series.

That same day Elway was about to start a 16-year career with the Broncos, where he would become the NFL's all-time-winningest quarterback with 148 wins, including 46 that featured game-winning drives in the fourth quarter.

"If the opposing team was up 13 points and had the ball, if the defense got a stop, we were going to beat them," Sharpe said. "We were going to score. He just had that belief. And it's funny, some people say when the game gets close, it would slow down. John would talk even faster. Sometimes, you couldn't understand him. But as his speech sped up, something inside him would slow down. It was such an unbelievable thing. It was hard to explain."

Every morning Elway woke up, it seems, was a day to compete for victory.

"I could see not only what he did on game day, but what he did in practices," said Jason Elam, the Broncos kicker and Elway's teammate from 1993–98. "I think he set the tone for what practices should be like. It wasn't goof around. It was game time on Wednesdays and Thursdays and Fridays. That spilled over because everybody had such respect for John.

"Not only was he a great player, I remember one thing that shaped a lot of my confidence was my rookie year—rookie years are tough on players. Just the length of the season. I remember, my goodness, after 11 games, counting the four games in the preseason and seven games in the regular season, you're not even halfway through the season yet. And you're ready to be done. I had some good games my rookie year, but there were a couple games I didn't play well at all. It was an emotional roller coaster, and I remember John coming over to my locker after one of the games and he said, 'Jason, the Denver Broncos drafted you for a reason.' He said it was because you are good, and because you are going to be with this team for a long, long time. He said, 'I've got faith in you. Everybody else in this organization does. Just sit and rest in that.'

"Every time I'm asked about John Elway, I think of that. He was a great teammate. He was encouraging, he was affirming. Not only was he a Hall of Famer, one of the best ever to play the game, but he was an awesome teammate as well."

Although, Elway had his share of impressive stats and honors—he was the league MVP in 1987, was named to 9 Pro Bowls, and had 12 passing seasons of at least 3,000 yards—his numbers don't necessarily compare favorably to the all-time greats, especially those who played in the following two decades.

He only once had a 4,000-yard passing season—in 1993, when his offensive coordinator was Jim Fassel. He never threw more than 27 touchdowns in a season. And his career completion percentage was 56.9.

Compare that to the 2016 season alone, when 13 NFL quarterbacks threw for more than 4,000 yards, 9 quarterbacks threw at least 28 touchdowns, and 28 of the 30 qualifying for the passing title completed at least 58.9 percent of their passes.

Elway, though, wasn't about the high-percentage checkdowns. What a waste of talent those passes would have been.

"He had a rocket arm," McCaffrey said. "He was incredibly intelligent. He made everybody around him better. Not just because of his physical ability at the quarterback position, but because of his leadership and his toughness.

"There weren't rules regarding hitting the quarterback back then. He used to get drilled. But he just wanted to be part of a championship team, which meant you had to be able to run the ball, you had to play good defense. That was a different era. If he was in an offense today that was spread out and he could use his football IQ to find open receivers and spread the field, he could have thrown for 5,000 yards multiple times. It's just a different era where that didn't happen.

"And most of the teams with huge passing stats were losing teams. There were a couple of good ones. Dan Marino had a lot of passing success in Miami, but they never won a Super Bowl. John was a guy who had the ability to put up huge numbers. He had the ability to put his team on his back in the fourth quarter and find a way to win. He had an incredible will to win. I mean, the helicopter spin in Super Bowl XXXII is obviously one of the statement plays in his career. It just shows you, 'Look man, I just want to win. I'm older, near the end of my career—I don't care about getting hit. I just want to move the chains, score points, and win the Super Bowl.'"

Elway became the first Denver Bronco inducted into the Pro Football Hall of Fame in 2004, his first year of eligibility. He didn't have to become eligible to go into the Broncos Ring of Fame—owner Pat Bowlen waived the five-year waiting period and inducted Elway in 1999, months after he had retired.

After his playing days, Elway never left the spotlight, but there were emotional struggles. He lost his beloved sister Jana to cancer and father Jack to an apparent heart attack, and he also went through a divorce—all within a two-year period, from 2001–03. As his personal life went through a difficult period, Elway at the same time joined Pat Bowlen as co-owner of the Arena League's Colorado Crush.

There were some car dealerships that succeeded and other investments that did not. While Elway gradually adapted to a life without playing, he was able to satisfy his unquenchable appetite for competition by becoming the Broncos general manager in 2011.

He inherited a team that went 4-12 in 2010. Under his front-office leadership, the Broncos won five consecutive AFC West Division titles in his first five years as GM, advanced to the Elite Eight of the NFL playoffs five consecutive years, won two AFC Championships, and one Super Bowl.

"He truly was the franchise," said Bill Romanowski, the Broncos strong-side linebacker during the team's back-to-back Super Bowl years in 1997–98. "One of the greatest players ever to play the game. It was awesome playing with him. He was a fantastic teammate, great guy. Another reason why the Broncos are having so much success is he knows how to do it the right way."

Terrell Davis, the great running back who helped push Elway from Super Bowl participant to Super Bowl winner, recalls a reunion of the 1997 Super Bowl team. The team was brought back for owner Pat Bowlen's induction into the Ring of Fame on November 1, 2015.

The night before, Halloween night, the team had gathered at Shanahan's mansion.

"Mike has that bowling alley downstairs," Davis said. "So we're having a friendly game of bowling with all the players. All of the sudden John challenges me to bowling. He wants to put money on it. I'm like, dude, we're just bowling. But John wants to make it competitive, so I'm like, 'You challenged me, I'll go for it.' So, we're going at it. And I can see what I've seen for a long time: This man does not want to lose. Even at this bowling thing that really didn't mean much."

And?

"He won," Davis said.

YRS	G	A	C	Y	PCT	TD	I	RTG	W-L
16	234	7,250	4,123	51,475	56.9	300	226	79.9	148-82-1

JOHN ELWAY STATS

POSTSEASON

A	C	PCT	Y	TD	I	RTG	W-L
651	355	54.5	4,964	27	21	79.7	14-7

2

TERRELL DAVIS

Running Back, 1995–2001

Terrell Davis has had his share of good luck and misfortune—not that he's dwelled on either.

He was born into a poor, dangerous neighborhood in San Diego, but he was also blessed with so much ability that he was a city sensation from childhood.

His first college football coach died unexpectedly and then his college dropped the football program, but adversity opened a path to the Southeastern Conference and the University of Georgia.

His NFL career was cut short by a knee injury, but he got to play for four years with a quarterback named John Elway and a coaching staff that knew how to scheme a running game like no other.

Davis never would have gotten those four sensational NFL seasons that eventually led to the Pro Football Hall of Fame had he not been unlucky enough to not understand the Japanese language.

A sixth-round draft pick—low enough to get cut without hesitation—Davis had just 1 carry for 0 yards against the San Francisco 49ers in the Broncos' first preseason game of his rookie 1995 season.

The second preseason game was against the 49ers again, only this time the two teams had to travel all the way to Tokyo to play in the American Bowl.

"We got there and it was a miserable week," Davis recalled 21 years later in November 2016. "It was hot. I felt like I came all this way and was spending all this time for no reason. I remember saying to Byron [Chamberlain, his rookie teammate]: 'Man, we're just camp meat.'

"And it did cross my mind in Tokyo—it was hot, practices were long, I hated being there, I wasn't doing well—so the combination of all things, I did think, 'I'm going home.'"

He called down to the front desk. How much is a flight? When does it leave? No, no, *fly. Airplane.*

"There was a language barrier," he said. "If I had spoken better Japanese, I might have gotten out of there. And then once I realized it wasn't easy getting out of there, cooler heads prevailed. I decided I might as well stick it out."

Davis lore would soon have another chapter. He didn't play in the first half of the Tokyo game. He ate a hot dog at halftime. He got in for the second series of the third quarter and got two handoffs from backup quarterback Bill Musgrave, gaining 5 yards. Musgrave finished off the drive with a touchdown pass to H-back Darrick Owens, who wound up the MVP of the American Bowl.

On the next play, Davis's career was born.

"Whenever I think of Terrell, I think of Japan in Tokyo," said Jason Elam, the Broncos Ring of Fame kicker. "He was a rookie. I kicked off and he was struggling to make the team. And he ran down and I had a cool little vantage point. There was a hole, and all the sudden Terrell closed that hole and just crushed that guy.

"And I remember thinking right then, 'Oh, he just made the team.'"

On the kickoff, Davis was lined up to Elam's right. As Elam approached the ball, Davis took off. The 49ers' Tyrone Drakeford caught it at the 8-yard line and ran up the middle right. He got to the 20.

BAM! Drakeford did not reach the 21.

"I was on kickoff coverage my whole life, going back to my Pop Warner days," Davis said. "I was actually the kicker, and sometimes I would make the tackle. So, this is familiar. I was in the [special teams] meetings, so I knew my alignment and a little bit of what to do, but the bottom line is, go make a tackle. I don't think it's that difficult. The key is to get through the blockers before they turn around."

A week later, Darrick Owens was released. He never played in another NFL game. Davis? He made it to the regular season where he never played on kickoff coverage again. He went on to become the greatest running back in Broncos history.

"Even then, I knew the impact that play would have," Davis said. "I didn't know exactly what it would do, but I knew it got me in the door. Because everybody came over and [running backs coach] Bobby Turner told me I was going in on the next series. I threw up after I got off the field. Bobby came over and said, 'You all right?' I said, 'I'm cool.' He said, 'Good, because you're going in next series.'"

After discarding the hot dog he'd quickly devoured at halftime, Davis wound up with nine more carries for 41 yards in Tokyo. He was the

Broncos starting tailback for the regular season opener against Buffalo, rushing for 70 yards and a touchdown in a 22–7 win.

He finished his rookie season with 1,117 yards to rank ninth in the NFL. In his second season, he rushed for 1,538 yards to finish a narrow second to NFL rushing leader Barry Sanders, who had 1,553 yards. Davis added another 91 yards on just 14 carries in the Broncos' second-round postseason game, a devastating loss to underdog Jacksonville.

Although Davis averaged 6.5 yards a carry against the Jaguars, it was the only time in eight postseason games he didn't surpass 100. It turned out to be one of the few regrets of Mike Shanahan's great head-coaching career with the Broncos.

"Did you realize we only ran T.D. 14 times in that game?" Shanahan said. "That's why we lost the game. We lost our toughness. They felt they were as tough as we were because we didn't run the ball. It was the worst game I ever called. For some reason, I got away from the running game. They felt they could beat us. After that game, I told myself I was going to make sure we were going to out-physical people."

In 1997, Davis rushed for 1,750 yards to again finish second to Sanders (2,053 yards) for the rushing title. But while Sanders was bottled up in his only playoff game that season, Davis led the Broncos to their first-ever Super Bowl title. He rushed for 184 yards and two touchdowns in a 42–17 rout of Jacksonville; 101 yards and two touchdowns in a hard-fought 14–10 win against Kansas City; 139 yards and a touchdown in an AFC Championship Game win at Pittsburgh; and 157 yards and three touchdowns despite a blinding migraine against heavily favored Green Bay to become MVP of Super Bowl XXXII.

"He took the pressure off John," said Broncos left tackle Gary Zimmerman. "When we didn't have a big-name back like that, they just teed up on John. So, once we had Terrell in there, they had two guys they had to defend. He definitely made a difference."

Davis was just getting started. He ran for 2,008 yards in his fourth season—this time Sanders was a distant fourth—to earn the NFL Most Valuable Player Award.

"If Mike [Shanahan] wanted to, he could have had T.D. rush for 2,400 yards," said Broncos tight end Shannon Sharpe. "But we wanted to win the Super Bowl, and we would have had trouble doing that if T.D. had too many carries; he wouldn't have been as fresh as he was come playoff time."

Davis would rush for 199, 167, and 102 yards in the Broncos' three victorious 1998 postseason games. That's 2,476 yards combined in a single season. Take that, Eric Dickerson. That 2,105-yard rushing season Dickerson had in 1984 did not include his 107 yard-game in the postseason. That's 2,212 yards combined—or 264 less than T.D.'s 1998 season.

Anyway, Davis's seven consecutive, 100-yard rushing games still hold as an NFL postseason record and are tied for the most overall, with Emmitt Smith.

"What I also remember about Terrell, he wasn't just a talented running back," Elam said. "He was very smart. He's articulate. He represents himself well, the organization, the community. He was basically the quintessential teammate to have. I think the world of Terrell."

Everybody did. Davis had made the quantum leap from unknown rookie to superstar in three years. For a guy who wasn't all that in high school, who had to scramble to play in college, who became a lightly regarded sixth-round pick who wanted to check out during his rookie season, Davis handled his ascension to the limelight with remarkable ease and maturity.

His upbringing helped.

"I know this is a whole different story, but when I was playing Pop Warner, in my eyes, it was kind of the equivalent," he said. "I was the biggest stud. I was called 'Boss Hogg.' I was kind of like a little celebrity. When I'd walk uptown, kids would know who 'Boss Hogg' was.

"So I went through it a little bit, but the difference was this: When I was little, I shied away from it. It drove me nuts. I didn't feel comfortable with that role at all. Now the NFL is a whole different world. But I leaned back to when I was young and remembered how I didn't embrace it, so I tried to embrace it when it came back.

"I enjoyed it, but I also could understand it comes with some responsibility when you become a player who is recognized and sort of one of the star players on your team. You've got to be consistent. You've got to bring it *every day*. People watch you. People watch you on your own team. So, I always tried to be accountable to my team. You can have bad games—that's almost inevitable; but you prepare yourself mentally and physically to do the best you can do."

Dad was a welder. Terrell Davis remembers going to the welding yard and watching Pops blow his torches.

Joe Davis was also a provider.

"The way I remember my dad growing up, we'd come home from school and there would be food already prepared," Davis said. "And all we had to do was fix our plate. That was it. But then when we got home, he wouldn't show up for another three or four hours. Homework, that wasn't his deal. Because he ran the streets. But the breakfast and dinner—we'd eat lunch at school—but the food would be prepared. And the clothes were prepared. So, it was kind of weird. All the stuff was done, but the quality time with my dad was absent."

It was a tough San Diego neighborhood. Joe Davis and his wife Kateree were separated. Mom took the two oldest boys, and Dad took the youngest four. Terrell was the youngest.

Dad almost always eventually made it home. Often drunk. Sometimes scary drunk. Chances are if you remember Terrell Davis running the football like no one ever did in the four-year period from 1995 to 1998, you are familiar with his story.

Terrell grew up sharing one bedroom with three brothers, two to a bed. A cousin had his own room. So did Dad.

"Dad came in one night and he'd have these moods where one day he'd come in and say, 'Don't call me Dad; call me Joe,'" Terrell said. "When he was intoxicated, it was, 'Call me Joe.' If you called him 'Joe' the next day, he'd probably knock your teeth in.

"So one day he came home, and he was always about lessons. 'Let me give you a lesson.' He came home, he was drunk, turned on the lights, woke us up. And he started going off on a tangent about something. And made us all sit up. When Dad got a little alcohol in him, he was going to preach to you. He was doing that, and then all the sudden he was saying how all our lives are only worth six cents. I guess that's how much a bullet costs. And he proceeded to fire shots over our heads. One by one: bam, bam, bam, bam."

If you had a parent like that, how would you turn out? T.D. turned out to be a warm, friendly, intelligent, highly successful person.

"The crazy thing—and you might have trouble believing this—but I wasn't scared," Davis said. "I wasn't nervous. I wasn't afraid. It was, like, he got his message across, he made his point. He left the room and we went back to sleep."

The youngest of six brothers, Davis knew his dad didn't have it in him to shoot his kids.

"Of course not," Davis said. "We knew he wouldn't do it, number one. When you know your dad, you know how he is, you know that's how he operates.

"I've seen my dad get in a fight on the streets. With guys at a liquor store. My dad wound up shooting his best friend at our house. That night, I remember cops coming in and pointing guns at us. Waking us up at, like, three in the morning, making us stand outside. I was about eight or nine years old. But it never affected my love for my dad. I loved my dad."

He so loved his dad that when Joe Davis died in 1986 from complications of lupus, 13-year-old Terrell slipped into a terrible funk. He didn't play football as a freshman or sophomore in high school. He then changed high schools, from Morse, where he was trouble, to Lincoln, where he again played football, although as a noseguard, kicker, and fullback. He finally got to regularly carry the ball as a senior.

He attended Long Beach State, where his brother Reggie Webb was playing. Davis redshirted as a freshman, but then head coach George Allen died after leading the program to a 6-5 record in his one and only season there. Prior to Long Beach State, Allen had been a highly successful head coach of the Los Angeles Rams during their Fearsome Foursome era, and the Washington Redskins during their Over the Hill Gang run.

"When he passed away, any hopes of playing pro ball were gone," Davis said. "Because we had a ton of scouts who would come to practice every day. George Allen would have them come there. The first time playing pro ball became more than just a thought was when my running backs coach told me that a scout had asked about me. I was like, 'Whoa!' I was a freshman on the scout team at the time."

The next year, under coach Willie Brown, Long Beach State went 2-9 and the school closed the football program. Davis played some, but tore up each ankle. He wanted to transfer to UCLA, but the Bruins only offered him a chance to walk on.

"And then while I'm waiting for UCLA to decide to give me a scholarship, on my voice mail in my dorm room, I get a message from some guy named Bob Pittard. He was a recruiter from the University of Georgia," Davis said. "I was like, 'What? Georgia?' My smile was as big as you can imagine. Georgia. So, I call him back and we arrange for a flight to bring me down and, man, when I saw that campus, I thought, this is it. I've got to come here."

Davis averaged 7.3 yards per carry as a sophomore for the Bulldogs, but only had 53 attempts as the backup to Garrison Hearst, who finished third in the Heisman Trophy balloting. As a junior, with Hearst gone to the NFL, Davis rushed for 824 yards, but then as a senior he missed a few games with a nagging hamstring injury, and split time with a running back named Hines Ward.

Four years into his career with the Broncos, Davis was on pace to become the number-one running back in NFL history. Look at it this way: Davis averaged 1,603 rushing yards through his first four seasons. Emmitt

Smith, the all-time leading rusher, averaged 1,425 yards through his first four seasons.

But Elway retired prior to the 1999 season and early in the fourth game that year, Davis tore knee ligaments while trying to make a tackle on an interception.

He was never the same, and wound up retiring prior to a 2002 preseason game. He finished with 7,607 yards—6,413 in his first four seasons, 1,194 in his next three. He became a unique candidate for the Pro Football Hall of Fame. Strong enough to become a top-25 modern-era semifinalist each of the first 11 years he was eligible; not quite enough to make it to the round of 15 finalists until his ninth year of eligibility.

Davis's candidacy was compared to that of Gale Sayers, who had five terrific seasons in the 14-game era before knee injuries prematurely doomed the career of the Chicago Bears great. In one way comparing Davis to Sayers is a disservice to Sayers, because the Kansas Comet was the first of his kind, a mesmerizing back with explosive speed and spellbinding cuts in the open field. In another way, the comparison was unfair to Davis, because Sayers—who is still the youngest player ever inducted into the Pro Football Hall of Fame, going in at 34 years old in his first year of eligibility, in 1977—never played in the postseason, while Davis may have been the best postseason running back of all time.

"I know I'm a special circumstance player," Davis said.

Davis was a top-15 finalist in 2015, and got inside the top 10 in 2016. In 2017, he broke through. It was a mild surprise he was elected, because another running back, LaDainian Tomlinson, was also on the ballot. Tomlinson was a first-time candidate and fifth all-time in rushing, with 13,684 yards.

The Hall of Fame voters, though, found room for two running backs.

L.T. was a regular-season great. T.D. remains the best postseason back in NFL history.

"And I appreciate that," Davis said. "I think what that says is people value big moments, and when the game is on the line you value how someone performs. I don't think Michael Jordan would have been Michael Jordan if he didn't perform well in the postseason. He could have been a great basketball player, but I don't think he would have been MJ if he didn't win six NBA championships. And not only win them, but hit clutch shots in those moments. So, the value they place on big moments and big games, I certainly appreciate that. It shows that when I played in games, I showed up. I'm most proud of that."

For the Hall of Fame induction ceremony in Canton, Ohio, in August 2017, Davis brought along his wife, Tamiko; their two boys, Jaxon and Myles; and daughter Dylan. His mom, all five of his brothers, and an adopted brother and sister were there too. It was the first time in nearly 20 years, Davis said, Joe Davis's six boys were together. And Terrell thought about his dad, Joe Davis.

For all the trouble his dad caused, Terrell saw good in him.

"My dad was a helluva man," Davis said. "Here was a black man trying to raise six black boys. His approach was, I'm going to be hard on you because this world is going to be harder. I will say this: I have five brothers and we're all alive. And growing up in the community we grew up in, that's a lot to say. That's a testament to our dad and how he raised us. He instilled in us that this world is not going to be kind to you, and you've got to be tough to prevail.

"Listen, he was a street dude. He wasn't a scholar. He was street smart. But he wanted to make his kids better than him. Yeah, I miss him dearly. To this day I always think, I always wonder—because he never saw me play—would he be proud of me? Because I was the youngest. And being the youngest, I always felt like my dad would be so hard on me. I was like, Damn, was he ever proud of me? He never told me he was proud of me. I kind of long for that. Hopefully, he's looking down and saying he's proud of me."

TERRELL DAVIS STATS

YRS	CAR	Y	Y/C	TD	REC	Y	TD
7	1,655	7,607	4.6	60	169	1,280	5

POSTSEASON

G	CAR	Y	Y/C	TD	REC	Y	TD
8	204	1,140	5.6	12	19	131	0

3

PEYTON MANNING

Quarterback, 2012–15

Peyton Manning may have been the smartest football player who ever lived, but brains alone didn't make him such an effective quarterback.

Yes, his gene pool and growing up around the NFL with his quarterback-playing father Archie helped, and so did Peyton's 6-foot-5 stature. There was so much said about Manning's cerebral preparation that his uncanny passing accuracy became underrated.

But after covering Manning during his four seasons as a Denver Bronco, what made him the first-ballot Pro Football Hall of Famer he is certain to become was his attitude.

Football is the ultimate team sport, and sometimes intelligence can be a hindrance to getting along with others. Manning was smarter than every single teammate he played with, at least in football IQ. He also worked harder than every one of his teammates.

Yet, Manning developed a tolerance for the naive rookie and crusty veteran. He got just a tad more out of the lazy but talented. He appreciated the try-hard but limited-skilled. He figured out no matter how many numbskulls or overly ambitious or partyers or do-gooders he shared a locker room with, it was his job as quarterback to make sure they all pulled in the same direction.

"The worst question some guys get, they ask these draft choices, 'What are you going to do with the money you just made?'" Manning said during his introductory press conference on March 20, 2012. "And they will say they're going to buy this and buy that. And I'm sitting there saying, 'I'm going to try and go earn it.'"

Loved that. Manning earned his keep, all right. Literally. When Broncos general manager John Elway asked Manning to take a $4 million pay cut from the $19 million salary he was supposed to make in 2015, he earned $2 million back by first leading his team past his good friends Tom Brady and Bill Belichick in the AFC Championship Game. And then

17

Manning received another $2 million bonus for helping the Broncos defeat the Carolina Panthers, 24–10, in Super Bowl 50.

You can guarantee him $19 million—or you can let him earn it. Manning wound up collecting $77 million of salary in his four years with the Broncos. He earned every dollar.

Given his four-year term with the Broncos, his No. 3 ranking on this list of the 50 Greatest Players may give pause. But here are the reasons why Manning received such a lofty ranking:

1. He single-handedly led the Broncos to a Super Bowl through his record-setting passing performance in 2013.

2. He came to the rescue in 2015 by coming off the bench to give his team a well-timed push toward winning Super Bowl 50. Remember, when ranking players on this list, Super Bowls trumped all. No one can dispute that the Broncos would have had six Super Bowl appearances, instead of eight, and two Lombardi Trophies, instead of three, had Manning not signed on with Denver as a free agent in 2012.

3. In Manning's four seasons, the Broncos won four AFC West titles, and earned four first-round playoff byes by posting regular-season records of 13-3, 13-3, 12-4, and 12-4.

4. He had the weight of the city on his shoulders when he signed up to become a Bronco, and he carried the city along for a thrilling ride.

5. The two years before Manning arrived, the Broncos went 4-12 and 8-8. The year after he retired, they went 9-7.

6. No Broncos quarterback played the position better than Manning did in the two and a half seasons from 2012 until halfway through 2014. Elway was great over 16 seasons, but he never passed with the efficiency that Manning demonstrated at his best.

7. Manning threw 37 touchdowns against 11 interceptions in 2012, 55 touchdowns against 10 interceptions in 2013, and 22 touchdowns against only 3 picks through seven games in 2014.

8. An outrageous 39-game run of 114 touchdown passes against 24 interceptions. If this book on the 50 Greatest Broncos is still on library shelves in 50 years, this run of 114 touchdown passes against 24 picks is not likely to be topped.

9. His 2013 season was the best NFL quarterback season of all time. His 55 touchdown passes and 5,477 passing yards broke single-season

league records that remain standing going on four years later. And those marks may hold up much longer than even Manning believes they will.

"I personally think all season records are going down, especially if they go to 18 games," Manning said. "And there won't be an asterisk next to them. Brady will probably break it again next year, if not the year after."

As someone who was a fan of the game long before he started dominating it, Manning holds in higher regard the 48 touchdown passes Dan Marino tossed in 1984 than any of the passing records set in the past 10 years or so, when the rules were changed to tilt heavily in favor of quarterbacks and receivers.

Still, defense was starting to adjust back to the wide-open offensive style in recent years. Manning's 55 and 5,477 marks not only have held up entering 2017, they were never threatened.

"Think about what he did: 5,500 yards, 55 touchdowns," said former Broncos tight end Shannon Sharpe. "See, when he broke Marino's record [in 2004], he broke it by one touchdown. When Brady broke Manning's record [in 2007], he broke it by one touchdown. Peyton broke [Brady's record of 50 touchdowns] by 10 percent. Imagine somebody breaking another record by 10 percent. They would have to rush for 2,315 yards. That's what he did. I think the record that may stand for a while is the 55 touchdowns."

It took a sequence of unusual events for the Broncos to land Manning after his long, successful run as the Indianapolis Colts quarterback.

Had it not been for a disc injury in his neck that took four surgeries to repair; had the Colts not spectacularly collapsed to the NFL's worst record without their superstar quarterback; had Stanford quarterback standout Andrew Luck not come out one year early for the NFL Draft—Manning never would have become available.

But each of those circumstances did occur, and when the Colts did release the most popular and successful athlete ever to call the state of Indiana home (with Larry Bird a close second), the Broncos were among the 11 teams who went after him.

Even though there was a risk that Manning at 36 years old was damaged goods, and even though Tim Tebow had just come off a wildly eventful run as their quarterback in 2011, the Broncos management team of Joe Ellis, John Elway, and John Fox believed it was worth pursuing the former Colt from New Orleans and the University of Tennessee.

During Manning's 13 playing seasons with the Colts, he had led Indianapolis to eight seasons of at least 12 wins, 11 years of at least 10 wins, two Super Bowl appearances, and one Super Bowl championship.

As he became a free agent in March 2012, Manning ranked No. 3 behind Brett Favre and Dan Marino on most of the all-time passing categories.

By the time he was through with the Broncos four years later, Manning was No. 1 in all of the significant categories of touchdown passes (539), yards (71,940), and wins (200, counting the postseason).

Manning was thorough as he went through the NFL recruiting process. He ultimately narrowed his choices to four: Tennessee, Arizona, San Francisco, and the Broncos.

He held a private passing audition for each team.

A Broncos contingent that included Elway, Fox, general manager Brian Xanders, offensive coordinator Mike McCoy, and quarterbacks coach Adam Gase watched Manning throw at Duke University.

Even if he was not quite Manning at full strength, he was close enough to convince the Broncos to take a chance.

"I just said, 'Here it is, guys. If you're not interested, you're not hurting my feelings,'" Manning said.

Fox told Manning during his visit to Broncos headquarters on March 9 that the quarterback would be in total control of their no-huddle, pass-moving offense.

Manning picked the Broncos, then set out to justify his decision.

Elway received disparaging pushback from loyal fans of Tebow, who was traded to the New York Jets the day after Manning arrived. The next four years, though, justified Elway's decision.

Manning's arm never did regain full strength. The problem with the disc injury in his neck is that it created nerve damage in his passing hand, which is why he took to wearing a glove on that hand. His ability to read defenses and anticipate his receivers coming open, however, reached new levels during his time with the Broncos.

"The Peyton Manning that put up 40 [points] on us was a better quarterback," said Broncos former defensive lineman Trevor Pryce, who is No. 23 among the 50 Greatest Broncos. "This Peyton Manning was smarter. He knew how to make up for whatever deficiencies he had with his arm.

"But the one that put up 40 against us, he threw missiles. And he put them on a dime and he'd throw them on a spot. I mean, Dallas Clark was just a guy. Dallas Clark with Peyton Manning was a semi–Hall of Fame tight end."

Manning went on to make the careers, never mind millions of dollars, for several Broncos pass catchers, too. See the careers of Eric Decker and Julius Thomas.

As a final chapter to Manning's legacy with the Broncos, he put his pride on the bench for the sake of the team. And received the ultimate reward for it.

As exquisitely as he played from 2012 to midway through 2014, Manning's skills eroded abruptly. The combination of injuries, age, and a change by new head coach Gary Kubiak to a more-conservative offensive system conspired to end Manning's career a year before his five-year Broncos contract was to expire.

After starting the 2015 season with a 7-0 record, Manning suffered a heel injury during the Broncos' Game 8 defeat at Indianapolis. He was so ineffective the following week in a loss to Kansas City, where he completed just 5 of 20 passes with four interceptions, that Kubiak pushed the proud quarterback to the inactive roster for the next six games.

When Manning's foot had healed enough to dress for the final regular-season game against San Diego, he did so as Brock Osweiler's backup.

It very easily could have worked out that Manning would finish his career on the bench.

But with the Broncos trailing early in the second half against the Chargers, Kubiak yanked Osweiler and inserted Manning. The Denver stadium sellout crowd gave him a standing ovation, and Broncos players fed off the fans' energy.

The Broncos won that game to earn the No. 1 AFC playoff seed, when a loss would have dropped them to the No. 5 seed. Manning played well in AFC home playoff victories against Pittsburgh and the favored New England Patriots in the championship game.

Manning didn't play particularly well in Super Bowl 50, but Von Miller and the Denver defense carried the day. Manning became the first quarterback in NFL history to lead two teams to two Super Bowl games and two teams to Super Bowl titles.

"I'm very proud of that," Manning said.

A month after Super Bowl 50, Manning formally retired. He and his wife Ashley and their twin children continue to make their home in the Denver area at the time of this writing.

"I thought about it a lot, prayed about it a lot, and it was just the right time," Manning said during a question-and-answer session following his emotional, 12-minute retirement speech. "Maybe I don't throw as good or run as good as I used to, but I've always had good timing."

PEYTON MANNING STATS

YRS	G	A	C	PCT	TD	I	RTG	W-L
4	58	2,170	1,443	66.5	140	53	101.7	45-12

POSTSEASON

G	A	C	PCT	TD	I	Y	RTG	W-L
8	309	196	63.4	11	6	1,950	85.0	5-3

4

SHANNON SHARPE

Tight End, 1990–99, 2002–03

Maybe it was 20 years of drinking well water in the boondocks some eight miles of country road outside the small town of Glennville, Georgia.

It could have been the hot dogs and hamburgers on white bread every Friday night that nourished the house of champions.

Or perhaps it was the one-and-a-half-mile walk to the nearest school bus stop every morning, cutting tobacco, or climbing through the chicken coops, where it was worth $1 for every 1,000 necks you could grab.

Then again, it could have been the lucky and loving draw of genetics that explains how two Pro Football Hall of Fame players came out of the same family, which would have been the case had the oldest son, Sterling, not been injured.

"I think all of the above," said Shannon Sharpe, the youngest brother who was inducted into the Hall of Fame in December 2016. "My dad was an athlete. My mom was an athlete. My uncles on my mom's side were athletes.

"Me, personally, I always played with everybody who was older. The youngest cousin I played against, he was two years older than me. My brother was three years older. Then I had cousins who were five and seven years older. I'm competing against them. So, when I go to school and compete against people my age, I was far more advanced.

"But growing up how we grew up—on a farm, and having to walk— my brother and I used to say it all the time: This wasn't living, this was surviving. To eat the way we had to eat. And to live the way we had to live.

"Working hard was something that was instilled in us at a very young age. Working the fields, cutting tobacco, picking pecans, whatever it was, whatever the manual chore was, you had to work hard. If you didn't work hard, you didn't have any money. So, for me, football was the easiest job I ever had."

Sterling Sharpe was a sensational receiver for Green Bay who averaged 85 catches, 1,162 yards, and 9 touchdowns over seven seasons. To lend perspective on that type of production, Jerry Rice, who holds every NFL career significant receiving record by wide margins, averaged 75 catches, 1,296 yards, and 13 touchdowns in his first seven seasons.

Had an abnormality between his top two neck vertebrae not brought a premature end to Sterling's career following the 1994 season, Grandma Mary Porter would have raised two Pro Football Hall of Famers in a tiny cinder-block house with concrete floors and a tin roof.

"Football was the sport I was least good at," said Shannon Sharpe, who broke the Georgia state triple jump record as a junior (48 feet, 3 inches), then broke it again as a senior (49 feet, 5 inches). "I only played football because my brother played it. I didn't think I was very good in football.

"Early on, I think I played out of position. I was an offensive lineman, I was a running back, I was a quarterback, I was a receiver. And then in high school, I was my brother's backup, because he was a senior and I was a freshman. And then naturally they had me play quarterback and running back like he did. But I never felt comfortable at running back and quarterback. That wasn't my heart. I did it because that's what he did."

At Glennville High School, Sterling played quarterback his first three years, and then two days before the opening game of his senior year, he inadvertently banged his hand on a teammate's helmet and dislocated the index finger on his throwing hand.

"So he moved to running back his senior year and he was player of the year at running back," Shannon said. "I always wanted to be like him. When he was number '3' in high school, I was number '19.' When he graduated high school, I took number '3.' When I went to Savannah State I told them I would only come if I could have the number '2,' because my brother wore '2' at South Carolina."

In the NFL, Sharpe had to wait until Ricky Nattiel moved on before he could switch from number "81" to "84"—Sterling's number with the Green Bay Packers.

Unlike Sterling, Shannon Sharpe made it to the Pro Football Hall of Fame because his numbers and accomplishments in a 14-year career—12 with the Broncos—could not be denied. When he called it a career following the 2003 season, Shannon Sharpe was the all-time leader among NFL tight ends in the Holy Trinity statistical categories of catches (815), receiving yards (10,060), and touchdowns (62).

Tony Gonzales, Jason Witten, and Antonio Gates eventually passed him in each of those three categories, but those three tight ends had three fewer Super Bowl rings combined than the three Sharpe had earned—two with the Broncos in 1997–98, and another with the 2000 Baltimore Ravens.

It took until his third year of eligibility, or two years too long, but Sharpe now has the right to annex the letters "HOF" to his autograph.

"Before it was three-time Super Bowl winner," Sharpe said. "Now it's Hall of Fame. It's funny how those three little letters, how much cachet they carry. They look at you in a different light. Because there are 24,000 men who have played this game, and at the time I went in, there were only 258 who could say they were Hall of Famers. And I think there were only 150 who were living. So, it's very, very elite company.

"It's still hard for me to absorb that I'm in the same building as Jim Brown, or Mean Joe Green. I grew up watching Mean Joe. And some of the guys I played against, I played against Reggie White and Derrick Thomas. Some of the all-time great, greats. Deion Sanders and I are in the same building.

"It's still hard for me to believe that a kid who wasn't drafted until the seventh round and started out on special teams, and they found a position for him, [made it to the Hall of Fame]. At the time, only three teams had an H-back position—the Broncos, the Chargers, and the Redskins. So, I went to one of the three teams that had an H-back position."

Sharpe was actually given the number "1" in his rookie 1990 training camp, a number that was befitting his 6-foot-2, 225-pound frame. He was a seventh-round draft pick in a 12-round draft, and it wasn't until Broncos head coach and football boss Dan Reeves nabbed Sharpe that he wound up with a starting player of more than two seasons.

"It was an unusual draft," Reeves said. "We had the Three Amigos (Nattiel, Vance Johnson, Mark Jackson), and we felt that Shannon could be a big receiver for us. And then when he got here, we started working drills and we could see that he was a mismatch for strong safeties and linebackers. And that's what you want from an H-back.

"Shannon was the exception, not the rule. You see a lot of guys with talent and settle on it. Shannon had a lot of talent, and he really worked hard."

After two seasons with limited playing time, Sharpe broke out in 1992 with 53 catches. Reeves was fired after that season, and new coach Wade Phillips brought in Jim Fassel to be his offensive coordinator.

Fassel's offense was tight end–friendly, and Sharpe had career bests with 81 and 87 catches in 1993–94, accounting for 995 and 1,010 yards. Later, with Mike Shanahan as head coach, Sharpe had career bests with 1,062 and 1,107 receiving yards in 1996–97.

Sharpe was on his way to the Hall of Fame. His bronze bust is in the Hall of Fame Gallery. They should also give him his own Hallway of Humor, or perhaps a Lobby of Levity.

"Mr. President! We need the National Guard!" Sharpe shouted into the red phone on the Broncos bench during a 34–8 whipping of New England in a 1996 game. "We need as many men as you can spare because we are killing the Patriots!"

Here's how Shannon Sharpe's fun-loving, gift-of-gab personality got its start. From the first time he put words together, he had a lisp, which can be difficult for a kid in the mean-spirited coliseum that is elementary school.

In third grade, Sharpe was put in a class taught by a speech therapist. One of her tactics was to have her kids read out loud. Whether the impediment was stuttering, lisping, or pronunciation, the therapist asked the other students to not help the assigned reader. Let them sound it out.

"And so Johnny got to a word and I knew it and I wanted to say it sooo bad," Sharpe said. "But she said, 'Don't help him. Now Johnny, sounds like . . . sounds like . . .'"

Sharpe could not stand it. Sounds like . . .

"Sounds like Johnny can't read," Sharpe said.

The other kids burst out laughing. The therapist threw Sharpe out of class, but it was too late. Sharpe's shyness evaporated.

"That was the beginning of where I thought I might be good at making people laugh," he said. "From that moment on, I figured out if I could poke fun at other kids, they wouldn't make fun of me and the way I talked. I had holey jeans and holey shirts and holes in my shoes and things like that. We didn't have sleepovers. We didn't want anybody to see how we lived. But if I could make people laugh, they wouldn't focus on what was wrong with me."

His remarkably quick wit landed him post-playing-career work as a studio analyst on CBS's *NFL Today* for 10 seasons, and in 2016 he joined Skip Bayless on a Fox Sports debate show called *Undisputed*.

"He was a guy that would keep levity in the locker room," said kicker Jason Elam. "He was constantly joking. But I never, ever heard him say a negative word about anybody. Not just the Broncos. He would joke and tease. He was incredibly competitive. I remember him and [Bill] Romanowski having some serious competitions in practice. That went on for years. It made them both better. It made our team better."

One of Sharpe's off-the-cuff remarks gave a young Elam the confidence he needed.

"It was my rookie year and I was in a big competition with David Tread-well and Brad Daluiso," Elam said. "And Wade after every practice had us end it with three kicks each. For every one we missed, the team had to run a gasser. One of the days, I don't know how long we were into it, but we all lined up and Shannon yelled out, 'Coach, let "E" kick all of them!'

"When he said that, that's when I knew I made the team. That's not a knock on Brad or David. But I knew that I had the confidence of my teammates. And Shannon was the most vocal leader. So, to me that was The Big Day of my rookie year."

The Broncos moment most vivid in Sharpe's memory?

"Third and six in Pittsburgh," he said.

It was the 1997 season AFC Championship Game at Three Rivers Stadium. The Broncos were up 24–14 at halftime, but the offense was sty-mied in the second half, while Steelers quarterback Kordell Stewart threw a touchdown pass with 2:46 remaining in the fourth quarter to draw within, 24–21.

The yellow Terrible Towels were waving. The fans were stomping and screaming. At the two-minute warning, the Broncos were backed up to their 15-yard line. Third and six. Fail to convert, and the Steelers would have got the ball no worse than their own 40, with plenty of time to at least tie the game with a field goal.

At the two-minute warning, Broncos head coach Mike Shanahan called "All pivot," which meant everybody would run a hook pattern, out of the "Cinco" formation, which meant empty backfield.

"Mike was the type of coach that if he put a play in during training camp and you ran it, at any point during the season, he felt we should be able to recall that play, whether it was five weeks ago or 10 weeks ago, or whatever it was," Sharpe said. "I'm looking at John and going, 'That's not in the game plan. What do you want me to do?' And he said, 'Go get open.' That was the first time he told me I could ad-lib."

Running back Terrell Davis went in motion to clear the backfield and the Broncos had three receivers to one side, two to the other. Cinco.

The Steelers surprisingly dropped their 3-4 pass-rushing linebacker, Jason Gildon, into coverage. He wound up backpedaling to cover Sharpe.

"All he had to do, if he would have just stuck his hand out, instead of trying to swipe the ball, it would have hit the back of his hand and hit the dirt," Sharpe said.

Sharpe caught it, turned, and picked up 18 yards. First down. You should have heard the silence. The Broncos ran out the clock.

"I had great numbers," Sharpe said. "I had been an All Pro. But I hadn't really had that signature moment. John was great, but he had The Drive. [Joe] Montana, he had John Candy and John Taylor.

"For a player, you must have a signature moment. You have to have a signature play. Up until that point, I had big games, multiple touchdown games, but I really hadn't had a signature play. And it's funny how that signature play happened, because we didn't practice that play."

SHANNON SHARPE STATS					
YRS	G	REC	Y	Y/C	TD
12	172	675	8,439	12.5	55

POSTSEASON				
G	REC	Y	Y/C	TD
12	47	505	10.7	2

5

CHAMP BAILEY

Cornerback, 2004–13

The first difficult, front-end decision for this project was choosing between Shannon Sharpe and Champ Bailey for the fourth-best player in Broncos history, or first player after the Big Three of John Elway, Terrell Davis, and Peyton Manning.

The argument for Champ: He was the best defensive player for a franchise that boasts more great defensive players than offensive players. Among our top 50, 25 were defensive players, 22 were offensive players, and three were specialists (kicker Jason Elam, and the versatile Rick Upchurch and Gene Mingo, who shared greatness as offensive players and specialists). So, it was past time to get a defensive player on the list.

As for splitting hairs between Bailey and Sharpe, we project Bailey to be a first-ballot Hall of Famer when he becomes eligible in 2019. He did, after all, earn 12 Pro Bowl berths, the most ever for a cornerback. Sharpe was inducted in his third year of eligibility.

However, we ultimately gave Sharpe the No. 4 slot because at the time of his retirement, he held all the tight-end records for catches, receiving yards, and touchdowns. In other words, he was the all-time best at his position. And again, the criteria that applied to placing Terrell Davis as high as No. 2; Peyton Manning at No. 3, despite playing only four seasons with the Broncos; and Von Miller at No. 6 was that Super Bowls trumped all tiebreakers.

Sharpe was part of two Super Bowl championship teams. Bailey got to two AFC Championship Games—he was *The Reason* they got to host the AFC Championship in the 2005 season—and one Super Bowl. But his Broncos fell short of a Super Bowl ring each time.

Ultimately, so long as Champ's in the top five, and the first defensive player listed, we felt good about his placement. If this project waited two more years, Von Miller might be placed ahead of Champ as the top defensive Broncos player. But as of this writing, there's no denying 8 Pro Bowls in 10 Broncos seasons for Champ.

"I appreciate you rating him that way," said John Lynch, a safety teammate of Bailey's from 2004–07, and another top-50 Bronco. "I think because of his quiet demeanor and lack of bravado, he's a severely underrated player. It's hard to say that about someone who everyone says will be a first-ballot Hall of Famer. I think people are missing the boat, though, on how good this guy was, how special he was.

"In my mind, he was one of the greatest defensive players ever to play the game. He combined an athleticism that was obvious. He ran—if you say 4.3 in this league, that's about as fast as it gets. But people forget Champ came in with a 4.2. He was one of the fastest players to ever play. He could jump out of the gym, change direction.

"But on top of all that, he was a student of the game. I fought hard at Fox [the network] to hire him after he retired. They said, 'Well, he's a quiet guy.' And I said, 'Yeah, but he's one of the most intelligent football players, one of the most cerebral football players I've ever been around.' He combined that intelligence along with the will to win.

"It irked me a little when people would put Darrelle Revis as the best cornerback in the league when Champ was in his heyday. I think Champ did all the things [Revis] did, but you also affect the game when you have all those interceptions. I felt like Champ was on a different level."

Bailey's best statistical seasons were in 2005, when he had 9 interceptions for 239 return yards—including a 100-yard pick return of a Tom Brady pass in a second-round AFC playoff game that amounted to a 14-point swing in the Broncos' 27–13 victory—and in 2006, when in the regular season alone he had 10 interceptions with 162 return yards.

Put those two seasons together and Bailey compiled an astounding 19 interceptions for 401 return yards, two touchdowns, and practically a third.

"It's funny thinking back about how great those two years were, because you don't see anybody having years like that now," Bailey said in November 2016. "You don't see guys having that number of interceptions and having that much of an impact on the defense.

"I'm not going to lie: It's a little harder on corners these days. It was hard back then, but the game is tailored to put up points now. With the rules, you can't find that shutdown corner like you used to. You have guys that are really good at it today, but to ask these guys to man up and do it every single play, it's very hard to do it."

To prove Bailey's point, after his 10-pick season in 2006, the NFL's last 10-interception season was a year later, in 2007, by San Diego's Antonio Cromartie. Which was a bit fluky, because Cromartie otherwise never had more than 4 picks in a season, and finished his career with 31 interceptions.

Bailey had 52 career picks (tied for 26th all-time), 34 in his 10 seasons with the Broncos.

Bailey's interceptions shrank drastically starting in 2007, when quarterbacks gave him the Deion Sanders treatment and stopped throwing in his direction.

"He was a shutdown corner in the truest sense of the term," said Broncos kicker Jason Elam. "After those two big seasons he had, teams didn't go after him pretty much. One of the most natural athletes I've ever been around. Talk about quiet and going about his business. He wasn't going to be all talk. He knew he was going to be prepared. He was going to be quietly humble and then tear you up on Sunday."

There was one other aspect of the cornerback position where Bailey was superior to Revis—tackling. Bailey had 699 tackles in his 15 NFL seasons, including 71 and 73 for the Broncos in his otherworldly 2005–06 seasons.

It was Bailey's willingness to tackle that puts him in the conversation for one of the best lockdown cornerbacks in NFL history. Sanders? Please. Receivers couldn't shake him, but he gave ball carriers the ole' treatment on his way to recording 200 less tackles than Bailey. Revis, who was still active at the time of this writing, had nearly 300 fewer tackles than Champ through the 2016 season.

"It was my attitude," Bailey said. "I wanted to be great at everything. If I was asked to tackle, I wanted to be great at tackling. If I had to block on an interception return, I wanted to be the best blocker. It was me wanting to be great at every part of my game. When there were special plays on offense, I wanted to be great at it. Punt returning. I don't know any other way to be."

Roland "Champ" Bailey Jr. grew up near the Okefenokee Swamp, in a small, if growing southeast Georgia town of Folkston (population 2,178 in 2000, but nearly doubled to 4,148 by 2010). He was the third of four children raised by Roland Sr. and Elaine Bailey.

"We were out there in the hot, humid climate, all day, every day," Champ said. "In the sand, throwing it around with our guys. That's what we did. Playing football, basketball, anything with a ball, we were doing it. We thought we could be gymnasts at one point. That's how country it was. It was awesome."

The three Bailey boys starred in football from an early age, led by Ron, the oldest, who was a two-year starting cornerback at Georgia before his career ended with a foot injury while representing the Tampa Bay Buccaneers in NFL Europe.

Boss, the youngest, also played at Georgia and had a nice NFL career, mostly with the Detroit Lions—and one special year with the Broncos and his brother, as a linebacker.

But there was no question Champ—a nickname his mom gave him when he was two, because of his natural affection for anything that was a ball and all the energy he displayed—was the best of the Bailey boys. In fact, at an early age, it was known he was the most sensational young athlete Folkston had ever produced. Larry Allen, who owns a hardware store and coached the Bailey boys at the 11- and 12-year-old levels, said Champ scored 92 touchdowns in those two years.

That doesn't mean Champ thought he would grow up to become the No. 7 overall pick in the 1999 NFL Draft or make $95.5 million in combined salaries in his 10 years with the Broncos.

"I was always among the best in my age-group, or my class," Bailey said. "I think it was the fact no one had really made it to this level from where I'm from that nobody gave it much thought [about making it]. People close to me knew I had a shot. But you never know, because they hadn't seen it. Those dreams usually fade away once you get to college. But things kept building and building and I kept grinding and grinding and people started believing."

At Charlton County High School, Bailey was not only a star defensive back, he was also the team's punter and quarterback until his senior season, when he gave way to younger brother Boss, who had a better arm. Champ wound up rushing for 3,573 yards and 58 touchdowns (even as a quarterback, he ran much more than he passed), and threw for 1,211 yards and 10 touchdowns.

At Georgia, Bailey should have been a stronger Heisman Trophy candidate in his true junior season of 1998, as he had 47 catches for 744 yards and five touchdowns as a receiver, three interceptions as a lockdown cornerback, plus he returned kicks and punts. Bailey did finish seventh in the Heisman balloting that year (Texas running back Ricky Williams was the runaway winner), but his case was perhaps hurt by the fact a similarly versatile player, Charles Woodson, had beat out Peyton Manning for the Heisman the year before.

Bailey thought he would go higher than No. 7 in the draft, but that was the wacky year when three quarterbacks—Tim Couch, Donovan McNabb, and Akili Smith—went one, two, three, and New Orleans coach Mike Ditka traded his entire 1999 draft—eight picks, including two in the first round—to Washington to move up and take the running back Williams.

Washington had another first-round pick at No. 7, where they took Bailey.

In his first game, he intercepted Troy Aikman of the Dallas Cowboys. Later in the year, he had a three-interception game against Arizona, with two coming against a quarterback named Jake Plummer.

When Bailey was traded to the Broncos in 2004, no one was happier than Plummer, who had arrived in Denver the year before.

"I didn't like Champ Bailey much when he played for Washington," Plummer said. "We played them twice a year and he picked me off five times. I rank highest on his list."

Carson Palmer later tied Plummer for Bailey interceptions with five. On one of Bailey's interceptions in his three-pick game against Arizona, he returned it 56 yards for a touchdown—a play that infuriated the competitive Plummer.

"I gave chase," Plummer said. "I was going to catch his ass. I knew I couldn't. And the last 5 yards he held the ball out like, 'Ha, ha.' Pimped me, kind of. It was the closest I've ever been to run up and slam him to the ground and start whaling on him because I was having a [bad] game.

"When he signed here with the Broncos, I told him that. I said, 'Man, I used to hate your guts.' And I told him why and he just kind of chuckled. And I loved him. Not the biggest guy, but he just made me better, day-in and day-out, because I knew he wasn't going to do anything half-assed in practice. He did his job; you didn't have to worry about it. He's going to lock the dude down, and he was a great teammate."

In his five seasons in Washington, Bailey played in all 80 games. He had five interceptions as a rookie, then one more in a first-round playoff win. He made the Pro Bowl each of the next four years, but Washington never made the playoffs after his rookie season.

At the end of the 2003 season, Bailey's rookie contract was up, and he was in position to become the highest-paid corner in NFL history. Meanwhile, the Broncos had a running back, Clinton Portis, who was making noise about holding out for a new contract after he started his career with back-to-back 1,500-yard seasons.

A trade was made with Bailey and a second-round draft pick going to Denver and Portis going to Washington. It's inconceivable to think now that the Broncos got not only the best cornerback in football, but also a second-round pick as a throw-in, which turned out to be running back Tatum Bell, who later went on to have his own 1,000-yard season.

Within five years after the trade, corners were considered a far more valued position than running back. The deal was the best thing that happened in Bailey's career, as it was not possible for any other fandom to have appreciated him more than those who bleed the orange and blue.

"But I can't say at the time I wanted to get traded," Bailey said. "I was a guy who was a Washington Redskin at 25 years old, who was starting to understand how big a market it was to play in Washington, playing in the NFC East. To be a part of an organization that was top five in value in the league. I didn't want to leave. There were endorsement opportunities.

"But after a year or two, I knew the difference was [Broncos owner] Pat Bowlen. You've got a guy who's running the team the way he runs it, you're going to have success. And I knew I had a better chance at having success in Denver than I did in Washington. And that was the best thing that happened to my career."

The highlight of Bailey's career? There were three he singled out. One was the chance to play with his brother Boss on the same defense in 2008. It didn't work out as he'd hoped, as both Baileys suffered injuries that year, and the Broncos blew a three-game lead with three to go to miss the playoffs. Still, playing together on the same NFL team was a rare achievement few families were able to share.

The second highlight was playing in the Super Bowl in Champ's final season of 2013. Bailey suffered from a Lisfranc injury (a midfoot injury affecting the Lisfranc joint or ligament, according to the American Orthopaedic Foot & Ankle Society) in his left foot during a preseason game that forced him to miss all but five regular-season games that year, and the Broncos were crushed in that Super Bowl, 43–8, by the Seattle Seahawks.

And we saved his number-one highlight for last. Champ fans won't need two guesses to come up with his favorite memory during his time with the Broncos.

"Obviously, the game against the Patriots in the playoffs," Bailey said of the 2005-season, second-round AFC playoff game at Invesco Field at Mile High. "[Tom] Brady was 10-0 [in the postseason]. They were running so hot. And to be able to eliminate them—that was a big deal. It gave us a shot to go to the Super Bowl. Even though we didn't, I could see people starting to give us that respect that we deserved, even for myself."

His two most heartbreaking defeats were in the next week's AFC Championship Game against underdog Pittsburgh, and in Super Bowl 48, which turned out to be the final game of his career.

"You know what, they both stunk, but when I look back—it's easy for me to be objective now because I'm away—but the way I feel about it is at least we got to those points," Bailey said. "Yes, I'm upset by the result. But I got there. I'm glad to say that I played in championship games and I played in the Super Bowl. Some guys don't get to experience that.

"I wish we could have won more. I wish I would have finished with two rings. But I can't dwell on it. People tell me to this day I had a great career. I feel like it was great. I appreciate every moment of it."

CHAMP BAILEY STATS

YRS	G	I	Y	TD	TCK
10	135	34	340	3	627

POSTSEASON

G	I	Y	TCK
6	1	100	19

6

— VON MILLER —

Outside Linebacker, 2011–Present

Every player contacted for this top-50 project was asked one common question among many others. When flipping burgers on the grill, what's the most vivid moment from their time with the Broncos that tends to pop into your mind?

The responses included plays, games, Super Bowls, disappointments, defeats, victories. The most unique perspective, though, came from the most singular personality.

As Von Miller was asked the question, he was also provided with possible answers. Wasn't it the combination of the 2015-season AFC Championship Game, in which he had 2.5 sacks on Tom Brady, and the 2015-season Super Bowl 50, in which he had another 2.5 sacks on Cam Newton, including two strip sacks that led to two Broncos touchdowns in a 24–10 win?

"All that stuff is good," Miller said. "I'm always going to remember Super Bowl 50. I'm never going to forget playing with Tim Tebow or Champ Bailey or Brian Dawkins, D. J. Williams, Elvis Dumervil."

But you could almost see Miller's mind whirring as he considered the question more deeply.

"But I think the defining moment for me, when I knew we were going to do some stuff, was when we got Peyton Manning," he said. "I think that changed everything for the whole organization. When we got Peyton Manning that made me feel like, 'Okay, all I've got to do is go out there and do my job and we would have the opportunity to do some things.'

"Yes, winning the Super Bowl was great, but when it changed for me was being around Peyton and seeing him, and seeing the way he carries himself. I think that rubbed off on me more than anything in my football career to this point."

How about that. The most vivid memory of Von Miller's career was not about a sack he made, or the MVP trophy he raised on the Super Bowl stage at Levi's Stadium on February 7, 2016, but about how his team signed another player in 2012. Now that's a selfless spirit.

"Obviously, the MVP of the Super Bowl was special, but I don't like to look back," Miller said. "I like to keep going. But as I was sitting back here and thinking about it, when we got Peyton Manning, it changed everything. We felt like, 'Now it's the Denver Broncos' time to go out and do it.'

"As a defense we felt like—I had sacks the year before, but now I've got to just go out and do what I do. That year for me [2012], my second year, was one of my most successful years. I don't know how many sacks I had [it was 18.5], but having Peyton Manning on my team, I think that sparked the whole team."

Listing Miller at No. 6 on the Broncos' all-time list might be a lofty ranking for a player who is still very much active and was only six years into his career. Perhaps it's a ranking that raised some eyebrows. He is there, though, because he made the greatest impact in the Broncos' winning Super Bowl 50. And he is there because he is already the best pass rusher in franchise history.

Stat-wise, Miller is tied for fourth with Rulon Jones on the Broncos' all-time sack list, with 73.5, a number he achieved in just 6 seasons and 88 regular-season games. Simon Fletcher in 11 seasons and 172 games had 97.5 sacks; Karl Mecklenburg in 12 seasons and 180 games had 79.0 sacks; and Barney Chavous in 183 games and 13 seasons had 75.0. Jones played in 129 games over nine seasons.

Based on Miller's average season, he is a half season away from surpassing Mecklenburg for second place, and two years away from supplanting Fletcher as the team's all-time sack master. If Miller winds up playing 10 seasons with the Broncos, he may well put up a sack number that would never be broken.

"He is, in my mind, the Broncos' best pass rusher ever, and if he can stay healthy and keep doing what he's doing, sooner or later Von Miller is going to prove me right," Fletcher said. "Then, that will be the happiest day of my life . . . because records are meant to be broken."

If Miller retired today, he would be the sixth-greatest Bronco of all time. Two or three years from now, he may be No. 2 behind only John Elway.

"I've got the same outlook I have on anything: I need to get better," Miller said, when told about his No. 6 ranking. "We all know what Mr. Elway and all those other guys did for this organization. It doesn't matter if it's five in front of me, or however many guys behind me. It's not about that.

We all have something special that we brought to the organization. It's not about a number or rank on a list. It's a list where you can look at individual performances and individual careers that these Broncos have had. Elway is Elway. He's done stuff for this organization as a quarterback and GM no one can touch. His legacy is secure. I'm not trying to compare my legacy to his. But I would like to do some similar stuff. I would like to have that type of impact on Colorado and the Denver Broncos like he had."

Von Miller was born and raised 16 miles straight south of Dallas in DeSoto, Texas. His dad, "Von 1," and mom, Gloria, started up Power Guardian Inc., a backup power system and battery supply company, before they had "Little Von" and his younger brother, Vins.

As a kid, Von could primarily be found outside, most likely on a track.

"I was always excited to run and do all the events all across the state and all over the country and Puerto Rico," Miller said. "That intrigued me. I never made it to the Junior Olympics, but that kept me in track and field from childhood all the way through high school."

He participated in every event he could, from the 110-meter high hurdles, to the 4-by-100-meter relay, the long jump, triple jump, high jump, shot put, discus. He competed in some junior heptathlon (seven individual events) competitions.

His main event was the 110 hurdles. As a junior at DeSoto High School, Miller was ranked No. 1 going into district finals, but tripped over a hurdle. He was ranked No. 2 as a senior, and placed third when only the top two finishers went to the state meet.

"All the disappointment I had in track and field, I never had that on the football field," Miller said.

Considering speed is such a big part of Miller's game as a pass rusher, it figures that his track-and-field skills translated to the football field.

"Running and all that speed work is all good, but I think where it helped the most is all that individual competition you had in track and field," he said. "You try to earn points for the team, but how successful you are in track and field is totally dependent on you. That individual competition, running next to your guy and finding something to pull away from him, you get that competition day-in and day-out in track."

Sure, Miller occasionally got into trouble as a youth and as a young adult. But there was so much goodness in this kid, how were Von 1 and Gloria, and John Elway and the Broncos, supposed to punish him?

As the story goes, Miller was letting his grades slip at Texas A&M to the point where coach Mike Sherman suspended him from the Aggies' spring game. Miller started to drive home, ready to quit, when Von 1 told his oldest son he was doing no such thing.

Miller got it together and posted 17.0 sacks as a junior and another 10.5 sacks as a senior. The Broncos made him the No. 2 overall pick in the 2011 draft—surprising, because most of the so-called draft experts didn't think a strong-side linebacker should be taken that high after Aaron Curry had been a bust a few years earlier.

Miller had 11.5 sacks as a rookie for the Broncos in 2011—10.5 before breaking his thumb in Game 11, an injury that required in-season surgery and a cast—to earn NFL Rookie Defensive Player of the Year honors. In his second season, Miller had 18.5 sacks and 6 forced fumbles to finish second to J. J. Watt for NFL Defensive of the Year honors.

But then Miller's career came perilously close to careening out of control before his third season when a positive test for marijuana led to a six-game suspension. Upon his return, he struggled with the extra 15 pounds of muscle he had put on from all the time spent in the weight room, and he had 5.0 sacks in eight games. Early in his ninth game at Houston, Miller suffered a torn ACL. He missed the final game of the season, and then the Broncos' 2013 postseason run to Super Bowl 48.

"After my first year and second year, I think I know everything," Miller said. "And then 2013 happened and I go from being the next Golden Boy to a totally different position."

To Miller's credit, his became a story of redemption. He stayed clean to the point where he was released from the NFL's drug program. He underwent strenuous off-season rehabilitation on his knee to have 14.0 sacks in 2014, despite wearing a knee brace.

Miller added 11.0 more sacks—plus another 5.0 sacks in the postseason—in 2015, then added 13.5 sacks in his first 12 games in 2016 to finish second again in the NFL Defensive Player of the Year voting.

"When I got suspended, where I was at in my career, nobody could help me right there," Miller said. "It was dependent on me. I had been on teams and I had been in situations that had stuff happen, but I had never been in a situation where it was totally dependent on me.

"In college, you look at transferring to another school, but they love you more when you're there. It's different in college. In the National Football League when you're suspended, it's like a death sentence. It was like, 'He's done.'

"You look at the history, and to be injured and suspended in the same year, it doesn't really pick back up for a guy. I wasn't going to let that happen to me.

"Going into year four, I have to prove myself beyond what you're really supposed to do. For me, I only count year one and year two and then year four as far as growth as a player. And then in year four I had that brace on. I always felt like I could make more plays if I didn't have to play with this knee brace. It changes your game. It might not hinder you. You can adapt to it, but it definitely changes your game.

"And then I go in year five, this is the last year of my contract. I no longer have to wear the knee brace. I have a full off-season where I can really work out. Year five, I didn't have to worry about all the stuff I worried about in the past. I didn't have to worry about the program and missing tests. I can just totally focus on football.

"In year five, we got coach [Wade] Phillips for his first year. It was like a new life. Coach Richard Smith, he was crucial for my career. But then we get another coach and he doesn't know me, but he does some things I needed and that helped me grow to another level and expand on what I really was."

The Broncos had to win their final regular-season game of 2015 against San Diego to earn the No. 1 playoff seed. Lose, and the Broncos would have the No. 5 playoff seed and open on the road.

The Broncos were losing at halftime against the lowly Chargers, and running back C. J. Anderson fumbled away their second-half possession deep in Denver's own territory.

Broncos head coach Gary Kubiak pulled quarterback Brock Osweiler and inserted the Hall of Famer, Peyton Manning, who was coming back from a six-week absence with a foot injury. The Broncos rallied behind Manning, won the game, and had home-field advantage through the AFC playoffs.

"We had been in that position before but I didn't get to play," Miller said, referring to the Broncos' Super Bowl run in 2013 that fell short in the Meadowlands. "I felt like I got a second chance to do it right. I always thought we would win a Super Bowl in my career, but I never, ever in a million years thought that it would be like that for me."

Miller from the left side and his pass-rushing partner Demarcus Ware on the right dominated the final two playoff games. Miller not only had 2.5 sacks on Brady in the AFC Championship Game, but also an interception that set up a Manning touchdown pass to Owen Daniels for a 14–6 lead. Ware had half a sack against the Patriots, plus an incredible 7 hits on Brady, not including the blast on his two-point, game-tying pass attempt with 17 seconds remaining.

In Super Bowl 50, the matchup of the 2011 draft's No. 1 overall draft pick, Newton, and No. 2 pick, Miller, was all about No. 2. Miller's strip sack of Newton in the first quarter caused a fumble that bounced in the end zone, where Miller's teammate Malik Jackson fell on it for a Broncos touchdown and a quick, 7–0 lead.

Later in the fourth quarter, with the Broncos clinging to a 16–10 lead, Miller clinched it with another fumble-causing sack of Newton, giving Manning the ball at the Carolina 5-yard line. Anderson eventually plunged in, and with the two-point conversion pass from Manning to Bennie Fowler, Denver had its third Super Bowl title.

I had one of the Super Bowl 50 MVP ballots. Obviously, I wasn't the only one who voted for Von Miller.

"Knowing where I had been in my career, I really wanted to take advantage of where I was at," Miller said. "So I did all that stuff in the off-season."

Off he went in the months after his Super Bowl 50 heroics, crisscrossing the country for one engagement after another. *The Ellen DeGeneres Show* one day, competing on *Dancing with the Stars* week after week. Through it all, he dealt with testy contract negotiations that ended with Miller getting a six-year, $114,500,000 contract that made him the highest-paid defensive player in NFL history.

"My sixth year, I'm thinking to myself, How can I take it to another level?" he said. "How can I make it even bigger than what it was? I'm thinking I'm going to go win Defensive Player of the Year. I worked for that and that didn't happen for me, but I think the type of football that I played off the off-season that I had—I mean, I wanted to win Defensive Player of the Year, but I felt I had a good year."

He lost the 2016 DPOY award to Oakland's Khalil Mack by one vote—no doubt because the Broncos, who lost Manning to retirement, missed the playoffs for the first time in six years with a 9-7 record, while the Raiders reached the postseason for the first time in 14 years, with a 12-4 mark. Team success is a huge predictor of individual honors.

"That one vote, that sticks with you," Miller said. "It doesn't really bother me, but when you see how close it was and then the off-season that I had, it definitely makes you want to do it, and the time for me to do it is right now. I'm 28 years old."

No. 6 on the Broncos' all-time list. On his way up.

VON MILLER STATS

YRS	G	S	I	FF	FR	TCK
6	88	73.5	1	20	5	339

POSTSEASON

G	S	I	FF	TCK
7	6.5	1	2	26

7

FLOYD LITTLE

Running Back, 1967–75

There was never a John Elway Day.

Not while he was playing, there wasn't.

Peyton Manning, Terrell Davis—they never had an official day in their name.

There was a Floyd Little Day, though, and it occurred in the prime of the running back's career. Before Elway became a teenager, long before Elway became the general manager who would sign Manning—well before the Broncos had a winning season, for that matter—Little was the most beloved athlete in Denver sports history.

So much so that Little has long been dubbed "The Franchise." So much so that Broncos fans—not players or coaches, but a couple of fans—carried Little off the field immediately after he played his final home game at Mile High Stadium in 1975.

So much so that during an October 29, 1972, game against the Cleveland Browns, Broncos owner Gerald H. Phipps arranged to hold a "Floyd Little Day."

Such celebrations were not uncommon for active players in Major League Baseball at the time, but it was the first—and last—of its kind by the Broncos. It was Little's rushing title, with 1,133 yards in the 14-game season of 1971, that inspired the day in his honor.

Years later, the first thing Little remembered about his day was that he played against one of his longtime favorite teammates who became a former teammate after Game 4 of the regular season. Floyd Little Day was Game 7.

"Rich Jackson had just been traded to Cleveland, and he tried to put a hurt on me," he said of the defensive end who was nicknamed "Tombstone," and later joined Little in the Broncos' inaugural Ring of Fame class of 1984. "The whole game. I got a note from the governor [John Love] and from the mayor [William McNichols], the YMCA and Boys and Girls Club. I got a car [Chevy Blazer] and all kinds of gifts."

Fittingly, Floyd Little Day turned out like so many other days in Little's career: He played extremely well. But the Broncos lost.

Even with fellow future Pro Football Hall of Famer Leroy Kelly running for the Cleveland Browns, Little was the game's top rusher, with 79 yards on just 14 carries. His 5.6-yard average suggests that Little should have got the ball more. Little also turned a short pass from quarterback Charley Johnson into a 19-yard touchdown in the game, and he also had a 23-yard punt return.

To this day, Little is the most versatile offensive player in Broncos history.

Yet, the Broncos lost to the Browns, 27–20. Inside the 2-minute warning, Little came through with a 25-yard run to the Cleveland 18, but Johnson was picked off with 1:12 remaining.

A fitting conclusion to Floyd Little Day? After nine seasons, all with the Broncos, Little was the NFL's seventh-leading career rusher, with 6,323 yards. He added another 2,418 yards on 215 receptions and 3,416 yards on punt and kickoff returns.

Little's 12,157 all-purpose yards held as a Broncos record for 30 years, and remains second in team history to Rod Smith's 12,488. But to reiterate Little's versatility, Smith got 91 percent of his yards as a receiver; Little got 52 percent of his yards as a rusher.

Yet, in Little's nine seasons, the Broncos' average yearly record was 5-8-1. If it's unfathomable to think any player on such dreary teams could be so popular, perhaps some context would help.

Prior to Little's arrival, the Broncos' average record was 4-10 through their first seven seasons, from 1960–66. Perhaps one reason for Denver's futility in the old American Football League was the fact that their first-round draft picks kept signing with the more-established National Football League.

It wasn't until the common draft of 1967 that Little became the first of Denver's first-round draft picks to sign with the team. Merlin Olsen, Kermit Alexander, and Bob Brown no doubt would have improved the Broncos' fortunes in the early- to mid-1960s had they not opted to play instead with the NFL's Los Angeles Rams, San Francisco 49ers, and Philadelphia Eagles, respectively.

Little was not just a first-round draft pick, but one of the most highly touted college prospects ever.

First, Little followed the great Jim Brown and Heisman Trophy winner Ernie Davis as running backs to wear the famed number "44" for Syracuse.

Then, Little from 1964–66 became the first, three-time consensus All American since Doak Walker pulled off the three-peat from 1947–49.

Little might have been a four-time All American except that freshmen were not allowed to play varsity sports at the time. He finished fifth in the Heisman Trophy voting in back-to-back seasons of 1965–66.

Walker later worked one year as a Broncos scout, and it happened to be in 1966—Little's senior season at Syracuse. Walker strongly recommended Little to coach Lou Saban prior to the 1967 draft.

So, when the Broncos selected Little, the franchise had its first star before his first carry. And he came along at a time when it appeared the Broncos were in peril of moving from Denver.

In part because of the excitement generated by Little's arrival, a local group of deep pockets with a community spirit bought Bears Stadium for $1.8 million and deeded it to the City of Denver. The venue was expanded by more than 15,000 seats to 50,000, and was renamed Mile High Stadium.

Thus, Little's nickname as "The Franchise."

Not a bad twist of fate for a guy who thought sure the Broncos would take guard Gene Upshaw with their No. 6 overall pick and leave Little for Joe Namath's New York Jets, with the No. 12 selection.

Had he become a Jet, Little likely would have been a Super Bowl champion in his second season of 1968. Then again, imagine what he would have missed with the Broncos.

All you need to know about Little's impact on the Broncos is that he was selected as team captain for each of his nine seasons.

Floyd Little Day? When asked about the most vivid memories of his playing days with the Broncos that have popped into his fertile mind over the years, Little's "Day" didn't even make the top two.

"One was when I was drafted," Little said in late June of 2016. "I didn't think I would be drafted by the Broncos; I thought I was going to the Jets. Two was the last home game; they carried me off the field. And three was Floyd Little Day."

Later, Little's number "44" was the second of three numbers that were retired, following Frank Tripucka's number "18," and ahead of Elway's number "7."

In 2010, after a 35-year wait that was perplexing in its length, Little was inducted into the Pro Football Hall of Fame. He became the third of four Broncos to earn football immortality, following Elway and left tackle Gary Zimmerman, and ahead of tight end Shannon Sharpe.

Little had to wait until his senior-citizen years to enjoy the elite distinction, but as he turned 74 on the Fourth of July in 2016, he was grateful for how his Hall of Fame election has positively impacted his life.

"Oh, yeah, tremendously," he said. "It's no longer Floyd Little; it's Hall of Famer Floyd Little. In fact, I'm on my way to the airport as we speak, going to a function at the Denver Convention Center. You say, 'How did it change your life?' Almost 180 degrees."

FLOYD LITTLE STATS

YRS	G	A	Y	Y/C	TD	REC	Y	TD
9	117	1,641	6,323	3.9	43	215	2,418	9

8

RANDY GRADISHAR

Inside Linebacker, 1974–83

No one exemplifies the Broncos Bias that has inflicted Pro Football Hall of Fame voters more than Randy Gradishar.

He is in the argument for number-one all-time slight by the Hall of Fame modern-era voters' committee.

With apologies to Jack Lambert, Gradishar was the NFL's best middle linebacker in the seven-year period from 1975–81. Lambert played at 225 pounds, spread over a 6-foot-4 frame. Gradishar was 6-foot-3, 240. Who would you rather get hit by?

"As good as there ever was," said Tom Jackson, who played on the outside right of Gradishar in the Orange Crush's four linebacker set. "And I don't say that lightly. His competitive spirit. His ability to tackle—I don't think there's anything more important in football. He also collected, out of a '30' defense, 20 interceptions. Over 100 tackles every single year of his life.

"And yet I hear the argument made in the secrecy of those rooms where the Hall of Fame committee argues whether someone should be in or not is that he could not have made as many tackles as he's statistically credited for. And I happen to know that's a lie. Because I not only watched every one of them on the field, I also watched him in film session the next day. It's just ridiculous."

The problem is not, as so many have claimed, an East Coast bias that plagues the Hall of Fame voting committee. It's a discrimination singular to the Broncos.

The Broncos have made 22 playoff appearances since 1977. They have appeared in eight Super Bowls, winning three. Yet they have just five Hall of Famers (John Elway, Gary Zimmerman, Floyd Little, Shannon Sharpe, Terrell Davis). Compare this to other franchises that have been considerably less successful.

The St. Louis/Arizona Cardinals, who have never been anywhere near the East Coast, have made the playoffs just eight times since 1960. They have played in just one Super Bowl and have no championships.

Yet they also have five Hall of Fame players who started playing after 1960.

The Buffalo Bills, who have 17 playoff appearances, four Super Bowl appearances—four less than the Broncos—and *zero* Super Bowl titles (although Lou Saban did coach them to two AFL titles in 1964–65) have 10 Hall of Famers.

The Kansas City Chiefs have 19 playoff appearances but only twice reached the Super Bowl, none since the 1969 season. Yet, they have 11 Hall of Famers, 6 more than the Broncos.

On the Left Coast, the Los Angeles/San Diego Chargers were in the AFL Championship every year from 1960–65 and have three Hall of Famers from that span. That's fine. But since 1965, they've put five players in the Hall, even though they have just 13 playoff appearances and one Super Bowl game—in which they got crushed by the 49ers.

The snub of so many Broncos players is so outrageous, the senior committee should nominate a Bronco every year for the next five or six years until the injustice is rectified.

Starting with Randy Gradishar.

"He had the best instincts of any football player I've ever been around," said Steve Foley, who played right cornerback and free safety during Gradishar's heyday. "He was phenomenal getting to where the ball was going. And never missed tackles. Just did not miss.

"And short yardage? Goal line? I don't care who was coming through, this guy—and I got to watch him firsthand, because I played a yard away and a yard back on short yardage and goal lines—he had free rein. I was supposed to help clean up the alleys, and I couldn't believe the plays he made. Going over the top, coming through, I don't care if the running back was 240 pounds, Chuck Muncie, 250—they weren't going anywhere."

In some ways, I understand how Gradishar has been overlooked by some of the older Hall of Fame voters. As someone who grew up in the Chicagoland area, when I think of Gradishar, I think of his playing days at Ohio State. The great Woody Hayes once said that Gradishar "was the best linebacker I ever coached."

"That quote came out after I had got here to Denver," Gradishar said. "Woody and I had a pretty neat relationship. I always said he was a good coach—of course, he was a legendary coach—but he was a teacher of character. That really stuck with me. He always talked about paying it forward.

And I talk about that today wherever I go. That was his motto. Getting that comment from him, we always had a special relationship. I always respected his teaching of paying it forward."

The NFL Draft in 1974 wasn't anywhere near the big deal it is today. It was held in late January, and Gradishar was in his Buckeye Village apartments, waiting for a phone call. Gradishar was expected to go as high as No. 4 to the Chicago Bears, or No. 5 to the Baltimore Colts in the 1974 draft, but he wound up sliding to the Broncos at No. 14.

"I had knee surgery after my junior year," he said. "Played my whole senior year with a 'Joe Namath' Lenox brace and played every game, never had a problem."

Still, several teams had medical concerns about Gradishar's knee until Broncos coach John Ralston called Hayes, who set up a conversation with the linebacker's orthopedic surgeon. Ralston was satisfied.

"After that I called my parents," Gradishar said. "I'm 21 years old, and my dad said, 'Randy, I never told you, I was born in Pueblo.' I found out that day my dad and his brothers and sisters and mom and dad were born in Pueblo. I didn't even know where Colorado was. I had to go see on a map where Pueblo was in relation to Denver. I still have cousins down in Pueblo. Gradishars."

One more thing about growing up in the Midwest: From that famous Orange Crush defense, I thought Tom Jackson was its best player. Dick Enberg and Curt Gowdy, the NBC announcers for AFC games in the 1970s and '80s, often spoke—and relayed more anecdotes—about the engaging Jackson than the reserved Gradishar.

It's not Jackson's fault he's so entertaining. He belongs in the Hall of Fame, too, for his 14-year playing career as a Broncos outside linebacker and 29 years as the NFL's top studio analyst. It's just that Gradishar was the key cog in Joe Collier's 3-4 Orange Crush machine.

"Randy was relentless," said Billy Thompson, the captain and safety of the Orange Crush. "He was a tackling machine. But it was the way we were set up. The 3-4, and we had some of the best linebackers: Tommy Jackson, Randy, Bob Swenson, Larry Evans, Joe Rizzo. And Randy was the key. He and Rubin Carter. Rubin Carter kept Randy clean, because they doubled Rubin. And when they doubled Rubin, that freed up Randy.

"And Randy led our team in tackling probably the majority of the time he was there. A tremendous athlete, a guy you could count on when the chips are down. That's what we always used to say: 'Who can we count on when the chips are down?'"

Gradishar was asked to describe his style of linebacker play.

"I always thought of myself as a diagnostician," Gradishar said. "My asset was the mental preparation for each game. The ability to take on a head-on blocker along with having the ability to go laterally, east or west, in pursuit and not getting knocked down or tripped up or held. Having that lateral ability to get to each sideline.

"I learned a lot at Ohio State, reading the offensive players. The initial read, and not guessing but anticipating where the ball was going, or who was getting the ball. Anticipating came from reading the guard or the tackle or the back in the backfield with the snap. I also had many times when you could tell if the guard was coming straight up on you, or if he was going to block down. You could tell if he was going to pull because his fingertips weren't all that red. Or a back would cheat a little bit to the right or the left. That was all part of the mental game preparation each week."

There were many flashback moments in Gradishar's career. A 93-yard touchdown interception return at Cleveland in a 1980 game against Brian Sipe, who would win the NFL MVP Award that year. That was the key play in the Broncos' 19–16 win.

There were all those goal-line stand tackles.

But to Gradishar, like all members of the famed Orange Crush defense, nothing topped the 1977 season, when the Denver defense allowed a franchise-best 10.6 points per game. The Broncos went 12-2 in the regular season and beat the mighty Pittsburgh Steelers and defending Super Bowl champion Oakland Raiders to earn the first Super Bowl trip in Denver history.

You had to understand Broncomania to understand what the team meant to the city of Denver and the Rocky Mountain region.

"Yes, that season was probably the highlight of my pro career," Gradishar said. "All of the sudden we're 12-2 and going in to our first playoffs. Playing the divisional game against the Pittsburgh Steelers, the whole Super Bowl champion mystique they had with Terry Bradshaw, Franco Harris, their Steel Curtain defense. We had no chance from the media standpoint. There was no way we could ever win that game.

"We end up winning that game and play for the AFC Championship. That was a memorable milestone game, playing against Ken Stabler—a 'Hate the Raiders' guy. Media-wise there was no chance for us to win that game, either, and certainly no chance to win the Super Bowl. Of course, we didn't win that game [they lost 27–10 to Dallas].

"But I always tell people we laid the foundation, our defense, for many years after '77, that Orange Crush. We laid the foundation for the John Elway era, and then eventually winning some games and winning some

Super Bowls, and where we're at currently. Took a lot of pride in that era. Because we played together six, seven, eight years. We weren't the Orange Crush for one year, but for seven or eight years."

There was a personal serendipitous moment in Gradishar's life that exemplifies how the bond from those Orange Crush teams was unshakable in both life and death. Norris Weese was the Broncos backup quarterback to Craig Morton during the Orange Crush era. Weese's signature play was his fake-field-goal pass to kicker Jim Turner that went for a touchdown in a Broncos romp at Oakland in 1977.

Weese also came off the bench in Super Bowl XII to lead the Broncos to their only touchdown against the Cowboys.

Weese had a beautiful wife and three children when he got a bum break. In April 1993 he was diagnosed with a malignant tumor in his lower spinal cord. He fought for nearly two years before passing away at 43.

But before he did, Weese helped an old teammate find a better life.

"I was out in California, so I went to his home to say good-bye," Gradishar said. "And my wife, Beth, was at that time a nurse taking care of him in home care. That's how we originally met."

Beth and Randy have been married 15 years as of October 2016. He has three children from his first marriage, Paige, Meredith, and Mark.

Gradishar wound up announcing his retirement in the training camp prior to his 10th season of 1983—Elway's rookie season—effective at the end of the year. It was a surprise, because Gradishar still had plenty of high-level play left in him. He earned his sixth Pro Bowl in 1982 and picked up his seventh in his final season of 1983, when Gradishar had a whopping 133 solo tackles.

"Originally, my first couple years, I thought if I could get to 10 years, that would be a goal," Gradishar said. "Eventually, I kept playing; I worked in the offseason, did some career planning in my eighth, ninth, tenth year, trying to figure out what I was going to do afterwards.

"And then I told Dan Reeves and Joe Collier and [publicity director] Jim Saccomano that my tenth year would be my last year. What went into that was I wanted to leave at the top of my game. Not losing a step, not being what I used to be. That whole mind-set today is completely different than what it was back then. From a physical, mental, emotional, and spiritual standpoint, I made the decision.

"I talked to Merlin Olsen, among other vets [Merlin played 15 seasons before retiring after the 1975 season]. Prayed about that; a lot of people close to me prayed about it. Went up to Greeley and made that announcement, and media-wise, some of them didn't believe me. The USFL started that year and my contract was up after that year, so they thought I was making my retirement announcement to maybe get more money from the Broncos. But that wasn't the deal.

"So that last year I had a lot of fun knowing I wouldn't have to run any more sprints, or lift any more weights, and physically I wanted to go out at top of my game—which every year I felt I improved in various aspects of my game. For me that worked, and I felt great about making that decision, and I have never looked back."

Today, Gradishar works in corporate communication for Phil Long, the number-one auto dealer in Colorado. The company branched out to the Mount Carmel Center of Excellence, which helps military veterans and their families in wellness and transitional services after they serve their commitment. Gradishar spends 70 percent of his busy schedule with this endeavor.

On game days, he serves as the Broncos uniform inspector.

"[Former Bronco] Greg Boyd used to do that for 15, 16 years," Gradishar said. "John Elway called and said, Would you like to do this? And I said, Sure. It's been a lot of fun going along with the NFL guidelines on uniforms, from pads to colors of socks to shields on their facemasks and chin straps and shoe logos and those kinds of things. It's just been fun. The Broncos have been very receptive of that, and it's a lot of fun to stay involved and keep cheering on the Broncos."

Gradishar was a top-15 Hall of Fame finalist in 2003 and 2008, but 25 years after he retired, he was transferred to the pool of "senior candidates." One or two are nominated each year, and hopefully one of these years soon, the senior committee will correct the wrong and place Gradishar up for induction into the Pro Football Hall of Fame.

"All I know is, it's not my responsibility to promote myself for the Hall of Fame," Gradishar said.

RANDY GRADISHAR STATS

YRS	G	S	I	Y	FR	TD	TCK
10	145	19.5	20	335	13	4	2,049

9
KARL MECKLENBURG

Linebacker / Defensive End, 1983–94

When the Denver Broncos first laid eyes on Karl Mecklenburg, they didn't know what to do with him. This was before they waited until the 12th and final round to take him in the 1983 NFL Draft.

"The Broncos sent two different scouts to the University of Minnesota," Mecklenburg said. "One of them came back and said he's too slow to play linebacker, maybe he can be a lineman. The other came back and said he's too small to play lineman, maybe he can play linebacker."

It wasn't the Broncos' fault. Mecklenburg was a 240-pound noseguard for the Gophers who had a knack for slipping through and penetrating the backfield. The very definition of a tweener.

Twelve years and six Pro Bowls later, the Broncos never did figure out what to do with Mecklenburg. He wound up playing every position in the front seven: Nose tackle, both defensive ends, both outside linebacker positions, and both inside linebacker positions.

No wonder he's slipped through the Pro Football Hall of Fame cracks. Voters don't know how to position his candidacy.

"Karl Mecklenburg, he's a Hall of Famer because I've never seen a guy and I've never heard of one that's in the Hall of Fame that could play inside [linebacker] and rush the passer," said Wade Phillips, who was Mecklenburg's defensive coordinator for four seasons and head coach for two. "It's just a combination that nobody else had. He was a tremendous pass rusher.

"I've never been around anybody that played inside backer as well as he did. He was great at it. And then on third down, you'd put him outside and let him rush. He could have been a defensive end all the time. His stats would have gone up where his sacks are concerned, but he made so many tackles you had to play him inside at an inside backer."

How about this for versatility: In 1985, his first season as a starter, Mecklenburg had 13.0 sacks, 4 pass deflections, 5 forced fumbles, and 65 tackles. The next year, he was second on the team with 127 tackles and added 9.5 sacks—an almost unheard-of near triple-double.

In 1989, there were a team-high 143 tackles and 7.5 sacks on his stat sheet.

"The interesting thing was, Karl was playing defensive lineman and he wasn't going to make it," said Steve Foley, who had made his own switch from corner to safety by the time Mecklenburg broke in. "You could tell he was light for a defensive lineman. But you could also tell he had good instincts. And you've got to hand it to [defensive coordinator] Joe Collier. I'm telling you, Joe's a genius."

It took a while for even Collier to see greatness in Mecklenburg. No one spotted it early. To give an idea on how Mecklenburg was considered a roster-filling afterthought, in recent years, Mr. Irrelevant, or the last guy picked in the draft, came in at No. 253 to No. 256 overall. Mecklenburg wasn't drafted until the No. 310 pick.

That's the same draft where a guy named Elway went No. 1 overall, and after a holdout threat there, and a trade here, the quarterback became the most famous Bronco of all time.

Only that's not how it was when Mecklenburg was finishing up. The NFL instituted free agency and its first-ever salary cap for the 1994 season—ill-timed for a pair of Broncos standouts who were winding down their careers. The cap was at $34.6 million for the 1994 season, and the Broncos payroll was at $33 million, leaving Mecklenburg and another popular defensive player, safety Dennis Smith, on the streets as unemployed free agents.

Two days before the 1994 season, the Broncos finally signed Mecklenburg; he was the NFL's first $1 million inside linebacker in 1993, but he accepted a cap cut to $612,000 to play one more year.

It wasn't difficult to find Mecklenburg a roster spot. All they had to do was cut their final-round, undersized rookie offensive lineman, Tom Nalen. Luckily, Nalen was re-signed to the practice squad and promoted back to the roster and starting lineup two months later, but that's another story for a few chapters later in this book. (Smith wound up coming back for the same prorated, $612,000 deal a month into the season.)

Back to Mecklenburg's final season. In pregame introductions before their season opener against San Diego at old Mile High Stadium, the Broncos made a splash of Mecklenburg's return during the pregame introductions.

First, the 11 starting Broncos offensive players were introduced, Elway going last. Naturally, Elway received a hero's welcome.

But then the Broncos introduced Mecklenburg, who upstaged Elway by receiving a far more uproarious ovation.

Mecklenburg remains No. 2 on the Broncos' all-time sack list, with 79.0, and his 1,145 tackles are fourth to Randy Gradishar and the safety tandem of Steve Atwater and Smith—an incredible career that far exceeded the low expectations even Mecklenburg once set for himself.

Growing up in Edina, Minnesota, he figured he was destined for medicine. His mom was a former undersecretary of the Department of Health, Education, and Welfare. Dad was a physicist. Karl got his degree in biology even after transferring to Minnesota following his first two years of playing at Augustana College in South Dakota.

"I was a premed major in college," he said. "I was hoping to squeak by for two or three years and make enough money to pay my way to medical school. But I knew I loved football. I still didn't know if I'd like being a doctor.

"To me the biggest difference between college football and pro football is mental. There are some guys gifted enough athletically to play pro football, but college, you do what you do; they don't have meeting time or practice time to change what they do week to week. In the pros, everything is new every week. You're making all kinds of adjustments every week.

"It doesn't matter how big or fast or strong you are, if you don't know where you're going, they've got no use for you. I had commensurate athletic ability, but now the mental side could take over. Pro football was my spot. I was better in the pros than I was in high school or in college."

In his first two Broncos seasons, Mecklenburg was primarily used as a special teams grunt. He had just one start, although he did get more third-down snaps as time went on, picking up 2.0 sacks in 1983, 7.0 in 1984.

"I remember when Meck came in and he had this old beat-up car," said Broncos receiver Steve Watson, referring to Mecklenburg's 1969 Chevy Impala he got from his father-in-law. "I just remember, twelfth-round pick, really as a defensive lineman. And you're standing there looking at him, and compared to the other guys we had, you go, 'He's just not very big.' And he was about on his way out the door and then [linebackers coach] Myrel Moore says, 'Hey, Joe, I'd like to stand him up and see what happens.'

"And then that off-season, I mean, Meck worked his tail off getting himself ready to play this stand-up position. Every time they'd put him in, he was making a play. They'd spot substitute and they'd put him in and he'd make a play, and you go, 'He's making so many plays, he probably needs to be on the field.'"

Mecklenburg said it was a torn ligament in his elbow that first forced his move from nose tackle to defensive end. In the Broncos' first preseason game of 1983, he tied Gradishar and Tom Jackson with a team-high four tackles. Mecklenburg also had a sack. He wasn't going anywhere but on the roster.

Mecklenburg may have been light as defensive ends go, but the truth is, Dan Reeves and the Broncos coaching staff were pleasantly surprised by his 6-foot-3 stature.

"I was the opposite of Ted Gregory," Mecklenburg said about the Broncos' 1988 first-round pick, who was a good two inches shorter than his listed height of 6-foot-1. "I was taller than they thought I was going to be. They had me at 6-1. I hadn't been 6-1 since eighth grade."

Mecklenburg is a motivational speaker now, and has always been heavily involved in programs that open educational paths for children. As he flips steaks on the grill in the summer, what play or moment frequently pops into his head?

"It's plays I didn't make," he said. "There was one play, we're playing the Cowboys. [Tight end] Jay Novacek, he had an option route against me, and he cut outside and I tried to cut in front of him and [Troy] Aikman threw it two inches beyond my reach and he turned it up for a big score, and we wound up losing the game.

"Another one was against Buffalo in the AFC Championship Game [a 10–7 loss]. I was covering the tight end, third-and-7; he made a little juke move right at the first-down marker and I jumped all over it. He turned upfield and Simon Fletcher was hitting [Jim] Kelly and he threw a horrible, wobbly pass and it still got there. If I would've just done what I was supposed to do . . . it was enough yards to where they wound up kicking a field goal."

It's easy to like a guy who is good at what he does but has this kind of humility. I've always thought of it this way with the Broncos: Elway had two segments in his career. The first was the Reeves era, when Elway was sensational in leading the Broncos to three AFC championships, only to get drilled in the Super Bowls. The other was his four years with Mike Shanahan, when Elway went out with back-to-back Super Bowl titles.

Karl Mecklenburg was the second-best Broncos player during the first part of Elway's career.

Since sacks became an official statistic in 1982, Mecklenburg is one of just five players who had at least 1,000 tackles and 70 sacks. Three of those five are in the Hall of Fame (Rickey Jackson, Bruce Smith, and Reggie White). The other, Cornelius Bennett, was an outside linebacker like Jackson. No one but Mecklenburg played inside linebacker and pass-rushing defensive end.

And while Mecklenburg has been a top-25 semifinalist six consecutive years, from 2012–17, he has never made the cut to the 15 finalists.

"The problem is, I played all those positions," Mecklenburg said. "If you call me a middle linebacker, then I don't have as many tackles and interceptions as I should have. If you call me a pass rusher, I don't have as many sacks as I would have if I was rushing the passer all the time. You want to define players, and unfortunately for something like this, a lot more players were defined more than I was."

On Christmas Eve 1994, Mecklenburg and Smith played their final game at old Mile High. The Broncos lost a close one to the New Orleans Saints, but with 2:19 left in the game, a graphic of Mecklenburg popped up on the scoreboard and he received a standing ovation.

After the game, as he walked into the tunnel toward the home locker room, fans in the south stands gave him another standing O.

Asked about what he was most proud of during his 12 seasons with the Broncos, Mecklenburg didn't mention a sack or an interception or a forced fumble that turned defeat into victory.

"The thing I'm most proud of was my relationship with the other players," he said. "The situation I was in with Joe moving me all around . . . was a challenge. When he put me in somebody else's position, he's basically saying I can do this better than that other guy. When you're playing all seven front positions, they're moving you all over the place and other people have to adjust, other people have to move.

"I'm sure if I hadn't handled it with tact and carried on in a way that showed I wanted to do anything I could to help the team, and this wasn't my decision, it could have gotten pretty ugly.

"And it never did. To me that connection, that brotherhood to survive that decision-making from the coaches, that's the thing I'm proudest of— that it never got out of hand."

KARL MECKLENBURG STATS

YRS	G	S	I	TCK
12	180	79.0	5	1,145

10
ROD SMITH
Receiver, 1994–2007

When I'm in a frivolous mood, I'll occasionally post on social media or a blog site a song that I always introduce as "a top 10 song of all time."

Over the years, I have come up with a list of well more than 50 songs that have made my top 10.

This 50 Greatest Broncos project presented a similar overload of worthy choices but a much firmer boundary. While working and reworking the Broncos 50-player list, at no place did I flip-flop more than at No. 10.

Besides my eventual selection of Rod Smith, I also had earlier top-50 versions where cornerback Louis Wright, safety Steve Atwater, and safety Dennis Smith took turns at No. 10. I also considered center Tom Nalen, whose accomplishments were deserving of consideration.

I didn't have trouble with my top 9 selections. There was some difficulty in the arrangement. I hated to place Floyd Little as low as No. 7. And as I stated, it was a struggle between Shannon Sharpe and Champ Bailey at No. 4. But there are the 50 Greatest Broncos of All Time, and there is the top 10.

In an informal poll, players from the 1990s predominantly went with Atwater and his eight Pro Bowls for the No. 10 spot. Players from the 1980s thought Dennis Smith was a better all-around safety than Atwater. Wright got the nod from many of the players from the 1970s.

But there was something about Rod.

"I don't know what the factors are in your ranking, but Rod was the greatest teammate," said quarterback Jake Plummer, who was No. 39 among the 50 Greatest Broncos. "He was so supportive of me. He took a lot of the leadership responsibilities off my plate so I could be me and not have to be that *guy* day in and day out. He knew when to step up and call guys out in the huddle. I always kind of leaned on him.

"He really was the epitome of an overachiever and a professional. I never doubted throwing the ball in his direction. I never doubted him being ready for a game."

Plummer recalled one week of practice when he was banged up and the Broncos backup quarterback was gimpy and they were low on passers.

"Rod went 9 for 9 one time in a 7 on 7 [drill]," Plummer said. "It wasn't checkdowns, either. He was hitting skinny posts and throwing comebacks. I said this guy knows the game so well he could probably play quarterback. He was such a student of the game. And he cared about his teammates. I wish I could have played 10 years with that dude. He was a phenomenal, phenomenal guy. Fun in the locker room. Laughed all the time."

Of the top four players I considered—again, it was Rod Smith, Wright, Atwater, and Dennis Smith—Rod Smith might have been the fourth best in terms of talent. But the combination of his overachieving production, leadership, longevity, and willingness to do all the little things for the sake of victory—namely, return punts after he was already an established star receiver, and block in the running game—is why I gave him the coveted No. 10 slot.

"I appreciate that," Smith said. "I wouldn't take anything away from any of those other guys if you put them in that spot. There's probably another five, six people you could have put in the top 10, just the way they carried themselves in their careers. We all played in different eras.

"I think what you've done with the people you've mentioned is, we tried to define—if you say Denver Broncos, you could mention one of those names every time. Each of those identified with the Broncos. Except for Peyton Manning, because he played so long with the Indianapolis Colts, and then he played with the Broncos his last four years. Of course, you can't deny that guy—he's a first-ballot Hall of Famer—but other than that, the other guys lived, breathed orange and blue pretty much the majority of their careers.

"I didn't grow up watching the Broncos, but I have studied them. A lot of those guys, I'd pick their brains, and they defined the Broncos organization during the tough times. Those 14, 15 guys you mentioned, they defined what the Broncos were about. Hard workers, blue-collar. Always play with a chip on their shoulders because we all felt our franchise was always disrespected. It's almost like we pledge allegiance. I appreciate them."

See there. What Smith just said is why he's a top-10 Bronco of all time. I also think he deserves a more-definitive symbol of immortality. Everybody has pet peeves when it comes to players inducted or not elected into the Pro Football Hall of Fame.

What's annoyed me is all this chatter about whether Terrell Owens and Randy Moss are Hall of Famers while Smith is not even dropped into the discussion. Even if T.O. did not make it past the 10 modern-era candidates vote in the first two years he was eligible, and Moss doesn't become eligible until 2017, their eventual election is certain.

Yet, through 2017, Smith has yet to make it to the semifinalist round of 25. Smith has been among the 100-plus players nominated for the Hall of Fame each year since he was eligible in 2012. Preposterously, he's never made it to the next cut.

Receiver seems to be the one position where it's mostly about stats. And numbers should matter. Stats don't lie about production. But stats should be at least equal, if not secondary, to how a player helps his team win.

And when it came to winning performances, Smith was the Tom Brady of receivers. Know how they give quarterbacks a win or loss for every game they start? I did the same thing for Smith, Owens, and Moss. Here are their records in games started, including playoffs:

RECEIVER	W-L	PCT	PLAYOFF STARTS	SUPER BOWL RINGS
Rod Smith	111-59	.653	12	2
Terrell Owens	124-89	.582	12	0
Randy Moss	112-96	.538	15	0

Smith had a better career winning percentage than John Elway (.645). And if you think Smith was beholden to Elway, know this: Smith only started two seasons with Elway. Both years ended with Super Bowl trophies. In the years without Elway, Smith not only had his best statistical seasons, averaging 84 catches and 1,075 yards in eight seasons, but he also helped the Broncos to a 77-52 record—a .596 winning percentage that still exceeds that of Owens and Moss.

Smith's career was epitomized by the fact he had zero catches in his first Super Bowl win to finish the 1997 season, and five catches for 152 yards, including an 80-yard touchdown reception that was the biggest play to win his second Super Bowl in 1998.

Smith was a willing blocker for Terrell Davis in one Super Bowl and the number-one receiver in the next. Smith is the Broncos' all-time leading receiver in catches, yards, and touchdowns, even though in 11 of his 12 playing seasons, the Broncos had a running back rush for at least 1,000 yards.

Yes, receiving stats should matter to a receiver's candidacy. But it shouldn't stop there.

"True story," said Tom Mills, Smith's longtime agent. "In early 2002, we were negotiating Rod's contract extension. The club wanted him to accept some performance incentives that were triggered by statistical thresholds. You know, catches, yards, those type of things.

"Rod could have reached those incentives without doing anything extraordinary. But he just couldn't get excited about the concept. He was coming off his best statistical season in 2001 [a league-leading 113 catches], but the team only went 8-8.

"In 1997, he caught 70 passes and the team won the Super Bowl. He much preferred catching fewer passes if it meant the team would win more games."

Smith's contract was adjusted so that his incentives were based on wins and playoff rounds, not stats.

About those stats. Smith is the Broncos' all-time leader in the Holy Trinity of receiving stats, with 849 catches (27th all-time in the NFL through the 2016 season), 11,389 yards (31st), and 68 touchdowns (42nd). Based on numbers alone, Smith probably does fall short of the Hall of Fame. The argument would be that if Smith goes in, does that mean every Irving Fryar, Derrick Mason, Henry Ellard, and Muhsin Muhammad are Hall of Famers?

No. But Michael Irvin had fewer career catches and touchdowns than Smith, and only a few more yards, and he went into the Hall of Fame. Why? Because Irvin, for all the controversy he stirred, had an impact on three Super Bowl title teams. Smith played a big part in two Super Bowl titles.

There is more to Smith's candidacy. Besides his borderline Hall of Fame stats and Hall of Fame–caliber winning percentage, he is a terrific story. Kurt Warner was elected into the Hall of Fame in 2017 in no small part because of his rags-to-riches story. An undrafted grocery-store stocker who became a Super Bowl MVP and two-time NFL MVP.

Smith was also undrafted. He spent his rookie year on the Broncos' 1994 practice squad. He finally got a chance to dress in the third game of 1995, and caught a 43-yard touchdown against Darrell Green for the game-winner at the buzzer for his first career reception. Yet Smith didn't get a chance to play receiver full-time until two years later.

Smith is still the NFL's all-time leader in receiving yards among undrafted players, and is second to Wes Welker in catches and touchdown receptions. Like Brady, Smith seemed to play his entire career with a chip on his shoulder. Brady, because he was a sixth-round draft pick. Smith, because he was undrafted.

"Those weren't chips, though," Smith said in a February 2017 interview. "Those were more like trees. My word was lack. L-a-c-k, lack. It was not having things I wanted, things I desired, things I felt I deserved—they drove me every day to this day. There are still things I want for my family, for my kids. I want good things for everybody. I just believed if you will your way to it, and work your way to it, it will happen."

That determined spirit was bred in the projects of Texarkana, Arkansas, where Smith and his three sisters and one brother were raised by their mom. He was an all-state high school quarterback who went to Division II Missouri Southern to play that position. He sat the bench as a freshman quarterback, then received a medical redshirt in 1989 because of a torn arch in his foot. In his sophomore year of 1990, he split time between quarterback and receiver.

As a junior in 1991, Smith became a full-time receiver, and wouldn't you know, he led the nation with 1,439 receiving yards off 60 catches. He tore his ACL early in the third game of his senior year and received a hardship exemption. So he returned for his second senior year—sixth year in all—at Missouri Southern and became a Harlon Hill finalist, with 63 catches for 986 yards and 13 touchdowns—all while finishing up three degrees. They weren't PE and recreation degrees, either (not that there's anything wrong with those studies). Smith's degrees: economics and finance, general business, and marketing and management.

"It was a struggle," Smith said of overcoming two season-ending injuries in college. "But six years was why I was able to get three degrees."

The brains and leadership he developed from school and the quarterback position were qualities he brought with him to the receiver position. Understand: Receivers are the most isolated members of the team, and therefore they can be the most selfish, stat-me players. Smith was an exemplary exception.

"The greatest teammate I've ever played with," said Broncos safety John Lynch, a Ring of Fame safety. "I don't say that lightly with some of the other guys I played with. What he did for a team in terms of his selflessness, the way he worked. Some people are leaders by virtue of the way they work, some are vocal leaders. Rod was all of the above. He was such a professional with the way he did things. His story, being an undrafted free agent, was inspirational. And then, he wasn't afraid to be vocal."

Smith believes his quarterback upbringing did help him succeed at receiver.

"One thing about quarterback, you have to know where everybody goes," he said. "You have to know what everybody's assignment is. The quarterback has to know everything. You've got to know down and distance. Personnel. Who's in what spot, what are the advantages, the weaknesses on certain plays if you're going to audible. Pretty much my whole career—pretty much my life—I always studied football as a quarterback. So if we came out of the huddle and the quarterback forgot what the play was or what his read was, I could tell him."

It took Smith a while to sell the Broncos. There were 29 receivers taken in the 1994 NFL Draft, 17 in the first three rounds. None of them were named Rod Smith. In fairness to the NFL, he probably would have been drafted had it not been for his two major injuries at Missouri Southern, in particular the ACL. It was Broncos scout Charlie Lee who most believed in Smith and signed him in 1994. The Broncos took a flyer on Smith, knowing they could stash him on their practice squad for a year so he could gain strength in his leg and body.

And then in 1995, Smith credits first-year receivers coach Mike Heimerdinger in developing him.

"If it wasn't for Charlie Lee and Mike Heimerdinger, there's no me," Smith said later.

After spending his rookie year on the practice squad, Smith still didn't have a catch two games into his second season, and 59 minutes and 54 seconds into his third.

It was the first NFL game Smith played in, and the score between the Broncos and Washington was tied, 31–31. It was fourth-and-10 with the ball at the Washington 43, and just 6 seconds remaining in regulation.

Elway didn't throw the ball up in typical Hail Mary arching fashion, but with 43 yards of zip. Smith snagged it away from Green, Washington's perennial All Pro cornerback, came down with it on his back, and hung on. Time expired as Smith fell backward into the end zone.

"It was the start of the greatest receiver in Broncos history," said receiver Mike Pritchard, who was double-covered on his fly pattern on the opposite side of the field.

It still took a while for the Broncos to believe in Smith as a receiver. He had just five more catches in 1995 and 16 in 1996, when he made his mark as a punt returner. It wasn't until 1997 that Smith had his breakout season, with 70 catches for 1,180 yards, and a career-best 12 touchdowns.

Smith was 27 at the time—a little old to be breaking out as receivers go—but it would be the first of nine consecutive seasons when he had at least 70 catches. Smith had an 80-yard touchdown reception from Elway in Super Bowl XXXIII that was the biggest play in the Broncos' whipping of the Atlanta Falcons, but of all his catches, he said his favorite was the first.

"My boyhood dream of playing in the NFL was always to play quarterback, to be honest," Smith said. "I played quarterback in the neighborhood and sandlot football games. Now it's the first game I'm active and John looked up and saw this guy he didn't know."

It was the only football game Elway had ever played in—high school, college, or pro—where he threw a touchdown pass on the final play to win the game.

"I pretty much went through everything with Rod," said Broncos kicker Jason Elam. "I remember me, Rod, and Jeff Campbell going up to grab lunch one day. And Rod is just hoping to make the team. We all saw it. He was in a competition with Mike Pritchard and Anthony Miller, they were Pro Bowl guys, and Rod was winning every single day.

"And then I remember that Redskins game in—I'm pretty sure it was '95. He was up against Darrell Green, one of the all-time best corners. And it came down to the end of the game and it would have been a 60-yard field goal. And I was running over to Shanahan, and I was right in Shanahan's ear, 'I can make it, Coach! I can do it! I can make it!'

"And Shanahan didn't even acknowledge me. He ran the play where Rod jumps up and catches it—I think it might have been one of his first catches ever—over Darrell Green. And the stadium explodes and I remember saying to Shanahan as he's taking off his headset: 'All right, that works, too.' That thrust Rod into an amazing career."

Smith started feeling pain in his left hip in 2004, an injury that didn't stop him from making his third Pro Bowl in 2005, but it eventually ended his career. Surgery following the 2006 season didn't take, but Shanahan kept him on the physically-unable-to-perform list until late November, when it was determined that Smith's career was finished.

"You could always tell, Mike Shanahan, he treated the game like a business, but yet there was a respect level and a love and admiration he had for Rod that was palpable," Lynch said. "You could feel it, and you could understand it once you played with him."

ROD SMITH STATS

YRS	G	REC	Y	TD
13	183	849	11,389	68

11

LOUIS WRIGHT

Cornerback, 1975–86

There was the pick six off the Snake when the Broncos finally broke through against the Oakland Raiders in that magical season of 1977, the year Louis Wright came into his own as a Pro Bowl cornerback and was named *Football Digest*'s AFC Defensive Player of the Year.

There was that fumble recovery for a touchdown in the opening seconds of the Monday Night Blizzard game against the Green Bay Packers in mid-October.

There was his game-winning, 60-yard touchdown return in overtime off Dennis Smith's blocked field goal against San Diego in 1985.

There were 26 interceptions in all and five touchdowns, including one off a lateral from linebacker Randy Gradishar, but when asked about the favorite play of Wright's 12-year career with the Broncos, safety Billy Thompson brought up one of his teammate's 846 tackles.

"I saw him make a play in Kansas City I'll never forget," Thompson said. "It was fourth down and a zillion to go and Kansas City came up with a fake punt. And the guy broke the line of scrimmage and was going for a touchdown. Louis came from the other side of the field, tracked him down, and tackled him on the 1. We held the four downs on the 1 and won the football game. That's one of the greatest plays I've ever seen."

It was the play Wright picked out, too, when asked in February 2017 to name his favorite moment. He went back 40 years to that great 1977 season. The Broncos were 8-1 entering Arrowhead Stadium against their AFC West rival and leading the Chiefs, 14–7, with about three minutes remaining.

It was fourth-and-17 at the Kansas City 48 and Chiefs interim coach Tom Bettis sent out punter Jerrel Wilson. The snap was to the upback, Mark Bailey, who handed off to Ray Burks, a linebacker. Even though the situation all but screamed for a fake punt, the Broncos were caught off guard.

Burks, in his first and only NFL carry, ran 51 yards. He needed 52.

"In those days you played those special teams," Wright said. "So I was outside and they do a fake, not a fumblerooski, but a fake to the upback, and he takes off running. So I'm looking across the field and I'm like, 'What's going on over there?' I started running over there, and pretty soon I realize he's got the ball and he started running for a touchdown.

"So I'm chasing him, but not fast enough. I can see the big red end zone coming up. I dove, grabbed his foot, tripped him up, and he fell at the 1-yard line. So everybody's coming out on the field, [Bob] Swenson, [Randy] Gradishar, Tom Jackson, and they think he scored and they're talking about blocking the extra point.

"They're coming out of the huddle, and meanwhile, I'm still trying to convince everybody it's not an extra point."

On first-and-goal at the 1, Ed Podolak rammed up the middle for no gain, stopped by Barney Chavous and Wright. Then it was Bailey up the middle. Gradishar nailed him. Again, no gain. Now there's 1:15 left in regulation.

There was a reverse to tight end Walter White. Jackson on the outside wasn't fooled, and the play lost 6.

On fourth-and-goal from the 7, quarterback Mike Livingston overthrew his intended receiver, incomplete. Denver's ball with 25 seconds left. Ball game.

"And that's when I knew we had something special," Thompson said.

"I'm really proud of that play," Wright said.

Before they used the term, Wright was one of the NFL's preeminent "cover corners." It wasn't until Deion Sanders in the early 1990s that "cover corner" came into vogue. By 2004, the Broncos' Champ Bailey made more than $7 million a year as a cover corner. The price was more than $10 million per in 2011, and the top corners were getting $15 million a year by 2017.

A tall cornerback at 6-foot-2, Wright never made more than $400,000, which was his salary in his final season of 1986. The rookie minimum salary in 2017 is now $465,000.

"Ahead of his time," said Jackson of Wright. "Ahead of his time not only in his skill set, but his size, his speed, his ability to cover. As complicated as the Orange Crush was, we went into a game with, 'You 10 guys have to be totally coordinated with everything you do—Louis, you take their best receiver. You take Lynn Swann, you take Steve Largent, John Jefferson, and you shut him down, and we'll win.'"

Wright made five Pro Bowls in his career, played in every game in 8 of his 12 seasons, 166 total, and helped the Broncos reach two Super Bowls (he started in "The Drive" game at Cleveland in the 1986-season AFC Championship).

He was elected into the Broncos Ring of Fame in short order, as he went in seven years after he retired. But surprisingly, Wright has not received much consideration for the Pro Football Hall of Fame. He and Gradishar are considered the top Broncos candidates in the senior pool.

Perhaps one reason why his bust is not bronzed in Canton, Ohio, is because his 26 interceptions are light compared to some other cornerbacks. The story sometimes told about the legend of Louis Wright is that if he had better hands, he would have had well over 40 interceptions.

"I've heard that," Wright said. "But I had one year, I think it was [1983], I had six interceptions that year. I made up my mind that's what I was going to do that year, and I made the Pro Bowl and all that stuff, but I gave up so many big plays and touchdowns, and I was like, 'No, no, the trade-off's not worth it.

"I took some chances on plays I shouldn't have. I had six interceptions—that was my best season total in 12 years. But I made too many mistakes."

So, does that mean interceptions are overrated when it comes to measuring a defensive back?

"It's not overrated, but I think if you put it into an equation and you plugged in numbers, the weight you'd give interceptions is too high," he said. "If it's third down and 8 at a critical stage and you force them to punt, you do that a couple times a game, I think that's worth more than an interception deep in your own territory. That year told me I'd rather have [fewer] interceptions and shut the receiver down."

Louis Donnell Wright lived one day of his youth in Texas and the rest in Bakersfield, California. The one day in Texas was his first day, in his parents' hometown of Gilmer.

"They were living in California, and in the 1950s, you know, black people couldn't just walk into any hospital and have a baby," Wright said. "So my mom went back home where she knew the doctor and had all three of her children. I have another brother and sister. We were all born there but we never lived there."

Back in Bakersfield, where the summer days could reach suffocating temperatures, Wright and his brother Fred grew up with a father-instilled work ethic. Glover C. Wright had moved from Gilmer, Texas, to Bakersfield to take a job delivering mail for the US Post Office.

"When he got off work he was a gardener," Wright said. "He'd go cut people's yards. He was a workaholic. So as soon as we'd get out of school, he'd load us in the truck and we'd cut yards till the sun went down. I think I was in third grade when he first started taking me."

Glover was a fair man, and would pay his kids. He kept a log of their hours in his truck.

"Back then it was $10, $15 a yard. But it was a little something," Louis Wright said. "Every day you had to go to work except Sundays. Unless you had a school activity. That's the only thing that could get you out of work. Naturally, I was in Student Council. I was in sports. I was in everything. 'Sorry, Dad—I have a track meet today.' 'Okay.' Whatever activity I could get in, I was there."

In sixth grade at Colonel Thomas Baker Elementary School, Wright won an officiated school sprint-off. Fastest kid in school. He played receiver and defensive end, believe it or not, in high school, and wound up attending Arizona State on a football scholarship for coach Frank Kush.

Gulp. The same taskmaster Frank Kush who John Elway didn't want to play for when he was drafted No. 1 overall by the Baltimore Colts in 1983.

"I know. But I kind of liked him," Wright said. "I don't know why, but I kind of liked him."

Maybe after being raised by Glover C. Wright, Frank Kush was a pushover. Wright took advanced classes above his head as a freshman, and while he didn't flunk out, the combination of struggles in the classroom and getting little attention from Kush led to a transfer back home to Bakersfield Junior College.

Where Wright sat on the bench his entire sophomore year.

"I think I wound up playing six or seven plays," Wright said. "The whole year. Bakersfield Junior College, I sat on the bench. I rode it out and went out for track. And I did really good at track, so I got a track scholarship to San Jose State. I had given up on football."

Know how almost every successful person wouldn't have made it if not for that one person who believed in him? For Louis Wright, that fateful person was Jim Colbert, a defensive backs coach at San Jose State.

Colbert came to a track practice in January 1973, seeking out Wright. He had heard, the coach said, that Wright was once a defensive back. A defensive back who, as Colbert looked around at his surroundings, could run.

"I said, 'Yeah, I used to play, but I haven't played in a couple years, really,'" Wright recalled. "He convinced me to come out. He said, 'If you don't make it, fine, but just give me an opportunity to work with you.' Which I did. I came out in August. If he didn't come out to track practice that day, I don't think I would have ever played football."

It was Colbert's only year of coaching at San Jose State. Talk about serendipity.

"He was a good coach," Wright said. "He taught me footwork and angles. He was really good."

In Wright's next season as a senior, he played well enough to earn a spot in the Senior Bowl. The North team's coaches were the Denver Broncos staff, led by John Ralston and Joe Collier.

Still, when Wright was the Broncos' first-round selection, No. 17 overall, in the 1975 draft—one spot behind New England tight end Russ Francis, and one spot ahead of Dallas linebacker Thomas "Hollywood" Henderson—he was surprised.

"I was like, 'What?'" Wright said. "They never said a word to me the whole week at the Senior Bowl. They never gave an inkling they even knew who I was."

He was still playing at a high level late in his career, recording five interceptions in 1985 and three more in 1986, for a combined total of 100 return yards. But he decided to retire around training camp, 1987.

"I thought about it, and you know what—there is no perfect time to leave the NFL," Wright said. "Or any sport. Whether you're Muhammad Ali or Michael Jordan. It's almost impossible to retire at the exact perfect time. Either you retire too early or you retire too late.

"I said, I'd rather retire too early than too late. I just made that decision. I didn't want the coaching staff to call me into the office and say, 'Hey, you're not doing it, and we're going to have to cut you.' And I didn't want to have to say, 'Those jerks, they cut me.' I didn't want any friction on either side. Thank you for 12 years. What more can a guy ask for?"

He went back to San Jose State to finish his degree, then got in the geology field for one and a half years, an occupation that paid well but too often took him away from home to desolate places. He wound up teaching and coaching in the Aurora and Denver school systems, professions he still held in 2017 at the age of 64.

"A lot of my friends and family at my age are retired," Wright said. "But I just love doing what I'm doing. I'm probably going to retire, but health-wise, I'm blessed. I've got a good job, I've got good kids. I say a prayer every day. I don't know what else I could ask for."

How about a nomination from the seniors' committee for the Pro Football Hall of Fame?

"It would be an incredible honor if it was to happen," Wright said. "The people that are in there, I have the utmost respect for, because you have to do a lot to even be considered to get in there. Some of the people that have been elected, especially in the defensive back category, I think—I'm not better than them, but I think I was as good as them.

"But I think the biggest enjoyment and satisfaction I have is my teammates and my coaches and people I was with for 12 years. I really think—and I could be wrong—but I really think they could depend on me. They can look me in the face and know that this was my assignment, this was my job to win the game, and I would come through. I felt I did everything I could for my teammates."

LOUIS WRIGHT STATS

YRS	G	I	Y	FR	TD
12	166	26	360	11	4

12 (TIE)

— **DENNIS SMITH** —

Corner/Safety, 1981–94

At no other position did the Denver Broncos have more great players than at safety. It started from the beginning, when Austin "Goose" Gonsoulin had six interceptions in the first two games the Broncos ever played, in 1960.

The great back-end performance continued with Billy Thompson in the 1970s, Steve Foley in the early 1980s, then Mike Harden, Dennis Smith, Steve Atwater, Tyrone Braxton, John Lynch, Brian Dawkins, and, more recently, T. J. Ward and Darian Stewart.

To show how strong Broncos safeties have been over the years, there are five at that position in the Broncos Ring of Fame (Gonsoulin, Thompson, Smith, Atwater, Lynch, and, one of these years, Foley should be the sixth), yet only four quarterbacks (Frank Tripucka, Charley Johnson, Craig Morton, and John Elway).

With apologies to the great Goose, it is generally agreed that Atwater and Smith were the models for the Broncos' proud safety tradition. Hotly debated is, who was better, Atwater or Smith, Smith or Atwater?

"You've got to put him in front of me," Atwater said. "We were in a game, I don't remember who we were playing, but I was running. I was full speed and I thought I was going to make the tackle and Dennis comes flying by me and slams into the guy. I'm like, 'Oh man.'

"He was an amazing athlete. And one of the finest I got to personally witness, and I saw how he played and practiced. He taught me a lot. It was an honor to play with him."

Atwater, though, played in eight Pro Bowls (only John Elway earned more berths among Broncos, with nine) to Dennis Smith's six (only five Broncos have more). Atwater has also been receiving stronger consideration for the Pro Football Hall of Fame.

"I always tell him if he ever gets into the Hall of Fame, I'll feel like I got there, too, because I feel like I was a mentor to him and I taught him the right way to play," Smith said. "That's what I'm most proud of in my relationship with him."

Smith or Atwater, Atwater or Smith. The subject has been debated many times in the Mile High Stadium press box over the years, especially from 1989–94, when Smith and Atwater were teammates. I decided they were so inseparable, they had to be ranked together. Tied at No. 12.

"I'm honored to be that high and be considered alongside Steve," Smith said in March 2017. "What I always tell people, the difference between us is, when I came into the league—a lot of people don't remember this—but I was playing corner. I was a third-down corner for almost the first half of my career. I was a nickelback. That would maybe separate us because I was a different type of player."

Smith was a more versatile defensive back, and he also played more of a quarterback role in the secondary. Atwater was a safety/linebacker. A big hitter. A huge hitter.

But you didn't want Atwater lining up against the slot receiver on third down. Smith was often asked to take on such a task. He went to a Pro Bowl when he was a safety / third-down nickel, and he went to multiple Pro Bowls when was strictly a safety.

Advantage, Smith.

"But also what I tell people what separates us overall is he played so well in the Super Bowls," Smith said. "He won Super Bowls and he played well in Super Bowls. Something I didn't do. I had my opportunities and that separates us, too. Those two things are what separate us."

Advantage, Atwater.

So, we're right back where we started. The first part, all-around play, goes to Smith. The second part, Super Bowl rings, goes to Atwater.

A tie for best safety in Broncos history. A bit trite? Yeah, well, so?

"I think I'll take the second part, though," Smith said. "The most important thing for every player is to win the Super Bowl. And that's something we never could accomplish. And we had three cracks at it, so I can't complain. I had my opportunities. Steve's teams were able to get it done. And that's what I always tell him, that's what separates us, is we won his Super Bowls. Not only that he was a big factor in the team winning them."

I polled other players who made the top 50 about the great safety debate, and those whose best years were from the 1970s and '80s picked Smith, because of his overall versatility and supreme athleticism. The players from the 1990s and those Super Bowl teams picked Atwater.

"If Dennis Smith had a memorable name he'd be in the Hall of Fame," said Karl Mecklenburg, a linebacker who retired with Smith following the 1994 season.

"Dennis could bait a tight end, let him get open, and then close the gap so fast," said Foley, who was Smith's starting safety partner from 1983–86. "He was a great cover. That was the difference. Steve was a big, in-the-box player. Obviously, he's bigger; he was built like a linebacker with defensive back speed, but really not a one-on-one cover guy.

"While Dennis played a little corner—Joe [Collier] liked to get you some corner experience just so you would know what the corners are going through when you've got to help them."

There was one game that encapsulates Smith's otherworldly skill. A 7-foot-2 high jumper at Santa Monica High School, Smith was also a 7-2 high jumper at USC.

"As high as I ever got," he said with a tinge of disappointment, but not a trace of conceit. "I couldn't clear higher than 7-2."

Geez. You've heard the expression, "rich people's problems"? Leveling out at 7-foot-2 in the high jump is a world-class-athlete problem.

Anyway, six days after the Broncos had defeated San Francisco, 17–16, in the famous "Snowball Game"—where a fan's decent aim with a thrown snowball distracted San Francisco 49ers holder Matt Cavanaugh enough for him to muff a snap on what would have been a chip-shot field goal—the Broncos won another improbable game on November 17, 1985, as Smith blocked two field goals in a 30–24 overtime victory against the San Diego Chargers.

Smith first blocked a 47-yard field goal by Ralf Mojsiejenko in the first quarter, keeping San Diego's lead at 7–0. The Chargers' Gary Anderson had returned the opening kickoff 98 yards for a touchdown.

With the score tied, 24–24 after four quarters, Dan Fouts led San Diego to the Broncos' 23-yard line on the first drive of overtime. Bob Thomas lined up for a 40-yard field goal, but his kick was blocked.

Many thought it was Smith who blocked it, but while he did storm up the middle with his arms raised, he said 32 years later: "I didn't block that one."

Daniel Hunter did. Didn't matter, because Broncos safety Mike Harden had called a time-out just before the snap because he thought that's what coach Dan Reeves was signaling from the sideline.

The Chargers got another chance to kick the game-winner. Improbably, Smith blocked the next one, too. Thomas's kick banged off Smith's forearm.

Broncos cornerback Louis Wright picked up the ball and ran it 60 yards for a touchdown as old Mile High Stadium trembled from the upper deck to the playing field.

Per the Broncos legendary public relations director Jim Saccomano, Smith was the only player in NFL history to lead his team in tackles (nine) and passes defensed (three) while blocking two field-goal attempts in the same game. It was also the only game in NFL history when the first and last touches of a game resulted in touchdowns.

"He did stuff other people couldn't do," Wright said of Smith. "He would say what he was going to do and then do it."

"I blocked a field goal earlier in the game, so I knew there was an opportunity there," Smith said. "The amazing thing about that play was, even on the one where we called a time-out, Louis Wright winds up with the ball. How did he know to be in position to get that ball every time it happened? Both times it happened, Louis Wright had the ball in his hands and was running toward the end zone. Then it happened for real and there he was again. How did he do that? There's a guy who should be in the Hall of Fame."

As you can tell from his praise-sharing comments, Smith was a heckuva teammate. He was raised well by Wilbert and Dorothy Smith in Santa Monica, a beach community 14 miles west, and a little south, of Los Angeles.

Wilbert was a big, country man from Texas who wound up providing for his family as a truck driver. Dorothy was from Louisiana until her dad, Dennis's grandfather, bought property in Santa Monica in the 1930s.

"Which is unheard of," Smith said. "My grandparents and my family still have the property today."

Growing up outside L.A., Smith was all in on John Wooden's UCLA Bruins, who won 10 NCAA basketball champions in the 12-year period, from 1964–75.

"I could name you the starting lineups of those UCLA teams," Smith said. "Bill Walton, Sidney Wicks, Curtis Rowe, Henry Bibby, Gail Goodrich. I knew all of them back then."

Through their fertile minds, Smith and his buddies brought those Bruins with him to his backyard.

"I was always outside," said Smith, a youth in the '60s and teenager of the '70s. "Back then we were outside. We had a neighborhood with a lot of kids. We had a basketball court in the backyard. A lot of kids in the neighborhood came over to our yard and played basketball.

"Basketball was my first love. I almost went to UCLA. I loved watching their basketball team. But I ultimately didn't wind up playing basketball, I played football. So, I said, 'Do I want to go to USC and get beat by UCLA [in basketball] every year, or do I want to go to USC and beat UCLA [in football] every year? That was a decision I had to make."

There were times when Smith played in the same USC secondary as Dennis Thurman, Ronnie Lott, Jeff Fisher, and Joey Browner.

"Think about that: Dennis Smith and Ronnie Lott on the same team?" said Steve Watson, a star Broncos receiver in the 1980s. "Lord. They were monsters."

Smith said Marcus Allen also started out as a defensive back, but in his freshman training camp, a bunch of Trojan running backs got hurt and he was switched to the offensive backfield.

Of all those USC stars, none meant more to Smith than Thurman.

"Dennis Thurman went to my high school and he went to USC," said Smith, who was three years younger than Thurman. "So it was not a hard choice for me to go to USC, because he was my hero when I was growing up. He was the first person I looked up to as an athlete. He's one of my best friends now."

Smith was the Broncos' first-round pick, No. 15 overall, in the 1981 draft. His buddy, Lott, went No. 8 overall to the San Francisco 49ers.

A right cornerback his rookie season, Smith shifted to safety in his second season of 1982, while also dropping down to the nickel position on third down.

"Dennis invented the nickel blitz," Wright said. "I shouldn't say Dennis; it was Joe Collier who came up with it. But Joe Collier had Dennis cover the wide receiver and then blitz the quarterback. Joe Collier invented that against the L.A. Rams."

The Broncos were playing the Rams in Anaheim in a December 1982 game. Vince Ferragamo was the Rams quarterback.

"Dennis started going out on the slot because people started going three wide receivers," Wright said. "He was such a good blitzer, he would be there. Sometimes you worry when you're on the blitz that there's no one back there to help. He would be there (on the quarterback). He did that against the Rams, and we won the game.

"So, like two weeks later, the Rams were doing the same thing. They started doing it. Pretty soon, the whole league was doing it. But it all started with that game against the Rams. That had never been done."

Smith said his best seasons were in 1989, the ninth season of his career, and 1991, his 11th season. The Broncos reached the Super Bowl for the third time in four years in 1989, although it ended poorly against Joe Montana, Ronnie Lott, and the 49ers.

Smith had 82 tackles, 78 return yards off two interceptions, 6 forced fumbles, and a blocked kick in 14 games in 1989, to earn his third Pro Bowl appearance.

"I always tell people I rode the bus to the first two Super Bowls. But I felt like I drove the bus to that third one," Smith said. "I was able to, for once, stay on the field. That was the biggest key to anybody's career. There's a saying: The best ability is availability. That year I figured out a way to stay on the field long enough to make an impact. I figured out how to stay on the field the last few years that I played."

In 1991 he started all 16 regular-season games for the first time in his career. He had 110 tackles, a career-best 5 interceptions, and numerous thundering hits. That season ended with a 10–7 loss at Buffalo in the AFC Championship Game, in which the high-scoring Bills' only touchdown came on an interception return.

"We always played the Bills tough but we never beat them," Smith said. "We didn't beat them that day either, but their offense had been scoring 50 points on everybody. Then we shut 'em down and I think we took their confidence away going into the Super Bowl that year. They thought they were invincible until we played them. And I think when they played the Redskins we showed the formula to beat them.

"That year our defense was good enough to win the Super Bowl. Had that game been in Denver, I don't think it would have been close."

Smith's storied career ended essentially as a salary-cap casualty. The Broncos didn't sign Smith or Mecklenburg until after training camp in 1994. They both finished out a disappointing 7-9 season, but in their final game at old Mile High, Smith and Mecklenburg both received prolonged standing ovations from the Broncos crowd.

"I mean, Dennis was a flat, stone-cold hitter," Mecklenburg said. "He would knock people out every third or fourth game. I was just hoping it wasn't me. He got me one time. He was just unbelievable. Joe Collier was so good at designing defenses around the skills of the people. He had Dennis playing strong safety and had no problem having him one-on-one with wide receivers. That doesn't happen with strong safeties. But Dennis was capable of it.

"Dennis was so smart, too. Dennis was doing my job in the secondary. He made sure everybody was lined up. He got things straight in their minds. There aren't many guys who are unbelievable athletes and can take it to that next level and become that leader and that coach on the field. Dennis was that guy."

DENNIS SMITH STATS

YRS	G	S	I	FR	TCK
14	184	15.0	30	17	1,171

12 (TIE)
— STEVE ATWATER —
Safety, 1989–98

We're all remembered for something. The class clown for his whoopee cushions. Willie Mays and Dwight Clark for "The Catch." The barber for his bowl cuts. Wilt Chamberlain for his 100. The chef for his spices.

Steve Atwater for his hit on Christian Okoye.

"It was definitely perfect timing because it could have gone the other way," Atwater said in October 2016. "The timing was right. I was kind of in a zone that night. I'm glad it happened that way versus the other way. Otherwise, it would have been people asking me, 'How did it feel to have Christian Okoye truck you?' I'd rather have it this way."

It was the second game of the 1990 season, a Monday night at old Mile High Stadium. The Broncos were up 21–9 with less than 10 minutes remaining in the game, but the Chiefs had just blocked a Mike Horan punt and had the ball at the Denver 17.

On first down, Okoye got the deep handoff from quarterback Steve DeBerg and had a big hole off the right guard. Okoye crossed the 15-yard line, churned past the 14, but one foot from the 13—*bam*! He did not touch the 13 hash.

Okoye, who at his listed weight of either 253 or 260 pounds was considered the largest of the successful running backs in NFL history—bigger even than Jerome Bettis—seemingly had his big body go limp as he fell backwards.

A Nigerian Nightmare, indeed.

Atwater looked down as his voice filled with competitive emotion.

"*Yeah*! You tried, baby!"

Those were the words NFL Films caught from a miked-up Atwater a moment after the hit. The slam became so iconic, it generated myths.

Myth 1: Okoye was knocked out of the game. Not true. He gained 8 yards on the next play to set up first-and-goal at the 6. After a penalty, the Chiefs scored on the next play to close to within, 24–23.

Myth 2: Okoye was never the same. Not true. He rushed for 122 yards the next week in a win against Green Bay. In the following 1991 season, Okoye rushed for 1,031 yards on 4.6 yards per carry and 9 touchdowns. It was a nagging knee injury that brought a premature end to his career following the 1992 season.

But that's just it with The Hit. Like anything that becomes truly legendary, Atwater's blast became exaggerated with time. It is unquestionably the most indelible bone-jarring hit in Broncos history.

In some ways, the hit made Atwater's career as the Smilin' Assassin. In some ways, the hit diminished Okoye's reputation as the league's most bruising, toughest-to-tackle running back.

Adding to the grandeur of the tackle was the fact that it occurred on *Monday Night Football* at a time when that was still the NFL's showcase game of the week. And Atwater, a first-round safety from Arkansas, was building on his brutal-hitting momentum in his second season. The week before in the season opener against the Los Angeles Raiders, Atwater had walloped Marcus Allen so hard that he'd given the running back a cut above his right eye that took 10 stitches to close.

Against the Chiefs in Game 2 of 1990, Atwater was all over the field. He had 14 tackles, including 11 by himself. Atwater did knock out one player in the game, but it wasn't Okoye. He sent receiver Robb Thomas to the locker room with a concussion. This was back in the day when it was rare for a concussion to knock a player from the game.

"Steve's play was outstanding," Broncos head coach Dan Reeves said after the game. "Eleven solo tackles is an incredible number for a safety. He's played extremely well since he came here, but last night had to be his best game, in my opinion, because it was so crucial."

When I got this project, before I started putting the 50 Greatest Broncos Players in order, I knew I had to put Atwater and fellow safety Dennis Smith back-to-back. They were a tandem for six seasons, with both earning Pro Bowl berths in 1990, '91, and '93.

I just didn't know who to put ahead of the other.

A simplistic comparison would say the primary difference between Smith and Atwater was about 20 pounds. Smith was a 200-pound safety who was more athletic. Atwater was closer to 220 pounds, and was often shifted into a linebacker position on first down.

A slight majority of former Broncos players and coaches I polled gave the edge to Smith.

"You've got to put him ahead of me," Atwater said.

It was hardly a unanimous call.

"Dennis Smith was the hardest hitter that I saw with my own eyes," said Broncos Hall of Fame tight end Shannon Sharpe. "But it would be hard for me to leave a guy with eight Pro Bowls outside the top 10. And he went to three Super Bowls in a 10-year span and he won two."

While Smith was a 7-foot-2 high-jumper type of athlete, Atwater wasn't just all hit. Born in Chicago, raised in St. Louis, Atwater was a good-enough basketball player to get invited to the McDonald's All-Star Classic (the chicken pox cost him the opportunity to play).

He was also a wishbone quarterback at Lutheran North High School. And a good one, too. So good he got a scholarship to play wishbone for the Arkansas Razorbacks.

Luckily for Atwater's long-term future, coach Ken Hatfield converted him to safety during his redshirt freshman season. Atwater set a Razorback record with 14 career interceptions, and he had 2 more in the Senior Bowl.

Selected by the Broncos with their No. 20 overall pick in the 1989 draft, Atwater was moved to the box by Broncos defensive coordinator Wade Phillips, while Smith played the free safety.

As a rookie, Atwater had an astounding 129 tackles and 3 interceptions, and he would have been the NFL Defensive Rookie of the Year if it hadn't been for the spectacular pass-rushing exploits of Kansas City's Derrick Thomas.

In his next four seasons, Atwater was credited with 173, 150, 151, and 141 tackles—unheard-of totals for a safety.

The eight Pro Bowls in Atwater's 10 seasons in Denver were tied with Champ Bailey for second-most in franchise history, just one behind John Elway's nine.

But Atwater doesn't consider the Pro Bowls and tackles the highlight of his career; nor was it his hit on Okoye.

"Super Bowl Thirty-Two," Atwater said without hesitation. "Having everything come together. We had a few injuries, nothing major. After going through some rough years, being with a group of special guys and being rewarded for your hard work was just amazing."

In Atwater's rookie year, the Broncos got to the Super Bowl, but they got humiliated by Joe Montana and the San Francisco 49ers, 55–10. In Atwater's second season, the year of the hit on the Nigerian Nightmare? It was a rare victory, as the Broncos finished 5-11.

The Broncos were 12-4 in Atwater's third season of 1991, but they lost a hard-fought 10–7 game at Buffalo in the AFC Championship. There were some 7-9, 8-8, and 9-7 years until Mike Shanahan got his Broncos machine rolling with three consecutive dominant seasons in 1996, 1997, and 1998.

The Broncos suffered a playoff heartache to Jacksonville to spoil their 13-3 season in 1996, but perhaps it helped to be the wild-card underdogs for the playoffs in 1997.

"We go to Kansas City, win a tough one, go to Pittsburgh, win a tough one," Atwater said. "It was crazy; it was an amazing ride. And then in the Super Bowl, I remember the third-down play, I knocked my guy Randy Hilliard out—knocked myself out. But the next play, John Mobley knocked the pass down from Brett Favre to Mark Chmura, the tight end, and we looked up and we're like, 'Wait a minute. This game is over.' Just that realization that we had won was the greatest experience I ever had, that moment right there. When John knocked that ball down."

The Broncos were up, 31–24, with 36 seconds remaining, when on third-and-6 from the 31-yard line, Packers quarterback Brett Favre attempted a pass to receiver Robert Brooks. A three-man collision wound up at the ball, with Atwater knocking out his nickelback Hilliard, Brooks, and himself.

On fourth down, with Atwater alert and watching from the sideline, Favre threw just enough behind Chmura for the linebacker Mobley to knock it down. It was the Broncos' ball with 28 seconds left, and Green Bay was out of time-outs.

Wait a minute. This game is over. On their fifth Super Bowl try, the Broncos had their first Vince Lombardi Trophy.

Atwater was tremendous in Super Bowl XXXII, registering six tackles, a sack, and two pass breakups. It was his last great year with the Broncos, as he was limited to a two-down safety in 1998 when the Broncos breezed to their second consecutive Super Bowl.

In a move that was highly criticized in the local press and in the locker room, Shanahan cut the ever-classy Atwater rather than pay him a $2.6 million salary. He went on to sign Dale Carter, who the Broncos had developed an intense hatred for because of his dirty, cheap-shot play during his time with the Kansas City Chiefs.

It wasn't just Elway's retirement that sent the Broncos into a tailspin for a while.

Atwater played one more year with the New York Jets, but after the 1999 season he called Broncos owner Pat Bowlen and asked if he could retire a Bronco. A one-day contract was rightfully arranged.

Atwater started in all 155 games he played in for the Broncos—15.5 per year in his 10 years—plus 14 more in the postseason. He was inducted into the Broncos Ring of Fame in his first year of eligibility in 2005, and while he hasn't received as much Pro Football Hall of Fame attention as his career deserves, he was a top-15 finalist in 2016.

Yet, for all his starts and two Super Bowl rings, and 24 interceptions and more than 1,000 tackles for the Broncos, Atwater is remembered most for his collision with the Nigerian Nightmare on a Monday night in 1990.

"I still hear about it," Atwater said, 36 years after his blast. "Not as much as I used to. But when people find out who I am, there will be, 'He's the guy who got Christian Okoye.' It's crazy that it's remained in people's minds for this long."

STEVE ATWATER STATS

YRS	G	S	I	Y	TCK
10	155	5.0	24	408	1,320

14

TOM NALEN

Center, 1994–2008

For this project, I briefly placed Gary Zimmerman ahead of center Tom Nalen as the first offensive lineman listed among the 50 Greatest Broncos.

There is a reason, after all, why the best left tackles get paid twice what the best centers make. The difficulty of protecting the blind-side outside edge against the world's elite pass rushers is no comparison to the tugging, pushing, pulling, and wrestling with the big heavies in a scrum.

But this is about the best of the Broncos, not the best of the NFL. Nalen played 14 seasons with the Broncos; Zimmerman, five. Nalen made five Pro Bowls with the Broncos and was a three-time All Pro, while Zimmerman had three Pro Bowls and one All Pro award in Denver.

Nalen was young in the late 1990s and was able to get that second Super Bowl ring to cap the 1998 season; Zimmerman wanted to come back after helping to win Super Bowl XXXII, but his beaten-down body wouldn't allow him to play for a repeat.

So here it is: Zimmerman was the best offensive lineman the Broncos ever had; Nalen was the best offensive lineman in Broncos history.

No one outside the football grunt rooms really knows for sure. Who watches blockers?

Maybe there is a way, though, to quantify the quality of a blocker. In the 12-year period from 1995 through 2006, there was one constant in the Broncos offensive line. Tom Nalen. In 11 of those 12 years, six different running backs had 1,000-yard rushing seasons: Terrell Davis (four times), Olandis Gary, Mike Anderson (twice), Clinton Portis (twice), Reuben Droughns, and Tatum Bell.

"It didn't matter who you plugged in back there," said former Broncos quarterback Jake Plummer. "With all due respect to John Elway or Terrell Davis or myself, or anybody who had success back there, Tom Nalen was the anchor of that line."

Wait. More evidence of Nalen's greatness is exhibited through his absence. The Broncos did not have a 1,000-yard rusher in the three seasons before Nalen became their starting center. And they did not have a 1,000-yard rusher in the 2007 season, when Nalen went down with a torn right biceps in Game 5, which turned out to be the final game of his career. Nor in the five seasons after did the Broncos have a 1,000-yard rusher.

Game, set, match. That alone should allow Nalen to cut in front of the line for induction into the Pro Football Hall of Fame.

"I watched a lot of football," said former Broncos safety John Lynch, who is now general manager of the San Francisco 49ers. "I studied a lot of football. But if you wanted to know how good an offensive or defensive lineman was, like in Tom's case, you talked to other D-linemen. Those guys used to say he was an absolute beast. So strong with his hands.

"Now, granted, he found the perfect system for what he did. But if you looked to central casting for an offensive center, Tom Nalen would be the guy. A crusty, funny, intelligent—in my mind, a Hall of Fame player—but certainly a special player."

Nalen has not received much consideration for the Pro Football Hall of Fame. He is a Bronco, after all. The Hall of Fame voters have demonstrated a puzzling bias against the Broncos, despite all their wins and Super Bowls. Nalen as of the class of 2017 had yet to be included among the top-15 modern-era finalists, much less receive consideration for the five elected each year.

He was inducted into the Broncos Ring of Fame, however, in his first year of eligibility, in 2013. His five Pro Bowls—the most for any offensive lineman in team history—are impressive, and he was also a first-team All Pro in 2000 and 2003, when he was also selected as the NFL's Offensive Lineman of the Year, and a second-team All Pro in 2002.

"It comes from the team," Nalen said at his Ring of Fame press conference in May 2013. "I spent 15 years here, and they felt like I was worthy of the 23 other guys that are in the Ring of Fame. That means a lot, because they knew everything about me—warts and all."

The signature moment for Nalen was Super Bowl XXXII. The Broncos had the lightest offensive line in the NFL, with an average of 290.2 pounds, and Nalen was the lightest of all at 286.

The Broncos had been blown out in their previous four Super Bowls, and the expectation was that their lighter-sized line would get blown out again by the defending Super Bowl–champion Green Bay Packers, who were 12-point favorites largely because defensive end Reggie White and nose tackle Gilbert Brown were considered mismatches.

White is arguably the best defensive end in NFL history. Brown was one of the NFL's most popular players in 1997, in ways similar to the phenomenon that was William "The Refrigerator" Perry in 1985. Brown was listed at 345 pounds, but he was probably closer to 375.

On nearly every snap, Brown was lined up directly across from Nalen.

White was held to one tackle in Super Bowl XXXII. Nalen abused Brown through techniques and angles. Brown wore down into a fatigued tub of non-factor in the fourth quarter.

Running back Terrell Davis rushed for 157 yards and 3 touchdowns off 30 carries, and was the Super Bowl MVP as the Broncos upset the Packers, 31–24.

Yet, Nalen never did get the credit he deserved nationally because of the belief that the sum of the Broncos' zone-blocking system was greater than its parts. As someone who always seems to be conflicted, anyway, Nalen both understands those who credit the system in one sense, but thinks it was an overrated factor in the team's success in another.

"[Offensive line coach] Alex Gibbs was here and didn't mind the fact that I was 280 pounds," Nalen said. "I know a lot of teams—you look at Dallas at that time—I wouldn't have been able to play for that team. I fit the ideology of the coaching staff.

"The whole zone-blocking thing is kind of crazy to me, because every team has run it. Obviously, Alex had a big imprint on how many times we'd run it during the game, but to be honest, we ran the same play over and over until teams stopped it. It just happened to be a zone play."

Thomas Andrew Nalen was born in Boston and grew up in Foxboro, Massachusetts (aka Foxborough), home of the stadium where the New England Patriots have played since 1971. During his days with the Broncos, Nalen didn't like to talk about whether he was a Patriots fan, but he did not hide his affection for the Red Sox and Bruins.

At Foxborough High School he was a three-sport star, serving as captain for both the football and basketball teams. He attended Boston College, where he was a highly decorated three-year starting football center and earned an accounting degree.

Yet, perhaps because he was undersized even for the 1990s, Nalen wasn't selected until the seventh round of the 1994 draft. He had survived the final cuts, but just before the Broncos' season opener, the team figured out how to fit the great Karl Mecklenburg under the league's new salary cap. Mecklenburg was re-signed for one more season and Nalen was waived onto the practice squad.

"I remember when he was on the practice squad as a rookie, the veteran guys coming in and saying, 'Man, that little Tommy Nalen is really good,'" said Broncos kicker Jason Elam. "He was just a guy that you knew was going to be solid every single game. He wasn't going to miss any assignments. He wasn't going to say a whole lot, either. He wasn't a rah-rah guy. But you knew he had your back."

At the halfway point of his rookie season, Nalen was called up to start at left guard in place of the injured Jon Melander. In his NFL debut, Nalen took on Sean Gilbert, who was coming off a 10.5-sack season. It was Nalen's first, and last, NFL start at a position other than center.

For the start of the 1995 season, Nalen was the Broncos starting center. He wound up playing center in 187 of his 188 starts—the second-most overall total in team history. Only John Elway, with 231 at quarterback, started more.

"When Tommy first got there we were hard on him," Zimmerman said. "[Brian] Habib really shaped Tommy. He was hard on Tommy. That's what helped me, was that guys shaped me. We were hard on Tommy and he did a good job."

Nalen gladly went along with the offensive line's media code of silence, instigated by Zimmerman and Habib and formally instituted by offensive line coach Alex Gibbs in 1995. Not that this meant a lack of publicity. In the media sessions leading up to the Broncos' back-to-back Super Bowl titles to cap the 1997 and 1998 seasons, dozens of stories were written about how the offensive line didn't talk to the media. They did talk during Super Bowl week because the NFL threatened to impose $10,000 fines to any player who didn't cooperate with the media.

After Zimmerman, Habib, and Gibbs left the Broncos, Nalen carried on the offensive line's no-interview policy, and could be brutally tough on a young blocker who was unaware of the internal rule. Young blockers were never unaware more than once.

"That's the way it works," Zimmerman said. "It's the players that shape the newcomers."

There was always talk of the Broncos shifting Nalen to guard—K. C. Jones was supposed to be the team's center in 1999, then Ben Hamilton in 2003—but it never materialized. The center serves as the quarterback of the offensive line with the way he calls out the protections at the line of scrimmage, and Nalen was simply too good at this to move over.

"Very, very smart," Plummer said. "Witty, humorous, dirty, nasty. All the good things that all linemen are. His feet were amazing. In this offense, it's not so much overpowering your guy, it's getting in position so they can't cut off a lane, and he was a master at positioning himself where he needed to be. But also directing that whole line. He directed everybody.

"I've said it before—that QBs get a ton of credit for being the most important player—but I truly believe that centers are right there. Without them the ball doesn't get snapped, number one. And two, they're calling all the protections, all the blocking schemes. People don't hear that. All they hear is 'Omaha, Omaha.' They don't hear the center directing traffic, and [Nalen] was the master at it. He knew it in and out.

"He was also a fiery, chip-on-his-shoulder competitor. He loved to mix it up. We were kindred spirits. If I had to pick a guy to go in a dark alley with, he'd be in my top five."

With Nalen at center, Terrell Davis went for 1,117 yards in 1995; more than 1,500 yards in 1996; more than 1,700 yards in 1997; and more than 2,000 yards in 1998. But the first time T.D. went down, some guy named Olandis Gary went for 1,159 in 1999.

Gary went down in 2000, and a 27-year-old rookie named Mike Anderson went from former Marine to nearly a 1,500-yard rusher and NFL Rookie of the Year.

Clinton Portis was drafted, and through his first two years he looked like the NFL's next great running back, rushing for 3,099 yards on 5.5 yards per carry and 29 touchdowns. Then Portis went to Washington, and while he was still good, he was far from great at 4.1 yards per carry.

A journeyman named Reuben Droughns and future cell-phone salesman named Tatum Bell also enjoyed 1,000-yard seasons while running behind a Nalen-based offensive line.

The kicker? When Nalen went down with a torn biceps injury five games into 2007, the Broncos 1,000-yard rusher disappeared. In Nalen's final season of 2008, when he didn't play at all because of a bum knee, no Bronco running back gained so much as 400 yards.

No wonder he was a first-ballot Ring of Famer.

"Hopefully this is the first step into another type of Hall of Fame," Plummer said. "He's one of the best centers to ever play the game, I believe."

TOM NALEN STATS	
YRS	G
15	194

15

GARY ZIMMERMAN

Left Tackle, 1993-97

My plane arrived in Canton, Ohio, at a time that presented me with the choice of either rushing to first check into my hotel and perhaps arrive two to five minutes late to the press conference, or go way early to the event.

I chose way early, but not nearly enough to beat the standards of Zimmerman Time.

It was August 1, 2008, the Friday before the Pro Football Hall of Fame class of Fred Dean, Darrell Green, Art Monk, Emmitt Thomas, Andre Tippett, and Gary Zimmerman was to be bronzed into football immortality.

The press conference at the McKinley Grand Hotel was scheduled to begin at 3:30 p.m. Thomas, appreciative for having to wait so long before going in as a senior candidate, walked in a few minutes early. A few others were there right on time, or a few minutes late. One or two must have had conflicts or didn't pay close enough to their itinerary, because they didn't show up at all.

I walked into the room around 2:20 p.m., and other than a hotel staffer or two setting things up, I was the second one there. Not the first. Already sitting stoically in a silent room in one of the chairs to the left of the podium was Zimmerman, a left tackle who played seven years for the Minnesota Vikings and five years for the Denver Broncos.

"In the NFL, if you show up late to a meeting you get fined," Zimmerman told me—and no one else for there was no one else to tell. "I never wanted to get fined, so I always show up early."

Yes, but a little more than an hour early? Of all the Broncos I have encountered over the years, few have fascinated me more than Zimmerman. In part because, by his own choice, so little is known about him.

His was a life not only of serendipity but reciprocity. He didn't like the East Coast, so instead of entering the NFL Draft, where he heard the Philadelphia Eagles would select him, he signed up to start his professional career with the Los Angeles Express of the United States Football League. The NFL came up with a more expansive supplemental draft in 1984 in attempt to combat the USFL, but the New York Giants weren't listening.

They took the East Coast–divergent Zimmerman with the No. 3 overall pick. Thanks, but Zim will stay out West with the Express.

After Zimmerman played guard and center at Oregon, the Los Angeles Express left tackle got hurt and Zim wound up converting to become one of the best left tackles in NFL history.

After the USFL folded, Zimmerman forced a deal from the Giants to the Minnesota Vikings, who were far enough away from New York.

He discovered the Vikings lacked decorum when it came to dealing with most of their players during those days of 10-person committee ownership, and when they personally insulted Zimmerman during a preliminary contract discussion, he retired, a sincere move that led him to the Broncos.

Although he spent more time in Minnesota than Denver, Zimmerman says his Hall of Fame bronze bust belongs to the Broncos. He accentuated this point by having Broncos owner Pat Bowlen present him during his Hall of Fame induction ceremony.

As you can now discern, one event in Zim's life became interrelated to another. Showing up more than an hour early to events? When time is a priority to a person, chances are work, or the obligation of work, is at the root. Zimmerman and his two younger brothers were raised by their father, Larry, an electrical engineer in the defense business who designed missiles and aircraft, and Mary, a stay-at-home, busier-than-Dad-ever-was mom, about 30 miles east of Los Angeles in Walnut, California.

From junior high on, Zimmerman and his brothers were home construction laborers.

"My dad, he'd buy old junker houses and my brothers and I, we'd help renovate them and turn them into rentals," Zimmerman said. "So even at a young age we were painting, landscaping. We used to hate Christmas vacation and summer vacation because while everyone else was sleeping in, we'd be up at six o'clock and work pretty much the whole vacation."

What they disliked as kids they came to appreciate later on. All that work helped shape Zimmerman.

"Without a doubt," he said. "It's a big, strong part of me, yeah."

And so there he was, at 46 years old—roughly 32 years after he'd hung his first sheet of drywall—sitting in an empty room, more than an hour early for a press conference in which he would happily serve a supporting role to the other lead characters, like Darrell Green and Art Monk. It wasn't work, but there was obligation.

The next day, there were six new football players enshrined in the Pro Football Hall of Fame, which meant six well-rehearsed speeches to the audience at Fawcett Stadium and many more watching at home.

Only one quoted the Dalai Lama.

"I chose Oregon because it was the only college that would accept me as a middle linebacker," Zimmerman said in his speech. "While dressing for the first practice, I thought how strange it was that I was number '75.'"

The crowd laughed. He learned after practice, he continued, the reason for his number. His coaches felt his future was not in tackling running backs and quarterbacks but in blocking for them.

Zimmerman continued: "As the Dalai Lama once said, 'Remember that not getting what you want is sometimes a wonderful stroke of luck.' The point I'm trying to make here is, nobody starts out wanting to play the offensive line position; it's just where we wind up."

He got some laughs and applause for that. Zimmerman's self-deprecating humor was laced throughout his 11-minute speech. His quarterback John Elway was among the already-inducted Hall of Famers sitting on the stage, enjoying Zim's speech.

Forgive the Denver fans and media who followed him if they found irony in Zimmerman's entertaining oratory. This was the same Gary Zimmerman who would not talk to the media during his five seasons in Denver.

"What happened in Minnesota was, we played a game we were supposed to win and we lost," Zimmerman explained in November 2016. "So a reporter came down and he said, 'What happened?'

"And I said, 'The offense didn't play well enough to win, the defense didn't play well enough to win, and special teams didn't play well enough to win.' So, the next day, the front page of the newspaper says, 'Zimmerman says the defense didn't play well enough to win.'

"And that was it. Not only am I in a hot spot with my teammates—I had to get this thing corrected—but I mean, there was a slant there. That's when I realized some of these [reporters] don't have your best interest at heart."

For a guy who wouldn't be quoted in any stories written about him, he had a few. Starting with how his pro career began.

Following his All-Pac 10 season as an Oregon Duck guard in 1983, Zimmerman had heard he was going to be drafted by the Eagles. The 1984 NFL Draft, though, wasn't until May—four months after the USFL held its draft, where Zimmerman was selected by the L.A. Express in the second round.

Zimmerman signed with the Express before the NFL's draft.

The NFL did hold a supplemental draft in early June for players who had signed with the USFL or Canadian Football League, and Zimmerman was the third player selected by the Giants—behind only his Express teammate Steve Young, who was taken by Tampa Bay, and running back Mike Rozier, who was taken by the Houston Oilers.

"I'm not an East Coast guy," Zimmerman recalled in November 2016. "I'm an L.A. guy, and the L.A. Express drafted me, so I was like, 'What the heck.' So, I go down there, and as it turned out the USFL was probably the most important piece of my career, because I learned how to play tackle. I was never a tackle before. I was a center/guard. So, I never played one snap of tackle, and I went to the L.A. Express and our left tackle got hurt in the first or second game, so I instantly became a left tackle. So, I got two years of training in the USFL and that kind of groomed the course for me."

The adjustment between center/guard and tackle?

"It's huge," Zimmerman said. "The center and guard play in a bunch, so a guy has to go straight through you, whereas a tackle, they can go around you, through you, cut inside on you.

"The tackle position, they always say you're on an island because you're out there by yourself. The tackle is more an angles-type of game, whereas center and guard is more about strength. You're firming up the pocket, where the tackle is containing the pocket. There's a huge difference when you're making the change."

After his second season with the Express in 1985, the USFL shut down, and Zimmerman was left with his rights owned by the Giants. The USFL's season ended in June, and most of its NFL-caliber players migrated to the more-established league in time for the start of the 1985 season in September.

But Zimmerman, who wasn't going to play in New York, sat out that season.

"I just told them I'd choose a different career," Zimmerman said.

He went back to his alma mater to watch the Ducks' spring football game in 1986, when he was approached by a Vikings scout.

"He asked me if I'd play in Minnesota and I said sure," Zimmerman said.

The Giants traded Zimmerman to the Vikings in exchange for two second-round draft picks that turned out to be cornerback Mark Collins and safety Greg Lasker.

In Minnesota, Zimmerman was a four-time Pro Bowler and two-time All Pro. He was a consummate professional even though the Vikings players understood they were not playing for a class organization. This was before the team was owned by Red McCombs, and long before Zygi Wilf.

"I enjoyed the people in Minnesota, I didn't enjoy the organization," Zimmerman said. "There wasn't free agency. It was a great group of guys. Our O-line was really tight. On our days off we all went hunting together, fishing together. It was like being in college again because we all had similar tastes.

"But the ownership was all about money. They had locks on the lights, timers on the showers. They'd charge you if you lost a sock."

Say what? Apparently, this is what happens when a 10-person board runs the team instead of one primary owner. It was also before Bowlen, who was heading the NFL broadcast committee, brought in the Fox network in mid-December 1993, a move that enhanced network competition for rights fees, and in turn multiplied the league's revenues exponentially. It was also before free agency.

Zimmerman's dismay with the Vikings organizational leadership crossed over to irreconcilable contempt when after the 1992 season, he sought to restructure his contract.

"I had deferred money that I asked to be advanced for tax reasons," he said. "So I went in there and ownership started belittling me. Told me I should shut up and take the money, because if I wasn't playing football I'd be flippin' burgers. I said, You know what, if that's what you think of me, see you later."

Zimmerman let it be known he would never again play for the Vikings. He wound up getting dealt to the Broncos prior to the last preseason game of 1993. Bowlen, frustrated that his team went through six left tackles in the five years since Dave Studdard had blown out his knee in Super Bowl XXII, went after Zimmerman on the advice of trusted scouts Jerry Frei and Jack Elway.

The Broncos sent a substantial haul to Minnesota—a first-, second-, and sixth-round draft pick—in exchange for Zimmerman.

"I had no input in that," Zimmerman said. "They were trying to trade me to the Jets to stick it to me because they knew I didn't like New York. But nothing happened there. They called me and said Denver would like you, and I was on a plane the next day."

A few minutes after he arrived at Stapleton Airport, Zimmerman knew he would enjoy playing for the Broncos and Bowlen much better than he ever did for the Vikings board.

"When I came from Minnesota, from day one I was shocked by how well I was treated," he said. "Jerry Frei came and picked me up at the airport, whereas in Minnesota they had some kid pick me up.

"Just the way I was treated, my family was treated, it was just unbelievable. And not just me—the way Mr. Bowlen treated everybody in that building as family: the equipment guys, the janitors, everybody who works for the Broncos are treated with kindness. That meant a lot to me. You wanted to play for him.

"Mr. B, he's so generous. He did a lot of stuff people didn't know about. He was a behind-the-scenes guy. We had similar perspectives because he always wanted to be in the shadows, never wanted to be in the limelight. I took notice of everything he did. He made the biggest difference in my career because where I came from, you were a piece of meat. We told the [Minnesota] owners, You've got to get new turf, and they said it would be cheaper to get new players. They just didn't care. And then Mr. B, he was unbelievable."

Upon his arrival in Denver, Zimmerman shook hands, put on pads, and went out to practice with his new teammates. Like everyone else, Elway was curious about exactly what the Broncos had in their new left tackle.

The quarterback figured it out the first time he dropped back to pass. Even if he was blind to what Zimmerman was doing on the left edge, Elway wasn't deaf.

"I remember the first day in camp after he came over from Minnesota, just the blow he delivered to those guys rushing the passer," Elway said. "It shocked me, the noise that it made when he struck the defensive lineman on a pass rush."

That old artificial surface at the Minneapolis Metrodome had taken a toll on Zimmerman's body, though. He was able to keep his parts together through his first three seasons in Denver, but he played the last two years with two damaged shoulders, a bum knee, and pain in his left hip that still bothers him today.

There was a moment in Broncos lore that will forever join Elway at Zimmerman's painful hip. In his final season of 1997, Zimmerman's shoulder was nothing more than a glob of excruciating, disconnected parts. After the season, doctors would tell him he either needed to stop playing or receive a prosthetic shoulder.

But before making his final football decision, Zimmerman had a Super Bowl to pursue. With the Broncos carrying a 9-2 record into their late-November game against the Oakland Raiders, Zimmerman encountered a problem.

"During warm-ups, his shoulder had slipped out of joint," said long-time Broncos trainer Steve "Greek" Antonopulos. "And I went to Mike [Shanahan] with Gary and I said, 'I don't think he's going to be able to play.' And Zim says, 'As long as number '7' is on the field, I'll be there.' He said: 'Don't you worry about me. I'll make it.' Zim is probably one of the toughest guys to ever put on a uniform."

The Broncos crushed the Raiders, 31–3, that day, scoring all their points in the second and third quarters. Elway came out in the fourth quarter. Zimmerman followed him to the sidelines.

Later that season, the Broncos won their first world championship by upsetting Green Bay in Super Bowl XXXII. Afterward, Bowlen uttered his everlasting line, "This one's for John!"

Elway felt sheepish about that proclamation, as it was the Zimmerman-led offensive line that destroyed the Packers for 179 yards rushing and four rushing touchdowns, and created a sizable advantage in time of possession. Broncos running back Terrell Davis was the Super Bowl MVP in some part because there was only one trophy, not five.

"The guys up front won Super Bowl XXXII, without question," Elway said.

Who got the better Zim, the Vikings or the Broncos?

"I've thought about this lots of times," Zimmerman said during his Hall of Fame weekend in 2008. "You got a smarter player. The Vikings had a more athletic, but dumber player. I talk about this all the time when I go talk to these classrooms. When you're young, you're surviving on your athletic ability and your quickness. Your recovery time is so quick. As you get a little bit older, your recovery time goes down and your smarts go up, and pretty soon your smarts take over. That's kind of where I ended up with Denver—the smarts were taking over."

Tom Nalen, a center, may have been the best offensive lineman in Broncos history, but that doesn't mean Zimmerman wasn't the best offensive lineman to ever put on a Broncos uniform. Nalen is the top Broncos blocker in part because he played three times longer with the organization than did Zim.

But there's a reason why the league's best left tackles make twice that of the best centers.

"The thing was, you'd say, 'Okay, Zim, you're by yourself. You've got D.T. [Derrick Thomas] by yourself. You've got Bruce Smith by yourself,'" said Broncos tight end Shannon Sharpe. "Think about it; he had to block Leslie O'Neal, who had 100 sacks. Greg Townsend, who had 100 sacks. Derrick Thomas, who had 100 sacks. And he had to play these guys twice a year. It wasn't one week you get J. J. Watt and then four weeks later he might play a Von Miller. He was playing these guys twice a year."

For Zimmerman, his football life would have a euphoric culmination. After playing both ways for Walnut High School—and both ways at Oregon for a bit as a sophomore—after two years with the L.A. Express and 12 years in the NFL, the best part of it all was his final game. He never experienced greater football joy than after the Broncos won Super Bowl XXXII.

The Broncos offensive line absolutely destroyed the front of the Green Bay Packers, who were 12-point favorites, largely because the NFC had won 13 Super Bowls in a row. Three of those AFC losses were on the Broncos.

"Everything just lined up in place because nobody gave us a chance," Zimmerman said. "We were too little to play and all that kind of stuff. All the moons aligned for that deal. We kind of felt two weeks before the thing, we kind of knew we were going to win. We didn't know how, but we knew we were going to win.

"The whole journey, it kind of capped my whole career. Twelve years and knowing how hard it is to even get to the Super Bowl. I only got there one time. A lot of guys never make it there. Just the journey from a little kid all the way through high school, college, USFL, 12 years in the NFL, and finally getting one crack at it and to be able to come out on top, it was kind of a storybook thing."

Today, Zim and his wife Lisa make their home outside New York City.

Kidding! The Zimmermans live outside Bend, Oregon. One of their daughters, Lindsay, was on the West Coast hiking, enjoying life at the time of this writing. The other daughter, Kelsey, has been working the last few years for the Broncos marketing department.

Many former Broncos players make some money by being a former Bronco. A card signing here, an appearance there.

"That's not me," Zimmerman said. "I'm out in the middle of the woods. I've got a 40-acre timber farm. So I got my hands full here."

But any time the Broncos induct a new member into their Ring of Fame, Zimmerman shows up for the ceremony. He also attends most of the Pro Football Hall of Fame ceremonies in Canton. He was so appreciative of the people for showing up for his big days, he couldn't stand not being there for someone else.

"The Hall of Fame was not something I ever thought about or was a goal for me," he said. "It was a great honor and stuff, but to me, the Super Bowl was more special because of the journey and all the hard work and all the people and teammates that brought you there."

GARY ZIMMERMAN STATS	
YRS	G
5	76

16

RICH "TOMBSTONE" JACKSON

Defensive End, 1967–71

It was Ring of Fame weekend and a steady stream of Denver Broncos greats were checking into the Inverness Hotel in the Denver Tech Center.

The lobby bustled as the likes of Floyd Little, Dennis Smith, Steve Atwater, and one of three guests of honor for the class of 2016, Simon Fletcher, passed through.

With much more tranquility, one of the roughest, toughest, strongest, and best Broncos of all time walked in slowly with a cane he didn't really use, wearing his trademark kufi cap.

Let me check in here, said Rich Jackson, and I'll give you all the time you need.

For a guy who was nicknamed "Tombstone," Jackson sure is a polite, soft-spoken gentleman of the highest order.

"I always wanted to respect people," Jackson said in his New Orleans drawl as he sat up in a lobby sectional, his two hands leaning forward on his cane. "My teachers, I would call Mister or Missus and their name. I wanted that to resonate with youngsters and have them pick up on that respect. I had a high school coach and he had a nickname, Zoo, and I would never call him that in any of our conversations. Zoo James. I called him Mr. James.

"I respected people so that I always wanted to make sure I was formal. I always wanted to make sure when people interacted with me, if they were having a bad day it would lead to a better day than had we not met. And if they were having a good day, I wanted to make sure I didn't take away from that day."

This would be a great day. For a guy who had just four healthy seasons in the NFL, Jackson's career reached mythical proportions. Perhaps, the most glowing tribute he received was from *Sports Illustrated*'s Paul Zimmerman. This was at a time when the Internet was just starting to take off and before the cottage industry of NFL bloggers and social media experts began to mushroom.

During this time, "Dr. Z" was *the* NFL opinion that mattered. In naming his NFL All-Century team in 1999, Zimmerman placed "Tombstone" as one of his three defensive ends, alongside Reggie White and Deacon Jones. Zimmerman once wrote of Jackson, "In his prime, he was the very best run-pass defensive end the game has seen."

Al Davis, the renegade Oakland Raiders owner, signed Jackson out of Southern University in 1966. But after playing sparingly as a linebacker in his rookie season, Jackson was traded to the Broncos in exchange for two of the best players in Denver history, receiver Lionel Taylor and center Jerry Sturm.

Several years later, Davis lamented trading Jackson away, saying "he was the best player they ever had."

"He had me. He tried to get me back," Jackson said of Davis. "I was with the Raiders. He said that was the biggest mistake he ever made when he traded me. [Broncos defensive line coach] Stan Jones saw me on some film. When they brought me here, again they tried me at linebacker—for one practice.

"And the next day they put me at right defensive end. I was there the whole year. And then the next year they switched me to left defensive end, and that's where I stayed my whole career. And Mr. Davis tried to get me back. We remained friends throughout the years. And I guess whenever they came to town I would contact him and go by and say hello to him."

Richard Samuel Jackson Jr. was born July 22, 1941, and raised with three sisters in New Orleans. His father, Richard Sr., died when he was seven or eight, as his son remembers.

"My mother raised us," Jackson said. "Catherine. It's ironic; my wife's name is Katherine. With a K. I called them both Miss Jackson."

Richard and the Jackson girls all attended L. B. Landry High School. All three sisters graduated with college degrees. Richard Jr. earned three degrees in physical education, secondary education, and administration from Southern University in Baton Rouge.

"I wanted to be a coach and principal," Jackson said.

In the 1950s, L. B. Landry was a joint junior high and high school. Jackson started on both the offensive and defensive lines on the junior high team, and he went both ways again as a junior and senior in high school.

He also ran the 100- and 200-yard dashes and anchored the 440 and 880 relay teams in track, and he was a state champion shot-putter.

It was in high school that his rare athletic blend of size, track speed, and strength brought on the nickname "Tombstone." He couldn't be blocked. A ball carrier couldn't run away from him. And no one could outsmart him.

"The termination of life. The symbol of death. The end of the road," Jackson said. "That's what 'Tombstone' means."

All of this earned him a scholarship to Southern, where he played football for the legendary A. W. Mumford, and again participated in the field events on the track team, throwing the shot put, discus, and javelin.

Shot put was his best event.

"I was a rinky-dink, 59-foot shot-putter," he said.

In football, Mumford started Jackson as an outside linebacker as a freshman. He also played some flanker, split end, and tight end.

"He was an outstanding coach," Jackson said. "Many of the things you see today, he created those. History will not tell you the outstanding black coaches that they had and the evolution of the outstanding things that are taking place today. He was ahead of his time."

As some of the more-established NFL teams were slow to diversify, the American Football League was signing dozens of players out of the National Association of Intercollegiate Athletics (NAIA) Southwestern Athletic Conference.

"Seriously, I don't think football would be, at all levels, what it is today, at the professional level, at the collegiate level, if it wasn't for the AFL," Jackson said. "When I grew up and saw football on TV, all I saw were white players in college. White ballplayers in the pros. There were a few black players in the Northern schools. For the Southern schools, you only saw white players. Texas, Alabama, same thing.

"The AFL had a great new pact. We'd go back and look at the basketball players, Zelmo Beatty, Willis Reed, Bob Love. Matter of fact, Bob Love was my roommate at Southern, and the guy who came along and broke all his records with the Bulls was a guy named Michael Jordan."

Jackson finished playing at Southern University in 1964, but he didn't sign with the Raiders until 1966. First, he went to grad school for a year.

"I didn't want to play football," Jackson said. "There was an AFL scout, he would sign a lot of the black ballplayers, guys with different teams. I didn't want to play, but this guy ran behind me. Every time I looked up here was this guy. Lloyd Wells."

Wells was a sports photographer and civil rights advocate who did most of his football recruiting work signing black college players for the Kansas City Chiefs, including Otis Taylor, Buck Buchanan, Willie Lanier, and Emmitt Thomas, to name a few.

Wells got Jackson signed up with the Raiders where he played some tight end and linebacker in an injury-plagued rookie season of 1966. When Lou Saban took control of the Broncos in 1967, he started reshaping the roster in his own vision. He dumped almost every good player from the Broncos' first seven seasons and started building his own team. Floyd Little, the first-round Broncos running back, and Jackson were the franchise players on each side of the ball.

Sacks didn't become an official statistic until 1982, so there's no doubt Jackson got robbed of some numbers. The Broncos, with help from New Mexico–based sack researcher John Turney, pieced together 43 sacks Jackson had in his time from 1967 until after the fourth game of the 1972 season, when he was traded to Cleveland.

The team acknowledges that Jackson had 31 sacks in the three-year span from 1968–70: 10 in 1968, 11 in in 1969, and 10 in 1970, when he became the first Bronco named to the NFL All Pro team. Remember, those double-digit sack totals were in 14-game seasons.

He also had seven sacks in 1967, three in just seven games in 1971—a season cut short by a knee injury that eventually ended his career. He had two sacks in his first four games of 1972 when he was dealt to Cleveland for a third-round draft pick that turned out to be offensive guard Paul Howard, who would go on to have a 14-year career with the Broncos.

There is historical dispute over whether Jackson or Deacon Jones invented the "head slap" pass-rush technique. Jackson also came up with the "Halo Spinner" move. After the Broncos upset the Super Bowl III–bound New York Jets, 21–13, at Shea Stadium in a 1968 game, Jets coach Weeb Eubank said, "87 wasn't blocked all day."

During the off-season, Jackson worked for a couple of years back in Baton Rouge as a deputy sheriff. He also was one of the few players of his day who believed in strength and conditioning. He could bench-press 555 pounds, dead-lift 600. He would do 50 chin-ups and 50 dips. And he swam.

Unfortunately for Jackson, he was the Terrell Davis of Broncos defensive players in that he was spectacular for three or four years, but a knee injury prevented him from going on to greater glory.

It also didn't help that Saban wasn't nearly the same coach with the Broncos as he was when he'd led the Buffalo Bills to back-to-back AFL championships in 1964–65. In Saban's five seasons with Jackson and Little, from 1967–71, the Broncos went 3-11, 5-9, 5-8-1, 5-8-1, and 2-6-1, when he was fired.

After cleaning house of so many Broncos greats like Lionel Taylor, Goose Gonsoulin, and Willie Brown prior to the 1967 season, Saban couldn't stop making unfortunate moves. In Jackson's mind, Saban's most glaring mistakes were trading second-round rookie Curley Culp to the

Kansas City Chiefs in 1968 and quarterback Marlin Briscoe to the Buffalo Bills in 1969.

"Nobody to this day could figure out why he got rid of Curley Culp," Jackson said. "I think Lou tried to make an offensive lineman out of Curley. We tried to tell him the man wasn't an offensive lineman. His love was for defense. He was the missing link for the Kansas City defense. When he went there they put him at noseguard. So, he complemented Aaron Brown on the outside. Buck Buchanan. Willie Lanier. Jerry Mays, Bob Bell. Curley was the missing link. That was the link we had.

"Can you imagine a defensive line with Paul Smith, Curley Culp, Alden Roche, and myself? Alden Roche, he lasted one year with us. They traded him to Green Bay. He was Green Bay's most valuable player. We got rid of him, too.

"Then the best quarterback we had was Marlin Briscoe. The time he had to prepare was nothing compared to what the other guys had. And he went out and did what he did. He was electrifying. We called him 'The Magician.' He was truly a magician. He could throw a nice spiral. He knew the game. He was very elusive. And he was tough. We had some quarterbacks—if you looked at them they passed out. He was a tough cookie.

"But I don't know, I enjoyed myself here. We had the teams. We were just missing that one ingredient—the quarterback. I wish I wouldn't have gotten injured."

Three weeks after he was dealt to the Cleveland Browns during the 1972 season, Jackson returned to play against the Broncos at Mile High Stadium. It was Floyd Little Day, and Jackson helped spoil his former teammate's tribute with three tackles in a 27–20 Browns victory.

Browns owner Art Modell hated the AFL. Never respected it, even after the 1970 merger. Floyd Little Day or D-Day, Modell didn't want to lose to the lowly Denver Broncos.

"After the game, he was so happy we won, he came up and kissed me on the cheek," Jackson said. "That was his response."

Jackson went to the Browns training camp in 1973, but soon realized his knee was shot.

"When I decided I didn't want to play, I called the New Orleans public school system and set up an interview the following Monday," Jackson said.

He was a physical education teacher, a high school football and track coach, and then worked nearly 20 years in administration. He was also an urban specialist for the City of New Orleans recreation department. Set up the schedules for all the youth sports, trained all the lifeguards. He handled those responsibilities in the summer and after school.

Many educators were let go after Hurricane Katrina hit in 2005, and Jackson has been retired since. His son Rashaad played against Eli Manning in high school before getting his degree from Southern University. Jackson's oldest daughter, Gina Jackson-Washington, also graduated from her dad's alma mater.

Jackson's wife is a graduate of Xavier University of Louisiana–New Orleans. Their youngest daughter, Aniika Jackson-Smith, is a dentist in Kansas City, having graduated from Xavier and Creighton.

"Education is pretty big in our house," Jackson said in an understatement.

He is a charter member of the Broncos Ring of Fame, joining Gonsoulin, Little, and Taylor in the class of 1984.

"I try to come back every year they have this Ring of Fame ceremony," Jackson said. "As I sit here and we see the Denver Broncos facility, that could not have happened if it hadn't been for us. We helped save the franchise. In '67 we were playing in a 35,000-seat stadium. And the next time we went to 50,000. And then we went to 75,000. This new stadium they have now, they only added [27] seats.

"As a matter of fact, we came out here in '98 and spent about two weeks out here, Floyd, a whole bunch of us, and we went around to the news media, TV, to the charity center ball and all that, campaigning for a new stadium."

The Broncos' current football stadium opened in 2001.

"We helped build the foundation for this franchise," Jackson said.

With that, Jackson and his son Rashaad headed up to their hotel room to get ready for the Ring of Fame ceremony that night, when the Broncos would induct kicker Jason Elam, pass rusher Simon Fletcher, and safety John Lynch.

It was a good day.

RICH "TOMBSTONE" JACKSON STATS

YRS	G	S
6	67	43.0

17

— BILLY THOMPSON —

Cornerback/Safety, 1969–81

Well before the Rev. Jesse Jackson became a civil rights activist, political orator, and US senator, he served as mentor to the future captain of the Orange Crush.

Jackson was a senior quarterback at Sterling High School in Greenville, South Carolina, when Billy Thompson was a freshman-in-waiting at the same position.

"I idolized him as a kid," Thompson said. "I followed him when he went to North Carolina [A&T] to play football and baseball. He was a great athlete. We still talk occasionally today."

Thompson also followed Jackson as a Sterling High quarterback and wound up becoming a leader of a different kind. A sensational rookie cornerback and punt returner for the Broncos in 1969, Thompson was the captain, strong safety, and inspirational leader of the 1977 Orange Crush defense that was chiefly responsible for Denver's first-ever Super Bowl appearance.

"I guess I would put it like this: In terms of leadership, Billy Thompson," said Tom Jackson, another Orange Crush starter at outside linebacker. "Our leader. If you could ever find tape of it, there was a press conference when he retired, everybody on the team cried like babies. Cried like babies."

Thompson became the first player to last as many as 13 seasons with the Broncos. He played, and started in, 179 games, missing only the final five games of 1970, his second season, and the first eight games of 1972. He started the last 139 games of his career, a streak exceeded in NFL history only by Tampa Bay's Ronde Barber and Green Bay's Willie Wood among defensive backs.

It was a career that began in spectacular fashion as Thompson became the first player in professional history to lead his league—the American Football League, in this case, in its last year before its merger with the NFL—in both punt returns and kickoff returns.

Thompson averaged 11.5 yards on 25 punt returns and 28.5 yards on 18 kickoff returns as a rookie. He also started all 14 games at right cornerback that year, leading the team with three interceptions, including one against the Houston Oilers' Pete Beathard that he returned 57 yards for a touchdown.

It was one of seven defensive touchdowns Thompson scored in his career—3 on interceptions, 4 off fumble recoveries. He recorded 61 turnovers in his career—40 on interceptions, plus 21 fumble recoveries.

"He wasn't one of these pompous-type players. He'd play wherever they needed him to play," said Broncos running back great Floyd Little, who played seven seasons with Thompson. "He started out as a corner, but they needed him at safety. He was the best defensive back on the team. What do you need? Return kickoffs. He'd raise his hand. That's what made the kind of leader you want in a player. I'd like to see him in the Hall of Fame in every way."

It was as at strong safety that Thompson made his mark as Bronco Billy. His defensive backs coach in 1969 was Joe Collier, who was also in his first year coaching the Broncos. Collier would stay through the 1988 season in Denver, and among his trademark strategies was converting some of his best cornerbacks to safety later in their careers.

"When Coach wanted to change me, I said, 'Why?'" Thompson said. "He said, 'Well, we're going to make you a better player. You're going to be my guy that moves on defense and you're going to be the run enforcer. And you've got to take care of yourself because you're going to be facing guys bigger than you.'

"Joe Collier taught me so much about football that I didn't know. It was incredible to learn under a guy like that. He's a guy that doesn't get much credit for that '77 team like he really should."

Steve Foley, Dennis Smith, Tyrone Braxton, and Mike Harden were among those who made the transition from cornerback to safety. The first was Billy Thompson, who after four seasons as a right cornerback became a strong safety in 1973.

"The biggest thing about B.T. was his fierce competitiveness and leadership skills," said Foley, himself a former quarterback and right cornerback who switched from right cornerback to Thompson's safety partner in 1980. "But he had a body behind him—6-1, 205—and he was a hitter.

"What's funny is you play a few years with a guy and you come away feeling like you know him for a lifetime. I got to play six years with B.T. Just a super player, very knowledgeable. Big hitter."

Even with all his talent, Thompson has repeatedly said his NFL journey with the Broncos would not have been possible without so much help from others, most notably his parents and Art Shell.

His dad was a jewelry apprentice, who spent his days building, repairing, and shining watches and rings. Mom stayed home raising and mentoring Billy, his older sister, and his younger brother.

"I had great parents," Billy Thompson said. "They didn't get the opportunities that I did. They sacrificed for us. I was the only one of the three of us to finish college and get involved in the things I did. Had I not been drafted by the Broncos, I was going to be a teacher and coach in Baltimore."

Thompson played basketball, baseball, and football in high school, and was successful in all of them. At Maryland State, now University of Maryland Eastern Shore, he played baseball and football. As you might have guessed, Thompson was a splendid center fielder. He would also catch the second game of doubleheaders.

Leadership positions.

"Art Shell got me into college," Thompson said.

Shell got through his South Carolina high school a year earlier than Thompson and had already been attending Maryland State when he went back to watch South Carolina's high school All Star game.

"He came over and introduced himself," Thompson said. "I didn't know who he was. He said, I need you to talk to my coaches. He said, I'm talking to you because they can't. He said, I'm going to take you out to dinner tonight. And the rest is history. I went to school there at Maryland State for four years and played with some great guys.

"At the time, I had offers from a couple other schools. I just felt good about them, the guys who picked me up and took me out to dinner that night. I felt comfortable with them. This is something I've never done, and they made me feel good, and they said, When you come to camp at the school we'll take care of you. And they did. They were like my mentors. Art Shell, Emerson Boozer, Earl Christy, Curtis Gentry, Charlie Stukes—these guys really took care of me."

A full-time defensive back at Maryland State, Thompson was twice an NAIA All American and—perhaps, more impressively—a three-time Central Intercollegiate Athletic Association (CIAA) first-team selection as a defensive back in football and center fielder in baseball.

In the 1969 NFL-AFL common draft, Broncos coach and football operations boss Lou Saban selected Thompson in the third round, No. 61 overall.

"Coach Saban asked me if the Broncos were my favorite team," Thompson said. "I told him no. He said, What about now? I said, You got me. He said, We're going to the Super Bowl."

That would not happen while Saban was in charge. The Broncos went 5-8-1 in Thompson's rookie year.

"I was on the College All Star team that played the Jets at Soldier Field," Thompson said, referring to when the college All Stars played the defending NFL champions, a series that kicked off the preseason schedule from 1934 through 1976. "They beat us, 26–24. Then we came to Denver in '69 and that was the [helmet to stomach] hit that Dave Costa had on Joe Namath. We upset the Jets [21–19]. This was my rookie year, and I said to myself, 'This is going to be easy.'"

The Broncos were 2-0 at time.

"And we lost the next three in a row," he said.

In that upset victory against Namath's Jets, Thompson played a part in the longest punt in NFL history. With the Jets backed up to their own 1-yard line, punter Steve O'Neal from his own end zone drilled a long, line-drive punt that got caught in the vortex of 5,280 feet above sea level. Thompson was standing near midfield, retreated to his own 35-yard line, and failed to make a difficult, over-the-shoulder catch. The ball bounced to the Broncos' 1—and stopped dead still.

The 98-yard punt is a record that can't be broken without a touchback. Thompson scrambled back to pick up the ball and returned it one yard, to the 2.

"The ground was a little hard," Thompson said 47 years later, in October 2016. "The wind took it and the ball hit on the nose of the football and just took off. I'd never seen anything like it. And that was the year I led the league in punt and kickoff returns.

"I'll never forget the look on Coach Saban's face when I was coming off the field. But what could I do? Steve O'Neal. As a matter of fact, he became a dentist in Bryan, Texas. Unbelievable punt. I remember when I came back to the bench Lou gave me that dead stare. I went the other way. Joe Collier said, Don't worry about it, Billy, it wasn't your fault. But Lou was furious."

The Denver Broncos can be separated into two historical segments—the first 13 seasons, when they never had a winning season, and the next 44, when the Broncos had just seven losing records, tying the Pittsburgh Steelers for the fewest losing seasons in that period.

Thompson was one of the few whose career overlapped both periods. It was those difficult first four losing seasons that helped him appreciate the Broncos' first winning season in 1973 (7-5-2 under John Ralston) and the great season of 1977, when Denver went 12-2 in the regular season, then won home playoff games against the mighty Pittsburgh Steelers and defending-champion Oakland Raiders at Mile High Stadium.

Between them, the Steelers and Raiders had combined to win the three previous Super Bowls.

"It was great, because it was the Raiders, and the Raiders had always dominated us at home, on the road, wherever," Thompson said.

Indeed, in the 14-season period starting with the 1963 season on through 1976, the Raiders had gone 24-2-2 against the Broncos, including a 17-0-1 run from 1963 through '71.

"And that '77 year we beat the Raiders twice," Thompson said. "We beat them out there [in the regular season]. And I'll never forget the looks on the faces of Al Davis and Art Shell after the AFC Championship. Art used to come up to me after every game and say, 'Billy, you guys just have to keep hustling. You've got a great team; it's just not your time.' And I went up to him after the AFC Championship game and said, 'I think our time is now.' And he just laughed. We shook hands and we moved on to the Super Bowl."

After he finished playing following the 1981 season, Thompson went to work for the Broncos in 1992 as their director of community outreach, a task that includes overseeing the team's alumni. That's 38 years combined employment as a player and administrator. Bronco Billy, indeed.

As the person who heads the Broncos alumni, Thompson keeps in touch with many of his former teammates. Floyd Little counts Billy Thompson as his closest friend.

"I got an honorary doctorate degree from Syracuse in May [2016], and Billy was there," Little said. "He flew cross-country to see me walk across the stage. He was the first to call me Dr. Little. That's the kind of friend he is."

Little was the team's captain from his rookie season until he retired after the 1975 season. In 1976, Thompson became the captain.

"Being tutored by Floyd and all the players before us, it was a responsibility that when we came out, we had to play our hearts out," Thompson said. "It was demanded. No matter what the score was, no matter if we were ahead or behind. We had to play, and we had to play hard.

"What I liked about it was, everybody wanted to be the hero. No one wanted to be the guy who was not hustling that would make a mistake in a crucial situation. And that's the way we practiced. The guys on that '77 team, we're still close today."

BILLY THOMPSON STATS

YRS	G	I	Y	TD
14	179	40	784	7

18

DEMARYIUS THOMAS

Receiver, 2010–17

To become familiar with the journey Demaryius Thomas took to the NFL is to wonder how many other athletically gifted people in this world never got a chance.

Perhaps the greatest receiver who ever lived never played football because at 11 years old, police officers stormed his home to take away his mother for the rest of his young life.

Maybe, the person gifted with the second-greatest receiving skills of all time never got a chance to use them because after his freshman year in college, a coaching change brought in an option offense where the quarterback ran more than he passed, where the team averaged 57 rushing attempts and only 12 pass attempts a game.

This is all part of the Demaryius Thomas story. His mom—and his grandmother, too—were imprisoned following a drug sting in Montrose, Georgia, as he watched the bust from his home before he was a teenager.

After not only keeping his life together but flourishing enough to later attend Georgia Tech, Thomas's new coach, Paul Johnson, instituted a highly successful option offense that generated only 74 pass completions (one by Thomas) in Thomas's sophomore season. Not 74 pass completions in two games. The entire season. Thomas caught 39 of the 74, or 53 percent.

As a junior, Thomas caught 46 of the Yellow Jackets' 78 completions (59 percent) for an incredible 1,154 yards—25.1 yards per catch. What few chances Thomas has had in life, he made the most of them.

There was good that came from adversity. Thomas grew up to become friendly, polite, drug-free, and respectful of others.

"I guess it was some of the ways I grew up," Thomas said. "Seeing so much stuff. Seeing what happened with angry people. I'm not saying it's a bad thing but just what happened with my family and stuff and being around people in college where they'd get angry. I just hate when people—I don't care who you are, I hate when people are disrespectful. My dad and my auntie and uncle would lean on opening the door for somebody, or saying thank you or 'Yes sir. No, ma'am.' It kind of grew on me as I got older, and as a man I found it helps you out. People look at you differently.

"I just try to stay out of people's way. I do my job to the best of my ability. I have my problems here and there, but I never try to let it come into my work or you guys [the media] who I see every day. If I got a problem, I'll leave it at the house."

Thomas also grew up to become a first-round draft pick of the Denver Broncos and one of the NFL's top two or three receivers during his best seasons, while his quarterback was Peyton Manning.

Thomas's celebrity no doubt helped to capture the attention of President Barack Obama, who commuted the sentence of Thomas's mom, Katina Smith, in 2015. And Thomas's direct plea on behalf of his grandmother, Minnie Pearl Thomas, to the commander in chief during the Super Bowl champion Broncos' trip to the White House in June 2016 led to another pardon. Today, both his mom and grandma are free.

"I've been blessed," Thomas said. "I could have gone a different way, but everything that happened to me made me a better person. And it made me the player I am today. I had a lot of good guidance along the way. I had people look out for me. I can't complain how it all turned out, but I've got more work to do. I want to win more Super Bowls. I want to become a better receiver. I want more catches, more touchdowns. I want to become the best."

This might have been my most difficult ranking, primarily because Thomas is still very much an active player. As former baseball union chief Donald Fehr once told me: History should not be judged by contemporaries.

Still, there is no doubt that even if Thomas retired today, he would still go down as one of the 50 Greatest Players in Denver Broncos History. Where to rank him was the problem.

Clearly, Thomas is the most talented receiver in Broncos history. No other receiver in team history had five consecutive seasons of at least 90 catches and 1,000 yards, as Thomas did from 2012–16—a streak he carried into the 2017 season at the time of this writing, by the way. Thomas *averaged* 98 catches for 1,374 yards and 9 touchdowns during that five-year stretch.

No other Broncos receiver ever had the ability to take a receiver screen along the line of scrimmage and go 70-plus yards for a touchdown, as D.T. did five times in his career.

"He reminds me a little bit of Brandon Marshall earlier in his career," said Broncos cornerback Champ Bailey. Marshall had three consecutive 100-catch, 1,100-yard seasons for the Broncos from 2007–09. "I got to know them both when they were puppies. It was just figuring out how to use what they had. They were both big guys, and one thing about

Demaryius, to me he was faster than Brandon Marshall. That's what made him a little scarier. He was very explosive; still is. He figured it out a lot faster than most young receivers because he was just trying to soak it up. He didn't have a lot of distractions. He's a consummate pro. I'm proud of the way he's handled himself up until this point."

You'll notice that Rod Smith is the highest-ranked receiver in this book. Even Thomas admitted in the final week of the 2016 season that he has not surpassed Smith as the top Broncos receiver of all time.

"I would like to be put in the situation where it's a toss-up between me and Rod once I'm done," Thomas said. "When I came in, that was a guy I looked up to and I actually worked with, and talk to him still. I watched him play, and at first he reminded me of [former teammate Eric] Decker. But watching him give his all, he taught me how to get off press on slants with a big body and be aggressive."

Smith has about three more seasons' worth of catches, yards, and touchdowns than Thomas had through the 2016 season.

Smith's career was about steady, sure-handed production. And leadership. But he couldn't flash the spectacular leap-up, reach-back, haul-in pass like Thomas does on a regular basis. And, again, the run after the catch? In 2013, Thomas led the NFL with 718 yards after the catch. He was second among receivers in 2012 (561 yards after catch) and 2014 (680 YAC).

So why isn't Thomas ranked higher? Because for all his catches and big plays—he already ranks third in team history behind Smith and tight end Shannon Sharpe in receptions, yardage, and touchdowns—Thomas has dropped a few. In his massively productive five-year streak of 90 and 1,000, he was also among the top eight in the NFL in drops each of those five years.

This is the problem with ranking active players, though. Ten years after Thomas retires, people will tend to remember only the great plays. He already has a team-most 34, 100-yard receiving games. He has already made four Pro Bowls, more than any other Broncos receiver. He set a Super Bowl record with 13 receptions.

Yet, because Thomas signed a five-year, $70 million contract following the 2014 season, more is expected. It's that way with all the top, active players.

"You know, he does get a lot of criticism about drops, and it's not fair, because everybody forgets he got 1,300 yards [in 2015]," said Thomas's receiver mate Emmanuel Sanders in the days leading up to Super Bowl 50. "Come on, man, he's got 1,300! Leave the man alone. Last year he got 1,600? Okay, last year he got 1,600, and he may have eight drops, but I'll take that.

"You ask any organization in the National Football League if they'd take Demaryius Thomas and they'll say, 'Yes, bring him over here.' I'm just happy to be a part. I'm happy to be his teammate. He's a baller. He works his butt off. He has great character."

As a kid, football was an afterthought for Thomas. He liked everything but the contact part.

"Growing up, my first sport was basketball," he said. "I never played on a traveling team. I always played in the yard. The first time I ever played on a team was my sixth-grade year. Basketball was the first thing. I tried out for football my eighth-grade year. I played defense. Didn't like hitting, so I stopped playing and stuck with basketball.

"And then track came around. I did the 4-by-100, triple jump, and long jump. As I got older, ninth-grade year, I still didn't play football—it was still basketball and track. Tenth grade, I made my mind up I was going to try it again because once basketball season was over with, all my buddies I was going home to play sports in the yard with . . . were playing football. I started off playing defense at first. The secondary with the high school team."

In that backyard, they used to play a game. "Throw 'em up, bust 'em . up," Thomas said. They would throw the ball in the air and up to a dozen kids from the neighborhood would fight for it. The kid who wound up with the ball would have to outmaneuver all the other kids from one end of the yard to the other.

"I was really good at that game," Thomas said.

He was born on Christmas Day 1987. One time, I asked him what it's like to have Christmas for a birthday.

"You ask me that every year," he said on Christmas Day 2015.

Come Christmas week of 2016, I forgot again. I asked him about having his birthday on Christmas Day. Again. Only this time it was in a small group of media. Thomas could have showed me up, rolled his eyes, dismissed the question, but he's not that type.

"It's not the best, but it's also not bad, either," he said with a smile. "You feel cool sometimes, but you get robbed when you're a kid. . . . The part that bothers me is when you have to buy gifts for other people on your birthday. I'm still trying to get over that. I'm buying Christmas gifts, but it's my birthday."

Thomas was the parting gift Josh McDaniels left for the Broncos. McDaniels's coaching term in Denver didn't go well, but he did have the foresight to make Thomas the Broncos' surprising first-round pick in the 2010 draft, No. 22 overall.

"Didn't expect to go there at all," Thomas said. "Everything was Dez. I didn't run much of the route tree in college, and then I broke my foot before my combine. I didn't think I would get drafted in the first round at all."

Dez Bryant was the highly touted receiver coming out of the draft, but he also had character concerns. After McDaniels clashed with Marshall the previous year, he wanted the coachable Thomas.

After easing into the NFL as a rookie, Thomas broke out in his second season of 2011, even though his quarterback was the passing-challenged Tim Tebow. Then again, Thomas was more accustomed than other receivers to producing in a run-heavy offense, as he did so at Georgia Tech.

He missed the first five games of 2011 to recover from an Achilles injury and then a broken thumb, but Thomas, in a 35–32 win at Minnesota, had 144 yards receiving and two touchdowns off just four catches.

It was the fifth of six consecutive wins Tebow had engineered for the Broncos that season, enough to win the AFC West with an 8-8 record that drew a first-round playoff game at home against heavily favored Pittsburgh.

In that game played at Sports Authority Field at Mile High, Thomas had receptions of 58 and 51 yards during regulation to help the Broncos forge a 23–23 tie against Ben Roethlisberger and the Steelers.

On the first play of overtime, Thomas came through with arguably the greatest single play in Broncos history.

The Broncos won the overtime coin toss and after a touchback, had the ball first-and-10 at their own 20. The call came in. Tebow was in the shotgun with Thomas split wide left, across from Pittsburgh's best cornerback, Ike Taylor. Tebow faked an inside handoff to tailback Willis McGahee, then drew back and hit Thomas in stride at about the Denver 38-yard line.

Thomas had beaten Taylor off the line and was a good step and a half in front when he snagged the pass about helmet-high with two hands—in the part of the field where the safety is ordinarily found to defend. The Steeler safeties, though, had crept up near the line of scrimmage prior to the snap in anticipation of a Tebow option-run play.

Taylor recovered and started wrapping his arms around Thomas's shoulders and facemask at the Broncos' 46. But Thomas warded off his defensive back with a ferocious left stiff arm.

The 6-foot-3, 230-pound Thomas had a head of steam around midfield, but safety Ryan Mundy seemingly had the angle on chasing down the Broncos receiver.

"He had the angle," Thomas said, "but he couldn't get it."

Thomas ran all the way to the right corner of the south end zone, and because the field was frozen slick, he kept running into the Broncos tunnel, Bo Jackson style. Touchdown.

It had eclipsed Champ Bailey's 100-yard interception in a 2005-season playoff game against New England as the most jubilant moment at the newer Broncos stadium, which opened in 2001.

The sellout crowd went berserk. "I'll never forget that one," Thomas said. "I look back and say that was my coming-out game because I had only four catches, but for 204 yards. I went up against Ike Taylor, one of the best corners at the time. To be able to do that with a guy everybody said couldn't throw in Tebow . . . but it was like, 'Man, this guy delivered.' That play started me off in the league.

"Breaking those records with Peyton [in 2013], playing in two Super Bowls, winning the Super Bowl [in 2016]—those were great, too. Those were probably bigger in the big picture. But when you're talking about one play, that catch from Tebow was probably the one."

Thomas is easily on pace to become the all-time leading receiver in Broncos history. Here's a look at the team's top four receivers:

PLAYER	YRS	G	REC	Y	TD
Rod Smith	12	183	849	11,389	68
Shannon Sharpe	12	172	675	8,439	55
Demaryius Thomas	7	101	546	7,704	52
Lionel Taylor	7	96	543	6,872	44

Thomas should move past Sharpe into second place in career receiving yards and touchdowns in 2017, and even if he doesn't supplant Smith as the number-one Broncos receiver, there's little debate that D.T. will go down as one of the more dynamic players in team annals.

If Sharpe and Smith are top-10 players in Broncos history, there shouldn't be much problem with Thomas getting a place among the top 20. The only question is whether D.T. winds up in the top 10 before he's finished.

DEMARYIUS THOMAS STATS				
YRS	G	REC	Y	TD
7	101	546	7,704	52

POSTSEASON			
G	REC	Y	TD
10	53	759	6

19
LIONEL TAYLOR
Wide Receiver, 1960–66

It's been a while since Lionel Taylor attended one of the Broncos alumni reunions.

"The older we get, the bigger the lies, the better we were," Taylor said shortly after his 81st birthday in the summer of 2016.

The truth about Taylor is he's one of the least-recognized great receivers in professional football history.

Let's begin the story on Lionel Taylor by getting it straight.

It's not quite true that he went from playing linebacker with the Chicago Bears in 1959 to setting a professional football record with 92 catches as a receiver for the Denver Broncos in 1960.

Actually, all that is true except for the part about the linebacker. After starting for both the basketball and football teams at tiny New Mexico Highlands University, Taylor did attend the Bears training camp as a linebacker in 1958.

"[The] only way I could get invited to camp was as a linebacker," Taylor said in a phone interview from his New Mexico home. "I ended up as a wide receiver, which I wanted to be. Because I've got news for you: I never hit anybody in four years in college and three years of high school. So, I wasn't going to play no defense."

It was different then. As a college linebacker, Taylor could cover would-be pass receivers extremely well—he was really more defensive back than linebacker—but the tackling he left to others.

Still, linebacker gave Taylor a chance to show George "Papa Bear" Halas what he could do. Only the Bears cut Taylor in 1958. He spent that year in Bakersfield, California, playing on the same semipro team as Tom Flores, the future quarterback and head coach of the Oakland Raiders.

Only Flores played defensive back in Bakersfield, while Taylor played the first half of games at receiver and the second half as a shotgun quarterback.

"We'd huddle and I'd draw up plays in the dirt," Taylor said.

113

In 1959, Taylor returned to the Bears training camp, this time as a receiver. He was cut again, but this time was re-signed after the Bears' second game. He didn't catch a pass in eight games that year.

"I was a starter those eight games," Taylor said. "You know why? I was on special teams, and you always start the game with a kickoff. I never was a starter with the Broncos."

Taylor went to a third training camp with the Bears in 1960. Again, he was waived, with Halas promising to bring him back after the second game. This time, Taylor was intrigued by the American Football League Denver Broncos. Dean Griffing, the Broncos' first general manager, was scouting for his Canadian Football League team when he spotted Taylor playing in Bakersfield.

During his two-week waiting period with the Bears, Taylor decided to visit the Broncos. At the time, the team was out east, opening their inaugural season with games at Boston and Buffalo. Taylor met up with the team at their New Jersey hotel the week the Broncos were to play their third game against the New York Titans.

"I didn't think the league was going to make it," Taylor said. "But I thought if I could come over and make a name for myself, I could go back to the NFL and get a little money, get a better deal."

Taylor's first game was the Broncos' third. It was at the Polo Grounds before a gathering of 20,462 on what was described in the official game book as a clear and mild afternoon.

Taylor didn't have a catch in the first quarter, but he wound up with six catches for 125 yards, including a 31-yard touchdown reception on a pass thrown by Broncos quarterback Frank Tripucka.

Taylor gave all the credit to his quarterback.

"I'll never forget that first touchdown he ever threw to me at the Polo Grounds," Taylor said. "I didn't start. I just joined them. I didn't know the terminology, I didn't know Frank. So I said, 'Hey can you throw me that down-and-in play?'

"And he didn't say anything to me. I went back to the bench and then in the huddle he said, 'Hey, you!' He didn't know my name. I said, 'What?' He said, 'Can you run that post pattern?' He threw it for a touchdown. He was something."

Taylor went on to have one of the most remarkable receiving seasons in American Football League–National Football League history in 1960. In just 12 games, Taylor had 92 catches—an all-time professional record at the time. The previous record, 84 catches by Tom Fears of the Los Angeles Rams in 1950, had stood for 10 years.

Taylor also ranked third in the AFL with 1,235 receiving yards and tied for second with 12 touchdowns.

Given the full 14 games the next year, Taylor in 1961 became the first-ever receiver to record 100 catches in a season. His 1,176 receiving yards ranked second.

"Frank got me started on the right track," Taylor said.

The Broncos media guide said that Taylor had "unquestionably the greatest hands in football."

"Lionel Taylor was not just a football player," said Gene Mingo, a team-mate of Taylor's from 1960–64. "He was a leader. You could ask him to do anything; he would do anything while playing his position. In my eyes, he should have been in the Hall of Fame."

Taylor went on to lead the AFL–NFL with 77 catches in 1962, 78 catches in 1963, and 85 receptions in 1965. His 76 catches in 1964 tied for second. To review, he led the AFL–NFL in receptions four consecutive seasons (1960–63), five of the first six.

Yet, although Taylor was part of the first class of Broncos Ring of Famers in 1984, and was also inducted into the Colorado Sports Hall of Fame, he is one of several AFL stars who have been overlooked by the Pro Football Hall of Fame in Canton, Ohio.

"No, no," said the humble Taylor. "They've got too many people up there in that lineup for me to be up there."

Taylor was born August 15, 1935, in Kansas City, Missouri, a miracle child as far as his parents were concerned.

"Out of three births, I was the only one that lived," Taylor said. "I was 3 pounds, 11 ounces."

He grew up in the coal-mining town of Lorado, West Virginia. His father, J. C. Taylor, was a coal miner for 45 years. His mother, Bertha, was a stay-at-home mom.

"We didn't have Little League or anything like that," Taylor said. "We all played sandlot with a Carnation milk can. That was our football. We just played street ball. If you couldn't throw a spiral with a Carnation milk can, you couldn't play quarterback."

Basketball was Lionel's favorite sport. He played football because that sport was so huge in the area; the Buffalo High School athletic department didn't allow its boys to play basketball unless they also played football.

Taylor played at the same high school as Charlie Cowan, who was three years younger. When Taylor wound up playing his college ball at New Mexico Highlands, Cowan did, too.

Where they separated was when the Broncos in 1961 selected Cowan in the fifth round of the AFL Draft, he instead signed with the Los Angeles Rams, who selected him in the fourth round of the NFL Draft.

Cowan wound up playing 15 years with the Rams as a left guard and right tackle.

Taylor at New Mexico Highlands was a shooting guard and small forward who once scored 30 points in a game against Air Force, and has the newspaper article to prove it.

He then set off on his unlikely journey to becoming one of the three best receivers in Broncos history, along with Rod Smith and Demaryius Thomas.

Like his good friend and teammate from the 1960s, Broncos safety Goose Gonsoulin, Taylor had six great years in Denver; got hurt, causing his production to fall off drastically in his seventh season; and then was dispatched by new coach Lou Saban prior to the 1967 season.

"My last year I [hurt] my thigh," Taylor said. "That's no excuse. We didn't throw it a lot."

He caught just 35 passes in 1966 from the quarterback likes of Max Choboian, John McCormick, Mickey Slaughter, and Scotty Glacken.

After that season, Taylor wound up with the Houston Oilers, where he would have just 24 catches in two years.

He then moved on to a lengthy coaching career, starting with a stint as receivers coach for the Pittsburgh Steelers, from 1970–76. He is the first to acknowledge that he became a much better coach starting in 1974, when the Steelers drafted both Lynn Swann and John Stallworth.

"I used to say that when I was coaching the Steelers, all I had to do was throw the ball out there and not say anything," Taylor said.

He then coached receivers for the Los Angeles Rams from 1977–81; Oregon State, 1982–83; Texas Southern 1984–88; and Cleveland Browns 1989–90; before doing a four-year stint in NFL Europe from 1995–98.

He then worked part-time with the International Management Group Academy, where on behalf of agents he would train the likes of LaDainian Tomlinson, Eli Manning, and Jim Kelly.

"We'd take them for two months, drills," Taylor said. "Adrian Peterson was the last guy I worked with."

Taylor now lives in Rio Rancho, a suburb of Albuquerque, New Mexico, with his wife of 58 years, Lorencita. They have two grown daughters, Loretta, and LaVern.

"Everybody's 'L.T.,'" Taylor said.

The most vivid memories he has of his playing days with the Broncos?

"You know, I can tell you every pass I dropped," he said. "I dropped one on the 3-yard line against Houston and we had 'em beat, and I ran a hitch pattern and it went right through my hands. I turned my head and started to run. I'll never forget that."

In that case, what Taylor needs is one more reunion with some of the other Broncos greats. The stories they all tell about Taylor, though, are no lie. If anything, they're understated.

"I don't know if any other team does as well as the Broncos with that Ring of Fame and bringing guys back," Taylor said. "They're fantastic about that. I haven't been back for years, but I hope to get up there this year."

LIONEL TAYLOR STATS

YRS	G	C	Y	TD
7	96	543	6,872	44

20

TOM JACKSON

Outside Linebacker, 1973–86

It was a special occasion, all right, and not only because it was the first playoff game in Denver Broncos history.

What made this game against the Pittsburgh Steelers special for Thomas Louis Jackson III was that his dad would be in attendance. Understand this was a different time. And Tom Jackson Jr. was no ordinary dad.

It was the 1977 season, and the Orange Crush hype machine was revved at full throttle. The biggest personality in Broncos history, and its second-best outside linebacker, Tom Jackson III was 13 years old, happily growing up with his sister and loving parents in Cleveland when he shockingly lost his mom, Katie.

"My mom went from being perfectly healthy to having a headache, and within days she had passed," Jackson said. "She had a stroke on Tuesday and she passed on Friday."

His father became a single parent who took on the roles of both mom and dad. Thomas Jackson Jr. provided by day, cooked by night, shaped his kids throughout life's twists, turns, and tragedies.

"Back in those days my parents had the traditional roles of a household," Jackson said. "My mom stayed home and cooked, my dad went to work. But watching my dad teach himself to cook is something that resonated with me as a person. He got to the point where his pot roast or his chicken was something he was so proud of. I watched him transition from man of the house to single parent and responsibility for me and my sister. That turned out to influence me in a great many ways as my life has gone on."

The nation's economy on Christmas Eve 1977 wasn't what it was today. Eating out was something families did on payday, not three or six times a week. And when people did go out, they rarely ventured beyond their neighborhood.

"Back then, parents didn't do what I do for my girls, which is travel around and watch them play soccer and getting on airplanes and going to watch the one [Morgan] that's in college play," Jackson said. "My dad saw me play in my 14 years probably a total of four times. But he was at that game. The Pittsburgh game. He came to our first playoff game."

Know how a player or coach or fan will say something like, "It was meant to be!"

With 4:30 left in the first half and the score tied, 7–7, Steelers future Hall of Fame running back Franco Harris was smothered by Broncos defensive end Lyle Alzado behind the line, and fumbled. Jackson picked it up and ran 25 yards to the Steelers' 10.

On the next play, Otis Armstrong ran it in and the Broncos were up, 14–7.

That's one turnover for Jackson. The Broncos were clinging to a 24–21 lead early in the fourth quarter, but the Steelers took over at their own 40. Two plays later, Jackson intercepted a Terry Bradshaw pass and returned it 32 yards to the Steelers' 9. The Broncos settled for a short field goal and a 27–21 lead.

There are two turnovers for T.J. Very next series, Bradshaw converted two third-down passes, and on first-and-10 from his 41, his pass to midfield was intercepted by—you guessed it—Jackson, who returned it 17 yards to the Steelers' 33. Two plays later, Broncos quarterback Craig Morton threw a touchdown pass to Jack Dolbin.

Three Jackson turnovers and returns that were converted into 17 points, the key as the Broncos emerged victorious from their first-ever playoff game by defeating the mighty Steelers (who were Super Bowl champs in the recent 1974 and '75 seasons), 34–21. It was, perhaps, the top individual highlight of Jackson's career.

"I always think of not only the importance of the game, but the fact my dad was there watching; that was of ultimate importance to me," Jackson said. "And to me, that's one of those moments I'll never forget.

"Now, obviously, the next weekend, when we punch our ticket to the Super Bowl [by defeating Oakland in the AFC Championship Game] that certainly looms large. But that game against a Steelers team that good, to beat them and get us on the right track, is a unique highlight for me."

Within those three defensive plays was the essence of Tom Jackson, the player. He was a tremendous athletic linebacker who not only made plays but also went on the offensive and returned them.

In 1976, as the Orange Crush was formulating, Jackson had seven interceptions with 136 return yards. As a linebacker. It's a single-season record among Broncos linebackers that will likely never be broken. Only one other linebacker in the 95-year history of the NFL has had more—Baltimore's Stan White, who had 8 interceptions in 1975.

More than one of Jackson's former Orange Crush teammates referred to him as the Von Miller of his day.

Besides 20 career interceptions, Jackson also had 44 sacks. And this was as Jackson was going out in 1986, as Lawrence Taylor was coming in to change the game, where outside linebackers became the league's preeminent pass rushers.

Jackson never got to pin his ears back and go after the quarterback play after play the way Miller, DeMarcus Ware, and Derrick Thomas did a few years later.

"No, our responsibilities back then were twofold," Jackson said. "You had to not only be a player who could pass-rush, but you had to play the run as well. You had to play well in coverage. I think as complicated as the game has become, it's also gotten a little bit simpler."

Really? Meaning, more specialized? Some guys are good against the run and play on first down while other guys are better going forward and play on third down?

"It's gotten specialized," Jackson said. "Guys in our day had to play every down. Guys don't do that anymore. I respect Von so much. What a superior talent he is. He's getting better and better. I don't think he's peaked."

I mentioned this in Randy Gradishar's chapter—that while watching the Broncos during their Orange Crush years from the Chicagoland area, and at college in Murray, Kentucky, I always thought Jackson was Denver's best player.

It wasn't until I moved to Colorado in October 1984 that I heard people occupying the local barstools state the case for Gradishar and Louie Wright as the best players on that famed Broncos defense of the late 1970s.

I came to realize why I always thought Jackson was the best. One, he was a great player. A first-team All Pro in 1977–78. A playmaking linebacker. The first player to play 14 seasons with the Broncos, as he lasted one more year than Billy Thompson and Barney Chavous.

"Tommy was my roommate. We'd just lay in bed and talk about football all night long," Thompson said. "One of the best weak-side linebackers I'd ever seen. Played with tremendous heart, tremendous effort."

The second reason was that Dick Enberg, Curt Gowdy, and Merlin Olsen, the NBC announcers for AFC games in the 1970s and '80s, often spoke, and relayed more anecdotes, about the engaging Jackson than any other Bronco.

One can only imagine how smitten the announcers must have been with Jackson during their production meetings on the eve of the Broncos broadcasts.

"He was the greatest storyteller I've ever been around," said Steve Foley, a cornerback, safety, and longtime Jackson teammate in Denver.

It's not Jackson's fault he's so entertaining. He belongs in the Hall of Fame, too, not only for his 14-year playing career as a Broncos outside linebacker, but also for his 29 years as the NFL's top studio analyst. Think about that. For more than 40 years—the period when football eclipsed all other sports as the game best suited for television—Jackson became the telegenic face of the league.

He was inducted into the Broncos Ring of Fame in his first year of eligibility, in 1992. There has to be a place for him somewhere in the bronze bust room in Canton.

"What you call flamboyant or colorful personalities, there were two guys," said Gradishar, who played inside linebacker alongside Jackson. "The first was Lyle Alzado. And also Tommy Jackson. They were the guys with the biggest personalities in my 10 years.

"Tommy stayed all 10 years I was there. He got in your face. He was always talking to the opponent, different players. He was yelling at coaches. He was our emotional, inspirational kind of guy. Tommy was a good outside linebacker. He competed. He was All Pro a couple of times. He was certainly the big voice and emotional voice of our team, with [Bob] Swenson and Billy Thompson."

In 1981, the Broncos started the Bob Peck Memorial Award in honor of the team's beloved public relations director who had died of brain cancer the previous year. The Bob Peck award would be given to the team's most inspirational player.

Jackson was voted by his teammates as the most inspirational player the first six consecutive seasons of the award. He had to retire before another player could receive the honor [Keith Bishop, in 1987].

"Tommy was the heart and soul and swagger of our defense," Foley said. "And he was a hitter. He wasn't that big, 215, 220. But he could run and he could hit. That legendary hit on, I think it was Clarence Davis, and he runs up to Madden—and I'm behind him, I'm playing right corner, and he's playing the weak side and I'm running up and I hear him go, 'How do you like that, Fat Man!' And the Raiders are ready to jump on him. But that was Tommy."

Ah yes, one of the most famous smack-talk moments in Broncos lore. It occurred during the 1977 regular season, on October 16 in the

Oakland–Alameda County Coliseum. Context is important here. Going into the 1977 season, the Broncos had won just 2 of their previous 28 games against the Raiders, going back to 1963.

In this game, the Broncos took out 14 years of Raiders frustration by dominating Oakland, 30–7. The Orange Crush intercepted Raiders quarterback Kenny Stabler not once, not twice, but *seven* times. The most stinging moment, however, was reserved for Raiders coach John Madden.

"There is a turnover that takes place right on the sideline," Jackson said in an interview for this project in December 2016. "And we kind of ended up rolling up on the sideline. And when I got up, John Madden was literally standing within four or five feet of me. It wasn't meant to be derogatory, but what it was, was this relief of all the things that had gone on with the Raiders' success and the Broncos' failures up to that time. And all of a sudden, here I was, face-to-face with the guy who stood for what the Oakland Raiders were about. I just remember standing up and saying, 'It's all over, Fat Man.' It was quite the moment."

Here's how Madden referred to that moment in his autobiography, *One Knee Equals Two Feet (And Everything Else You Need to Know about Football)*:

> Tommy Jackson of the Broncos wasn't very big, but he was a quick linebacker before there were quick linebackers. And he was the wildest linebacker I've ever seen. You never knew where he was going to turn up. He was tough, but not disciplined, which made him that much harder to figure out. Against a disciplined linebacker, you knew that if you did this, he would do that. But with Jackson, you had no idea. One time he might run in there, the next time he'd run out there. And for some reason he didn't like me.
> "Take that, fat man," he would yell.
> He was the only player who ever yelled at me like that.

Jackson admits that his passionate competitiveness wasn't completely innate. He credits much of his ambitious aggressiveness to his John Adams High School wrestling coach, John Bianchi.

"A little Italian guy who weighed all of about 155 pounds," Jackson said. "He taught me how to compete. And how to train. And how to transfer your passion to the wrestling mat. I think his influence was great to me because he taught me how to go out and care about what you're doing beyond a score, beyond what the referee might say, and to be unafraid."

Jackson wrestled in the heavyweight division even though it wouldn't have been difficult for him to shed one or two pounds and compete in the 185-pound division. As a 187-pound heavyweight, Jackson was always wrestling against larger opponents.

"Part of what Coach Bianchi had to get through to me was you have to be unafraid when you go out there to wrestle," Jackson said. "Well, that carried over to the undersized linebacker. And not worrying so much about my size, or lack thereof, and being able to go out there in the NFL and compete.

"He influenced me in a great many ways. But he was also a guy who had great character. Typical of the coaches back in those days, he loved us. I don't mean to get too sappy, but the man had us over for meals. The man loved us. I don't think many of us who wrestled for him will ever forget that."

The Orange Crush years were to the Broncos what Neil Armstrong was to astronaut moon walkers. The first. We take the Broncos for granted now because they've been pretty much winning every year since the mid-1970s. But there was a time when they never won. As in their first 13 seasons.

The Broncos' 14th season featured a rookie from Cleveland and the University of Louisville named Thomas Louis Jackson III. It also marked the franchise's first winning record. Jackson's final season was 1986, otherwise known as the year of "The Drive."

It's no coincidence the Broncos took off during the Tom Jackson years.

"Earlier you asked me about the highlight of my career," Jackson said. "The highlight really is that we managed to go from losers to winners. The hardest thing to do in sports is to try and figure out how to take a losing mentality that has existed for 13 years and turn that into a jumping-off point for winning. It's something we believe we're part of to this day. We figured out how to teach this franchise to win. That's probably something we're most proud of."

TOM JACKSON STATS

YRS	G	S	I	Y	TD
14	191	44.0	20	340	3

21

AUSTIN "GOOSE" GONSOULIN

Safety, 1960–66

From the press box at the Denver Broncos stadium there is a wonderful view of half the names bannered in the team's Ring of Fame.

Some of the names are from the early years when the Broncos were often terrible and never the winner. Occasionally, there are whispers from cynical scribes sitting suggesting that given the context of more time—as the Broncos became frequent winners from the mid-1970s to the present thanks to bringing in dozens, if not hundreds, of better players—some of those early Ring of Famers wouldn't have been worthy of such distinction.

Let the record show that Austin William "Goose" Gonsoulin was one original Bronco who could have excelled in any era. In the first game the Broncos ever played, a road win on September 9, 1960, against the Boston Patriots, the rookie Gonsoulin had two interceptions.

Nice professional debut, kid.

After the Broncos had played their second game, a road win at Buffalo, Gonsoulin had six interceptions. Goose was the first NFL–AFL player ever to have a four-interception game, and to this day, no one has had five.

Do we have to look up the NFL–AFL record for most interceptions two games into a career? Six picks in two games will stand forever.

"It's a shame for some of the players in the 1950s and '60s who set records, they only played so many games," said Nickie Gonsoulin, Goose's wife of 50 years. "He got those interceptions right off the bat. Nobody broke it until they started playing more games. And then they started to get no-cut contracts."

Gonsoulin added a seventh interception in Game 3 against the New York Titans' Al Darrow and finished his rookie season with 11 interceptions. In 14 games.

The Broncos have played 56 more seasons since that inaugural season of 1960—39 since the regular season was expanded from 14 to 16 games. They have had cornerbacks like Champ Bailey and Louis Wright, safeties like Dennis Smith, Steve Atwater, John Lynch, and Brian Dawkins.

No Broncos defender has ever picked off more passes than Gonsoulin's 11 in his, and the team's, and the AFL's, first season of 1960.

"Goose played center field and he played the ball really good," said teammate Lionel Taylor, a star Broncos receiver in the early 1960s. "And he was a big safety; he could hit, too."

What did Gonsoulin do after that magical first season? He spent six months serving in the Army Reserves, which he did again after the 1961 season. After his third season of 1962, Gonsoulin worked on teammate Bud McFadin's Texas ranch.

While playing during this time, Gonsoulin once got a strange visit from, shall we say, one of the AFL's all-time unique guys.

"One of the best stories he ever told me—Al Davis was an assistant coach with the Chargers," said Bob West, sports editor of the *Port Arthur News*, who got to know Gonsoulin after his playing days. "And the Broncos had played the Chargers, and Al Davis had come up to Goose in the locker room after the game and claimed he was a reporter writing a story about defensive backs.

"And he said, 'I'd like you to diagram the toughest plays for you to cover.' Goose knew who he was, so he diagrammed one of the easiest plays for him to cover. About the time he finishes diagramming the play, a Broncos assistant coach comes over and says, 'Al Davis, you don't belong in our locker room; get your ass out of here.'

"The coach asked Goose if he knew who he was talking to, and Goose, said, 'Yeah, I know who that is,' and just laughed."

Six years into his career, Gonsoulin had an astounding 43 interceptions—by far the most of any AFL player through 1965.

Unfortunately, Gonsoulin's interception production stopped with the end of that 1965 season for the Broncos. After starting the first 61 consecutive games in his career, and 83 of his first 84, the hard-hitting safety—who was also known as one of the best safety blitzers in the game—may have been experiencing the effects of a battered body in his seventh season, when in 1966 he missed four games because of injury and didn't record an interception.

"I remember how tough Goose was," said Gene Mingo, a Broncos halfback and kicker through the team's first four and a half seasons. "Our trainer Fred Posey used to carry these tongs as part of his sideline medical bag. Once Goose got hit so hard he nearly swallowed his tongue. Thank God we had Fred Posey there, and he pulled it out. It was quite a sight to see. Goose Gonsoulin to me—I put him in the same category as Lionel Taylor. Goose loved the game. He played the game hard."

Just as significantly that season, the Broncos coaching staff was a mess. Mac Speedie started that 1966 season and was fired after an 0-2 start. Ray Malavasi became the interim, and the Broncos finished up 4-10. Malavasi so trusted his star safety, he let Gonsoulin call the defensive plays on the field.

To begin the 1967 season, Gonsoulin was still a team captain, but as he drove from his Texas home to Denver for training camp, he learned that he had been waived. Gonsoulin had played out his option the previous season and was hoping to negotiate a no-cut clause in his contract upon arriving.

New head coach Lou Saban, in one of the first of his many questionable decisions, decided instead to cut Gonsoulin. That same off-season, Saban traded cornerback Willie Brown to the Raiders.

Gonsoulin was picked up by the San Francisco 49ers, who held his rights after drafting him in 1960 in the 17th round. (Gonsoulin was also a 17th-round pick of the New York Giants in 1959, until it was discovered that "Goose" still had to complete his senior year at Baylor.)

He recorded three more interceptions in just seven starts for the 49ers in the National Football League, and retired after that season.

Had Gonsoulin, who averaged a whopping 7.2 interceptions through his first six seasons, recorded just four more picks with the Broncos, he would have gone down as the all-time AFL interception leader.

As it is, Gonsoulin finished tied for third with Kansas City safety Johnny Robinson, and trailed only David Grayson and Jim Norton. (See chart at the end of this chapter.) Incomprehensibly, none of those four AFL interception leaders are in the Pro Football Hall of Fame. Gonsoulin was a first-team, all-AFL selection in 1960, '62, and '63, and was named to the second team in 1961 and '64.

When the All-AFL team was selected after its final 1969 season, Gonsoulin was a second-team safety.

Gonsoulin was born June 7, 1938, in Port Arthur, Texas, to Gilman and Audrey Gonsoulin. An outstanding football player at Thomas Jefferson High School, where he was a classmate of future Broncos teammate Carl Larpenter, Goose could have gone to LSU or Texas but instead went to Baylor, where as a senior he was a halfback (27 carries, 72 yards), end (18 catches, 235 yards, 2 TDs), defensive back, and team captain.

"Goose came from a very, very poor family," West said. "Texas and LSU recruited him real hard, but the reason he went to Baylor was because when he visited Texas and LSU, everybody had on suits. And he didn't have a suit. And he wouldn't feel comfortable at either one of those schools. He knew he would be more comfortable at Baylor wearing blue jeans.

"In fact, whenever he would come home from Baylor to visit his parents, he would have to hitchhike."

In 1960, Goose was not only drafted in the 17th round by San Francisco, but also by the American Football League Dallas Texans. He signed with the Texans but was quickly traded to the Broncos, along with end Don Carothers, in exchange for Jack Spikes.

In his first day of Broncos training camp at the Colorado School of Mines in Golden, Colorado, head coach Frank Filchock put Gonsoulin at safety. An AFL All Star was made.

Gonsoulin was single through his first four NFL seasons, then married Nickie on Monday, September 28, 1964. The date was mentioned because it was a Monday, the day after the Broncos lost at Bears Stadium to the Houston Oilers. Goose broke up two passes and had three tackles.

The next day, teammate and fellow Texan Bud McFadin was his best man, and Bob Scarpitto—a Broncos do-everything running back / flanker / punter—also stood up in the wedding.

The Gonsoulins had two children, Angela and Greg, and four grandchildren when he died at 76 on September 8, 2014, in Beaumont, Texas, after a long battle with prostate cancer.

After football, Gonsoulin ran a successful construction company and invested in land. He wound up with a 167-acre farm outside Port Arthur.

"He loved having a farm to handle," Nickie said. "It was a lot of hard work, but that's what he loved. He loved the outdoors."

He was huge in his community, starting the NFL Punt, Pass, and Kick competition in the Port Arthur area, and serving as spokesman for the Julie Rogers Gift of Life program that benefits prostate cancer research. He helped organize Bum Phillips's celebrity golf tournaments that raised money for the Hughen School in Port Arthur.

"When he got sick we talked quite often," West said. "He put up a helluva battle against cancer. He went through a lot. And while he was going through all that he then had a quadruple bypass. I mean, it was unbelievable the guy survived as long as he did. He was just a bighearted, unbelievable fighter.

"And he loved the Denver Broncos. He went to every function that he could go to. He spoke glowingly of [Broncos owner] Pat Bowlen. I know Bowlen took care of the old players. Goose always thought highly of him because he did that."

When Bowlen started the Broncos Ring of Fame in 1984, Gonsoulin was one of the four original inductees.

"Pat Bowlen and his wife were so nice, the way they treated the former players," Nickie Gonsoulin said. "Thank God they brought in the Ring of Fame. Everybody said people would always have something to look back on with these players like my husband."

AUSTIN "GOOSE" GONSOULIN STATS

YRS	G	I	Y	TD
7	93	43	542	2

AFL INTERCEPTION LEADERS (1960-69)

NAME	TEAM	1960-65	TOTAL
Dave Grayson	Dal/KC/Oak	22	47
Jim Norton	Hou	33	45
Goose Gonsoulin	Den	43	43
Johnny Robinson	KC	14	43

22

CRAIG MORTON

Quarterback, 1977–82

It doesn't matter how many misfires he had, how many games his team didn't win, or that he isn't among the 310 men inducted into the Pro Football Hall of Fame.

Craig Morton proved to be the ultimate gamer when the stakes were highest. Deep inside an elite athlete's heart and soul, there is no greater achievement.

"That's a nice way of putting it," Morton said. "I'll take that."

Morton played in 222 games over 18 NFL seasons, including 77 games and 6 seasons with the Denver Broncos. He threw for more than 29,000 yards and 190 touchdowns.

That he played in one particular game for the Broncos, and played like a champion, was the stuff of legend.

In that first, great Broncos season of 1977, Morton famously and literally winced and hobbled out of his hospital bed to play in the AFC Championship Game on a frigid January 1, 1978, at Mile High Stadium. Not only play, but he threw two touchdown passes to Haven Moses in a 20–17 win against the hated, and defending-champion, Oakland Raiders. The Broncos were going to the Super Bowl.

Broncomania was never more manic.

"Now all the information that came out after the game and as history has gone on, I know what happened," said Broncos cornerback Louis Wright. "But then, I did not know. I knew he was hurt and might not play. Norris Weese was taking all the snaps, and we thought Norris was going to be the quarterback. And then all the sudden there was Craig. I didn't know what I know now. I know he played, but now that I know the circumstances of how he played, it was pretty incredible."

Morton had been the former Dallas Cowboys quarterback who then spent two and a half desultory seasons with the New York Giants before he became the final missing piece for the Broncos in 1977. He had a fantastically steady regular season, posting a 12-1 record before a left hip injury and little to play for had him playing just one, three-out series in the final regular-season game against his former Dallas Cowboys. The Broncos lost, 14–6, in what turned out to be a preview to Super Bowl XII.

But first, the Broncos had to get there. And there were six and a half days between playoff games when it looked like they might have to try to get there without their quarterback.

Which would have meant the Broncos probably wouldn't get there, no matter how good their Orange Crush defense.

Morton's hip kept getting worse to the point where after he threw two touchdowns without an interception in the Broncos' 34–21, first-round AFC playoff win against the Pittsburgh Steelers, he spent the following week in the hospital. As in Monday through Sunday morning.

Blood kept building up in the hip and doctors had trouble draining it out. It left his leg grotesquely discolored from the upper left hip down to his knee. Weese took the first-team practice snaps that week, and most of the Broncos players figured he would play in the AFC Championship Game against the Raiders.

Then Morton left the hospital on Sunday morning and was driven to Mile High by a friend, Oren Hawley.

"Morton was a warhorse," said Broncos right cornerback Steve Foley. "When I saw his body black and blue like that, I had never seen anything like it. I'm like, 'What is that?' I didn't know a body could bruise that bad. And then to play like that in the championship game—it was just a special time for us and the city."

About an hour prior to the game, Broncos coach Red Miller asked Morton how he felt. Morton said, "Red, if you'll tie my shoes, I'll play."

Miller bent down and in front of the entire, team, tied Morton's shoes.

"I said, 'Let's go,' Morton said. "I said, 'Don't let 'em hit me and we'll win this thing.' I didn't want to fall on my left side. I only got hit a couple times and it wasn't on that side, so it was great."

Morton's injury leading up to the AFC Championship either was not revealed to the press, or the press didn't find out until after the game. Miller had taken the unusual measure of closing off the practices to the media that week. The extent of Morton's injury still wasn't known to the masses until former *Denver Post* sportswriter Terry Frei published a book in 2007 entitled, *77: Denver, The Broncos, and a Coming of Age.*

Such a covert quarterback operation would have never happened today. One, the Broncos would have been heavily fined and perhaps would have been ordered by the league to surrender a high-round draft pick for not properly disclosing the injury. Two, there are no secrets in today's Twitter-equipped media with their loose-lipped sources.

And three, they don't make 'em as tough as Craig Morton anymore.

He was the son of a World War II veteran who fought Japan in the New Guinea campaign.

"He never talked about anything regarding the war," Morton said about his father, Ken. "Now that I'm watching all these documentary shows about World War II, New Guinea was not a nice place to be. He never talked about anything, and in watching these documentaries, nobody talked about anything because the fighting was so brutal."

Ken Morton was a strict father. He sacrificed for his family, his country. He wanted things done a certain way. And that meant the people around him did it a certain way, too.

Morton's mom, Maxine, "was a great mom," Craig said. "She was very protective of us."

She was a housewife, then became a secretary, as the position was called then, to Campbell, California, school district principals and administrators.

Morton starred in baseball growing up in Campbell, a town not far from San Jose. There were about 12,000 in Campbell in 1960, and about 40,000 living there now. Morton was a second baseman in high school and outfielder at Cal-Berkeley. He had a good arm in baseball, but not a pitcher's arm.

"That was always my best sport, I thought," he said. "When I graduated from high school [in 1961] I got some offers from the Yankees and Detroit."

This was before Major League Baseball's first draft in 1965. He was offered $50,000 signing bonuses.

"Which was a lot of money in those days," Morton said. "But I always wanted to go to college and play college football. So, I went to Cal to play both football and baseball. I never was not going to college. I had my goals and dreams, and one of them was to play college football, be captain of a football team, and play in the Rose Bowl. I accomplished a couple of those, but not the Rose Bowl. But no regrets."

He wound up at Cal after taking a formal visit to Notre Dame. Dad was a strict Catholic and he wanted his son to go there. Morton remembers it was cold with snow on the ground when he visited South Bend, Indiana, in April 1961. Joe Kuharich was the Fighting Irish's coach during the lean years prior to Ara Parseghian.

None of those factors explains why he didn't go to Notre Dame.

"I mean, they had curfews and everything," Morton said. "I said, 'Shoot, I'm not going there. I've already been through all that.' I was sitting in my room at 10 o'clock every night [in high school] because I got a 'C' my freshman year in English. My dad said I needed more discipline. So, I was in my room every Sunday through Thursday at 10 o'clock. So, I broke loose close to my senior year; I told him I'd had enough."

Morton may have been feeling his oats, but he still loved his parents. He chose to play at Cal primarily because he wanted his mom and dad to watch him. It may be difficult for the modern-day parent to understand, but in the 1960s, only the most fortunate American families took one- or two-week vacations each year away from home.

For the Bears, Morton was a two-and-a-half-year starter for head coach Marv Levy and his staff that included Bill Walsh and Mike White. Morton broke all of Cal's passing records for some pretty bad teams. He showed enough to become the No. 5 overall pick of the Cowboys in the 1965 NFL Draft—after the Chicago Bears took Dick Butkus with the No. 3 overall selection, and Gale Sayers at No. 4.

That the Cowboys took Morton with their first pick was a mild surprise considering they already had a good young quarterback in Don Meredith, who had just finished his fifth year in the league, second as a starter.

Morton would sit four years behind Meredith before the latter surprisingly retired at 31 while coming off three consecutive Pro Bowl seasons.

"Great mentor, great friend," Morton said of the man who later became known as "Dandy Don" on *Monday Night Football*. "One of my dearest people, one I always loved. After he retired—he retired when he was 30 or 31—I didn't expect that. I was a quarterback a couple years before Roger came."

In 10 years with the Cowboys, Morton fell between Meredith and Roger Staubach. Morton was 10-2-1 as a starter in 1969 and 8-3 in 1970, when his Cowboys finally made it through the NFL playoffs and played in the first merger Super Bowl, or Super Bowl V.

Cowboys coach Tom Landry infamously had Morton and Staubach alternate plays for a Week 7 game against the Chicago Bears in 1971. It didn't work, and Staubach became the quarterback the rest of the season. Morton went 10-4 in 1972 after Staubach suffered a separated shoulder.

"Boy, we had great competitions," Morton said. "It switched every year, it seemed like. He's still one of my great friends. We were always really good friends, but boy, we were competitors. The competition never got in the way of our friendship."

Midway through 1974, Morton asked for, and was granted, a trade when he was again replaced by Staubach. But his two and a half seasons with the Giants were miserable, as Morton played down to the level of his team.

After the 1976 season, Giants head coach John McVay—who later became enormously successful while helping to build the San Francisco 49ers into a dynasty from 1982–94—informed Morton on March 7, 1977, that he had been traded to the Broncos in exchange for Denver quarterback Steve Ramsey and a draft pick.

"I said, 'Thank you very much,'" Morton said. "I was so relieved. One of the last games I played with the Giants was against the Broncos. [The Giants lost to Steve Ramsey and the Broncos, 14–13.] I knew they had a great defense, and I knew they had a quarterback that would not make any mistakes. They were really a good team."

The Broncos were 9-5 in 1976, but 12 of their veteran players—nicknamed the Dirty Dozen—led a revolt against head coach John Ralston. Broncos owner Gerald Phipps supported Ralston, although the coach resigned because of his players' actions and Red Miller was hired.

Miller was well received. Morton's arrival drew mixed feelings.

"We were skeptical," said Rick Upchurch, who was coming off a punt return season for the ages in 1976. "We're saying, Wait a minute. You're bringing in a guy that's been in the league, what, 12, 13 years already? And he's not in the best of health. People who saw him were like, 'Check his legs out.' But what you couldn't account for was his savvy, his smarts, and his ability to throw the ball in the right place."

Defensive lineman Lyle Alzado greeted Morton by saying, "Now we'll win a championship."

"When we got Craig, I was glad because he had experience," said nose tackle Rubin Carter. "And that means a lot. He had been there. He took his bumps and bruises but he was still there, and he still had his mental capability and he was able to run an offense and run a team and make audibles at the line of scrimmage.

"I felt good about it. Until then, we had young guys at the quarterback position. Craig gave us a chance. Don't turn the ball over. You know, let the defense win the game."

"He was the missing ingredient," said Broncos safety and captain Billy Thompson. "He had an immediate connection with Haven. It was a tremendous year for both of them."

Morton threw for 1,929 yards and 14 touchdowns in 1977. Just as importantly, he only threw 8 interceptions.

In the two AFC playoff games—the first two playoff games in Broncos history—Morton threw two touchdown passes in each. He beat the Steelers, the team of the 1970s, and the Raiders, the defending Super Bowl champs. That's all.

"He had that leadership where he could calm everybody down and take control," Wright said. "He gave us that feeling everything would be all right."

Morton played well again in 1978, when the Broncos again won the AFC West and made the playoffs. Miller flirted with the more-mobile Weese in 1979, but with the Broncos down, 34–10, midway through the third quarter in Game 4 against Seattle, Morton was sent in.

In the span of seven and a half minutes, Morton threw touchdown passes to tackle-eligible Dave Studdard and Moses late in the third quarter, and Upchurch early in the fourth, to make it 34–31.

Morton then engineered a 40-yard touchdown drive capped by Rob Lytle's 1-yard touchdown run to give Denver a 37–34 victory in one of the greatest comebacks in NFL history.

"We got a lot of breaks," Morton said of that game. "Upchurch made some great plays and Haven made some big plays. The defense started getting turnovers. It just turned. It wasn't just me. Defense created good field position and guys were making plays and then we just thought, 'Well, this could be fun.'"

Morton's best season with the Broncos, at least statistically, was 1981. At the age of 38, Morton threw for a career-best 3,195 yards and tied his single-season best with 21 touchdowns while posting a 10-5 record as a starter.

For Broncos fans, though, Morton's signature season will always be 1977, and his signature game will always be the AFC Championship.

From the jump, Morton had an instant connection with Moses. Thus, the M&M connection.

"Haven saw the same thing I saw from his perspective downfield," Morton said. "It got to where we knew what the other one was going to do."

They almost got their biorhythms intercepted by Raiders safety Jack Tatum early in the 1977 AFC Championship Game.

"The first series, Haven was going across the middle and Tatum stepped in front of it, but it was thrown so hard it bounced off his chest," Morton said. "Otherwise, he might have taken it for a touchdown. So, I said to Haven, let's go dig corner. So, he faked in and Tatum came in and Haven took off for the corner and nobody was around."

Injured hip and all, Morton delivered a perfectly thrown down-and-out pass to Moses, who caught it around midfield and sprinted the rest of the way for a 74-yard touchdown that gave the Broncos a nerve-settling 7–3 lead.

Midway through the fourth quarter, after the Raiders made the Mile High Stadium sellout crowd nervous with a Kenny Stabler–to–Dave Casper touchdown pass that narrowed the score to 13–10, Morton and Moses came through again.

This time Moses made a diving catch in the end zone for a 12-yard touchdown and a 20–10 lead that was enough.

"Haven made a lot of great catches in that game," Morton said. "It was just a wonderful moment."

Super Bowl XII, not so much. The Broncos offensive line was no match for the Cowboys defensive front. Morton was sacked twice and intercepted four times.

"We couldn't beat the Cowboys, maybe once in 10," Morton said. "They had a great defense. It was a horrible game. I played horrible. I never really had a bad game the whole year until the Super Bowl. Their defensive line, we just couldn't match up against those guys. We had no running game. All we could do was throw interceptions, which I did well that game."

After his terrific 1981, when Morton helped break in a young, tall receiver named Steve Watson, the NFL endured a strike-shortened season in 1982. Morton played in two games before the strike, but after two months off, his battered knees and 39-year-old body had had enough.

Following his playing career, he stayed in the Denver area to first co-own a successful drug-and-alcohol rehabilitation center. He got talked into the restaurant business, which wasn't so successful.

He then worked for an oil company, coached the Denver Gold in the USFL, and wound up helping his alma mater raise $321 million to renovate 90-year-old California Memorial Stadium. Since that project was completed in December 2010, Morton has been retired.

"If you retire, you've got to get a dog," he said. "So you have something to do. I can't golf anymore. I have a left shoulder that went seven years ago. They wanted to replace it. I said, I'm not having any more operations; I'll live with it."

He's had 23 surgeries from football, maybe 24. It's hard to keep count. All Broncos fans know is when they needed him most, Morton managed to get his battered body to show up.

CRAIG MORTON STATS

YRS	G	A	C	PCT	Y	TD	I	RTG	W-L
6	72	1,594	907	56.9	11,895	74	65	79.1	41-23

23

— TREVOR PRYCE —

Defensive Lineman, 1997–2005

Trevor Pryce was 6-foot-5 and looked taller, weighed 285 pounds and seemed heavier, a third-team All American college player who wound up better than the first-teamers when he walked into the Denver Broncos locker room for the first time in 1997.

"I was intimidated," he said.

The Broncos were not the defending Super Bowl champions quite yet, but they should have been. They were the NFL's best team in the regular season of 1996, only to lose their opening playoff game to Jacksonville.

The Broncos were so stunned they would win the next two Super Bowls. A first-round draft pick out of Clemson, Pryce was the new kid on a team already loaded with championship talent before they realized they were champions. The best kind of talent. So talented, Broncos boss Mike Shanahan didn't waste much time drafting for more.

"I was one of only three players in my draft class," Pryce said in an interview for this project in March 2017.

Indeed, Pryce in the first round, guard Dan Neil in the third round, and safety Cory Gilliard, who never played in the NFL, made up the entire 1996 Broncos draft class.

"I think it's different now, with teams balancing out their payrolls with young, minimum[-salaried] players," Pryce said. "The Broncos had a great roster. They had a great team the year before, and they didn't have a lot of need. So, I was in a locker room full of grown-ups.

"I was shocked at first by how big everybody was. I was used to being the biggest. I was used to hearing, 'This kid has this, that, and the other.' And then I lined up and their offensive linemen were some of the biggest human beings I had ever laid eyes on."

Pryce remembered how inferior he felt the first time he tussled with Broncos veteran right guard Brian Habib during practice.

"He looked like he was covered in granite, but he was 300 pounds," Pryce said. "It was physically difficult at first, and the game moved way too fast at first. I remember our first practices: We practiced without pads, but we practiced at full speed. There was no difference between practicing with pads and practicing with T-shirts. It was full speed. That first minicamp was eye-opening and it was exhausting and it was really difficult. And I thought there was no way I could do this."

Pryce was so raw, he was inactive through the first eight games of his rookie season. He had played just one college season as a defensive lineman. He played outside linebacker at Michigan before transferring to Clemson after two seasons. Still, they don't sit first-round draft picks for half a season anymore, unless they're quarterbacks. And even then.

Fast-forward a year to 1998. The Broncos were defending Super Bowl champs, heading for one more Lombardi Trophy. Only this time Habib was traded to Seattle, replaced by Neil. And Pryce was now a third-down specialist / part-time starter who was ready for the fast-paced NFL.

Two of the Broncos' regular-season games in 1998 were against Seattle.

"I made sure I lined up against Brian Habib every play," Pryce said.

Pryce had a sack in each of the two games the Broncos played against the then AFC West Seahawks.

This was not the easiest of rankings for the 50 Greatest Broncos. At one point, I had Pryce ranked as low as No. 33. He mostly hovered between the late 20s to late 30s before I decided Pryce deserved to be ranked a tad higher than Rulon Jones, who was one of the best two-way (stop the run and pass rush) defensive linemen in Broncos history.

Pryce ranks seventh on the Broncos' all-time sack list, and first among pure defensive tackles, with 64.0 in 121 games. Jones is tied for fourth on the Broncos' list, with 73.5 sacks in 129 games.

Had Pryce's four full additional seasons with the Baltimore Ravens been included, he would have been a top-15 selection. In 2006, the year after Broncos coach Mike Shanahan and general manager Ted Sundquist made the egregious error of releasing Pryce, the defensive tackle matched his career high with 13.0 sacks for the Ravens.

"The way I used to learn about the guys up front is to talk to the guys they played against," said Broncos Ring of Fame safety John Lynch, who is now general manager of the San Francisco 49ers. "By that measure of talking to opposing offensive linemen, they really feared playing against Trevor. He had a rare combination. I think he was 6-6, but he had great leverage where he had long arms that could get underneath people. Long arms and slippery hands."

Pryce may well have been the most physically gifted defensive lineman the Broncos ever had, with Rich "Tombstone" Jackson the only consideration. For all of Jackson's greatness, though, he only played four full seasons with the Broncos, and parts of two others. Pryce played eight full seasons with the Broncos, missing most of another because of a back injury that required surgery.

Know this about Pryce: He's the only Broncos defensive lineman who finished second in a Florida district high school meet in the 110-meter-high hurdles with a time of 15.0 seconds.

Pryce is also the only Broncos defensive lineman who was drafted in the first round after playing just one college season from the three-point stance.

He also is the only defensive lineman whose sister, Nandi, was one of the best soccer players in the country in the early 2000s, becoming an All American at UCLA and a fixture on several US National Teams.

Just to further emphasize the type of athleticism that ran through Trevor Pryce's gene pool.

"A natural. Unbelievably natural guy," said Broncos kicker Jason Elam. "I wish I would have had a chance to play with him longer. When he wanted to dominate, he could do it. Once he kind of figured himself out and figured out how good he could be, he was dangerous. I don't think early on he realized how good he could be. Just a dominating player."

Problem was, the Broncos always seemed to want more from Pryce. He lived through the expectations of first, a first-round draft pick, and then, a record-setting contract.

"I don't know where you have him ranked, but I think there is a little bit of a notion that potentially he should have been in the top 10," Lynch said. "That's how good he was. I think a lot of that, after having played with him, I learned he was a great teammate.

"Maybe it was perception rather than reality. He was a little nonchalant. That's not what people are used to in football. They want guys gritting their teeth. And that just wasn't his personality. Trevor is a very intelligent guy. A very intelligent player. I think sometimes that intelligence . . . he was kind of a relaxed guy, and he wasn't a 'yes' man. He'd question things, and so he sometimes would clash with coaches."

Pryce did occasionally land in coach Mike Shanahan's doghouse, especially after the Broncos made Pryce the NFL's highest-paid defensive player with a seven-year, $60 million contract in April 2001. He earned it after registering 13.0 sacks in 1999, when he was selected first-team All Pro, and 12.0 sacks in 2000—unheard-of sack totals for a defensive tackle, at least until J. J. Watt came along a decade later—while drawing the first two of four consecutive Pro Bowls.

But after that 2000 season, Shanahan fired defensive coordinator Greg Robinson. Pryce's next two defensive coordinators, Ray Rhodes and Larry Coyer, devised schemes that were not suited for the defensive tackle's pass-rush abilities.

"My first two years it was, go rush the quarterback," Pryce said. "Don't worry about whatever happens. Our first defensive coordinator [Robinson] was, 'You go get the quarterback, let the linebackers play the run. You play the run on the way to the quarterback.' It was perfect for me because my job was to go straight as fast as I could. And it worked. We won Super Bowls two years doing that.

"And then the Ravens won a Super Bowl [in 2000]. What I remember was, the NFL is a follow-the-leader kind of organization. Whatever works, everybody is going to do. All the sudden for a few years there, pass-rushing took a backseat because the Ravens defense was so dominant against the run. The Ravens back then, they had pass rushers, but they didn't have defensive tackles who could get to the quarterback. Their job was to keep blockers off [middle linebacker] Ray Lewis.

"So we tried to do that, but I was 285 pounds. This doesn't work. It didn't work at all for me. We tried to do what the Ravens were doing, but we didn't have guys that looked like that. We were all long, and athletic and kind of lean. Not the 350-pound fire hydrants. The Broncos were paying me like an elite defensive lineman, but the job they wanted me to do was not an elite defensive lineman's job."

Late in the 2002 season, after the Broncos lost back-to-back overtime games and four of five to fall from 6-2 to 7-6, Pryce may have taken a passive-aggressive stab at the coaching staff by saying Denver had "the most talented roster in the NFL."

Pryce didn't intend that as a knock at Shanahan, but the coach took it that way, and he singled his star defender out in a local radio interview. We're not paying you to evaluate talent, Shanahan said. We're paying you to make plays.

Pryce didn't engage in a war of words. He still managed 23.5 sacks in the three seasons after Robinson was fired.

"He kind of reminded me a little bit of Von [Miller], and a little bit of J. J. Watt," said Broncos cornerback Champ Bailey. "Maybe not as great as they are, but he was that disruptive. I think he was a little unappreciated. Because when he left Denver and went to Baltimore, he was still doing some of the same things. I'm not sure what Trevor's mind-set was, because he had a lot of interests outside of football. Kind of an interesting guy.

That's not a knock. The fact he not only loved football and loved other things maybe even more, and still performed at a high level—it shows you the type of talent he was."

Pryce was born in Brooklyn, New York, but at eight years old, his dad, Trevor Sr., and mom, Jackie, moved to the Orlando, Florida, area. Dad, a telecommunications engineer for AT&T, was given a choice with his transfer order.

"We had to decide between Florida and California," Pryce said. "One had Disney World, the other, Disneyland. We went to both. I think we decided on Florida because Florida didn't have earthquakes."

Thinking outside the box may be an irritant to controlling NFL coaches, but it can help a guy adjust when the cheering stops. Pryce's last NFL season was in 2010, but after a stint as a Fox Sports 1 TV sports panelist, he settled in Carroll County, Maryland—about equidistant between Baltimore and Washington, DC—with his wife Sonya, daughters Khary and Kamryn, 14; and son Trevor III.

His stimulated mind wound up writing a trilogy entitled *Kulipari: An Army of Frogs*, which is in the genre of *X-Men*, *Avatar*, and *Teenage Mutant Ninja Turtles*. Netflix won a bidding war for the rights to adapt the story into an animated series. Pryce became a writer and TV producer.

"Netflix wants a season two, so I'm working on it now," Pryce said in March 2017. "That's what I do with my days. It's a pretty big deal in our household."

About his nine seasons with the Broncos, Pryce said he remembers most the two Super Bowl titles; the transition in defensive coaching philosophies; and the number of quarterbacks Shanahan went through following the retirement of John Elway after the 1998 season and second Super Bowl.

In his final season with the Broncos, Pryce was a stalwart on their defensive front in 2005, when the Broncos won the AFC West with a 13-3 record and beat New England in a second-round playoff game to earn a berth in the AFC Championship Game. There were times that year, though, when Pryce was frustrated by his task of holding up blockers. It's not that he didn't do it; he fulfilled his task without complaint, at least not publicly. It's just that holding up blockers was not properly utilizing Pryce's skills.

He had just 4.0 sacks in 2005, and was surprisingly released as a salary-cap casualty after that season, along with 1,000-yard rusher Mike Anderson and "receiving" tight end Jeb Putzier. The Broncos promptly wallowed in mediocrity for the next six years until Peyton Manning came to the rescue by joining the team in 2012.

Those 13.0 sacks Pryce had in 2006 with the Ravens? Pryce's defensive coordinator was Rex Ryan. Was Pryce glad to leave the Broncos? Bitter about his release?

"Bitter? No. Not at all," Pryce said. "Glad to leave? That wasn't the case, either. I liked Denver. My kids were born in Denver. While I played in Baltimore, we still lived in Denver. For four years, we'd come back to Denver for six months. I had no hard feelings whatsoever. The Broncos made me one of the highest-paid defensive linemen—at one point I was the highest paid in the league. So I didn't have any animosity.

"It was just a difference in philosophy with the coaches. When I got to Baltimore and I had that big year my first year there, it's because they made a clear line in the sand as to what they wanted me to do: 'Your job is to go get the quarterback.' Rex Ryan coached with less handcuffs. If you want to go that way, go make the play."

TREVOR PRYCE STATS			
YRS	G	S	TCK
9	124	64.0	391

24

HAVEN MOSES

Receiver, 1972–81

One day, while scanning for research on the Denver Broncos' Orange Crush defense, I bumped into a replay of the 1977-season AFC Championship Game.

Not just snippets or highlights of the game, but the entire game. Every play, cut up without commercials. Dick Enberg was the play-by-play announcer for the game, televised on NBC, and Len Dawson, the former Super Bowl champion quarterback for the Kansas City Chiefs, was the color commentator.

I had watched that game live on television from my home in Oswego, Illinois, during Christmas break my freshman year in college, but I had not remembered it as I thought I did.

In compiling this book, 14 Broncos players who participated in that AFC Championship Game against the Oakland Raiders, including nine on defense, made our top 50. What I thought I remembered about that game was how rabid Broncomania was at the time—the sea of orange in the Mile High Stadium stands—and how much the nation was captivated by the Orange Crush defense.

But while watching the event again nearly 40 years later, and knowing what I know now as a more ardent football observer, it became obvious Haven Moses won that AFC Championship Game. It was Moses who came through with the best performance of his life to bring the first-ever Super Bowl game for Denver.

"Yes, he did," said Tom Jackson, a Broncos outside linebacker in that memorable victory against the Oakland Raiders. "He comes to us from Buffalo and we used to always say, 'Moses, take us to the Promised Land!' He was an amazing talent. Yes, he dominated that game, and right at the beginning. It started as soon as the game started. Just a tremendous player and tremendous athlete."

Haven Moses had his share of explosive games while averaging a stunning 18.1 yards per catch in his 14-year career. He was remarkably consistent, as he averaged 18.0 yards per reception in four and a half seasons with the Buffalo Bills, and 18.1 yards per catch in his nine and a half seasons with the Broncos.

He had 16 games of at least 100 yards receiving, but never before, and never after, did he have 168 yards receiving as he did in that AFC Championship Game against the Raiders. He once had three touchdown receptions in a 1973 victory against the Houston Oilers, and later that same year he scored two touchdowns to single-handedly lift the Broncos past the Kansas City Chiefs, 14–10.

But it had been more than four years since Moses' last multi-touchdown game when he scored on receptions of 74 yards in the first quarter of the 1977 AFC Championship to give Denver a 7–3 lead against the Raiders and 12 yards midway through the fourth quarter to move the score to 20–10, Broncos.

"Haven was absolutely determined going into that game," said Broncos returner and backup receiver Rick Upchurch. "He was the one guy who said we were going to win this game. That's what he said, 'We're going to win this game.' He took responsibility for it and accountability for it and he came through big-time."

After recording a relatively modest 27 catches during the 1977 regular season—if for 539 yards and a robust 20.0 yards per reception—Moses in the AFC Championship had five catches for 168 yards and two touchdowns in one of the most clutch receiver performances in Broncos history.

"That game was the culmination of what I had put into it, showing my talents on a major stage," said Moses in an interview for this project in February 2017. "Which we didn't get too often during the course of the first 10 years in the league.

"We didn't have the sophisticated game plans that they have right now. You didn't have the creativity. Obviously, the time we're living in now wants to have more touchdowns, more excitement. We were evolving in the '60s with the AFL. In my 14 years, I went through quarterbacks every two years. I never had an offensive coach that gave me the opportunity to do more things as these guys are now.

"However, my numbers—however small they might look now—if you look at them, they were impactful."

Haven Moses is doing well, thank you very much. In 2003, at the age of 56, he suffered a debilitating stroke that was brought on by high blood pressure and for years cost him the use of his left side. You couldn't tell through his two-handed snags but Moses was left-handed, exaggerating his struggles.

"I couldn't hold a club, couldn't do anything for five or six years after that," said Moses, a left-handed golfer. "In 2008, I decided to go out on the driving range. I was doing so much rehabilitation and sitting around. It was suggested I get out and start doing things that I was comfortable or familiar with, and golf was the one thing I had enjoyed prior to that."

He started going regularly to the Fox Hollow driving range in Lakewood, Colorado, to begin the slow process. The workers there allowed Moses to work by himself as he endured the physical and mental struggles with the game.

This went on for about four years.

"Golf is about balance," he said. "From the neurological damage I had suffered in my brain this began to redirect those electrons back to where I could function. It's been an uphill battle, but I've had some wonderful support from family and community on this journey, and I continue to count my blessings. I still limp and have limited use in some things, but for the most part my life has been one I'm very proud of, more so than what I accomplished as a player."

What the stroke couldn't do was paralyze the determination that poured through every fiber of Moses from the start. He was born Haven Christopher Moses Jr. on July 27, 1946. I used to pretend I was Haven Moses during imaginary games in the backyard while growing up on the outskirts of the Chicago area. That name was so cool, so hip, in my own fertile mind, I just had to be Haven Moses.

"I was named after my father, Haven," Moses said. "He was named after a Baptist minister in Arkansas. It was an interesting name to grow up with in Los Angeles."

Moses was the oldest of six kids raised Catholic by their mom and aunt in Compton, California. Dad had died at an early age. Across the street was Centennial High School, a state football powerhouse coached by Aaron Wade.

But mom wanted her kids to have a Catholic school education, which meant Haven and his siblings taking a bus trip 25 miles one way each day, with transfers along the way, to San Pedro, California, where he would graduate from Fermin Lasuen High School.

"The Catholic schools, especially the elementary schools, provided not just the academic side but also the spiritual side, which was a very strong element with our family," Moses said. "My siblings and I all attended Catholic grammar school and high school for 12 years. I think it served our purpose well."

He attended Los Angeles Harbor Junior College where he played both ways, but was considered better as a safety. So much so that USC legendary coach John McKay recruited him with the idea of Moses becoming the Trojans starting safety. And Moses reciprocated with a verbal commitment.

But Moses' quarterback during his freshman year at Harbor Junior College, Don Horn, had moved on to San Diego State and invited his former receiver down for a visit. Among those meeting Moses during his visit to San Diego State were head coach Don Coryell, offensive line coach Joe Gibbs, defensive coordinator John Madden (remember, Moses was a two-way player), and grad assistant Rod Dowhower. And then some of the Aztec players.

"Growing up in L.A., it was every athlete's dream to play for either SC or UCLA," Moses said. "But when I took my visit, there was something about the players when I went to SC. There was so many of them, number one, on scholarship. And nobody seemed to be happy. It was like a business.

"I wasn't all that into football. I was trying to get an education, and football afforded me that opportunity because we couldn't afford it. I just felt more comfortable at San Diego State. On the way back, I felt, 'This is where I belong.' There were 18,000 students, beautiful campus. But it was one where I just knew I could accomplish what my parents set me out to do, and that was to get that education.

"It never entered my mind that football was going to evolve into what it did. Even in college. Not until my senior year when Coryell made a reference. He said, 'You know, you're going to be a top draft choice?' I looked at him like he was crazy."

Moses was the No. 9 overall selection of the Buffalo Bills in the 1968 draft, and in his rookie year, he had 42 catches that held as a career high until 11 years later with the Broncos, where he had 54 receptions in 1979.

Moses' time in Buffalo was humbling, to say the least. After winning a state championship in high school, going undefeated in his two seasons of junior college and winning the equivalent of what is now a Division II national championship in Moses' junior season of 1966 at San Diego State, the Bills in his first four seasons went 1-12-1 (with the only win against Joe Namath and the eventual Super Bowl champion New York Jets), 4-10, 3-10-1, and 1-13.

For the 1972 season, the Bills hired back head coach Lou Saban, who after leading Buffalo to back-to-back AFL titles in 1964–65 had failed to make the Broncos a winner at any point from 1967–71. With the Broncos, the dictator-like Saban discarded all the established stars he had inherited, repeating this trend with Buffalo in 1972, when he couldn't make it through six weeks into the regular season with a talent like Moses.

"Lou Saban didn't want me," Moses said. "We had drafted O. J. [Simpson] in '69, and it was about running the ball, and rightfully so. But that meant receivers were obsolete, pretty much."

Meanwhile, Dwight Harrison, a receiver turned defensive back for the Broncos, had engaged in an extremely volatile argument with Lyle Alzado early in the 1972 season. Management sided with Alzado, and with the Broncos wanting to get rid of Harrison and Saban not wanting Moses, a player-for-player swap was conveniently arranged.

"I was Buffalo's number-one pick in '68 when Joe Collier was their head coach," Moses said. "He drafted me. When he was let go in Buffalo, he came to Denver to be their defensive coordinator. So when I become available he knew me, and John Ralston knew me from when I was at San Diego State and he was at Stanford. So they knew what they were getting."

Was the trade the best thing that ever happened to him?

"I'm still here," he said.

He married his college sweetheart, Joyce, prior to his rookie year in Buffalo. Moses, Joyce, and their three children will celebrate their 50th wedding anniversary in June 2018. Denver meant they were considerably closer to their families and friends in California.

And Moses raved about the sunshine, the pristine blue skies and white clouds that were part of living in a city settled at 5,280 feet above sea level.

Moses' first full season in Denver was also the first winning season in Broncos history. They would have six more before he retired following the 1981 season.

"Haven was our Fred Biletnikoff," said Broncos safety Billy Thompson said. "Tremendous hands. Great teammate. He was a guy you could count on in the clutch."

Never did the Broncos play a bigger game than the first time they played when winning meant a trip to the Super Bowl. On the second play of the Broncos' second series against the Raiders on January 1, 1978, quarterback Craig Morton, who had spent the week in a hospital because of a leg injury, threw a deep out pattern. Moses beat his man, Raiders cornerback Skip Thomas, by a step and a half, gathered the ball around the Oakland 40, and raced in.

The Raiders were accustomed to playing in big games; the Broncos were making their big-game debut. Moses' big play let his teammates know the stakes were not too high. The best team would win.

"What made him great was he knew he was great," said Steve Foley, a member of the Orange Crush secondary that day. "He didn't have a cockiness to him, but you get him near the ball and he's bringing it in. He's catching it and he had great moves. I mean, great moves. He was a superb route runner and had good speed. Not blazing. Not one of those guys like Cliff Branch who was, 'oooh man, don't let him get too close.' But you didn't want him to get up on you."

In the fourth quarter, with the Raiders closing to within 14–10, Moses beat the Raiders heralded cornerback Lester Hayes by making a tremendous diving catch in the end zone for a 12-yard completion on third-and-5, giving the Broncos a 20–10 lead.

"I don't think I ever remember Haven dropping the ball," said Broncos cornerback Louis Wright. "He must have. But you look at some of the receivers—and I love Demaryius Thomas, I think he's incredible. I really like him. But he drops more balls in one game than Haven dropped in his entire career."

It's too bad Morton didn't come along sooner. Veteran quarterback Charley Johnson had one superb year with the Broncos, in 1973, but then his body started wearing down. Morton was beat-up, too, when he arrived, but he had the savvy, leadership, and arm strength to push the Broncos from good to Super Bowl contender.

"I had not had a quarterback that could throw past 15 yards or a game plan that had any electricity in it," Moses said. "But Craig had the arm. He could stretch us. He wasn't very mobile, but we had a decent-enough line, and he had a quick and strong arm that gave us an opportunity."

The M&M connection had its best run in 1977 and '78, and then Moses had to wait for coach Red Miller to first give the more-mobile Norris Weese a try in 1979 before realizing that Morton was still the more-effective quarterback.

It was in 1979, at the age of 33, that Moses set career highs with 54 catches for 943 yards. He retired No. 3 on the Broncos' all-time list, with 302 receptions, No. 2 in receiving yards with 5,450, and tied with Lionel Taylor for the club lead in touchdowns with 44.

"Haven wasn't a blazer but he was smooth," Upchurch said. "Because of his long strides he would get up on you so fast and get you in a situation where you had to make a decision. Not only that, he was so quick out of his breaks. And plus, Haven was a competitor. And he had great hands."

During his playing days with the Broncos, Moses worked during the off-season. Not work out, although he did that, too. But work. He worked for Olympia Brewing Company one year as a sales rep. He worked four years for Samsonite in various capacities. He then hooked up with Coors, where he worked 15 years in marketing, distribution, and sales.

He was working for a nonprofit group that fund-raised for the arch-diocese for Catholic elementary schools when he suffered his stroke. Then he worked for the Denver Health Foundation for five years after the stroke before retiring.

"My life has been full," Moses said. "I retired two years ago, my wife retired three years ago. We live downtown. I can see the lights of the [Broncos] stadium. I'm living in a dream right now at this point in our lives. You don't know where it's going to go when you're playing, and you see so many things happen to others afterwards, but for Joyce and I, I can't say it enough—we are truly blessed."

HAVEN MOSES STATS

YRS	G	REC	Y	Y/C	TD
10	140	302	5,450	18.0	44

25

RULON JONES

Defensive End, 1980–88

One of these years, the Denver Broncos are going to induct Rulon Jones into their Ring of Fame.

And when that moment occurs, the overwhelming response among Broncos fans will be: Wait a minute; Rulon Jones wasn't already *in* the Ring of Fame?

Jones was one of the most popular Broncos players in the 1980s, a defensive end who was the AFC Defensive Player of the Year in 1986, and recognized as the team's all-time sack leader with 73.5 when he retired after his 1988 season.

It's possible that Jones simply fell through the Ring of Fame cracks. It wasn't until Pat Bowlen came along as owner in 1984 that the Ring was established, and by the time the Broncos finished honoring their backlog of stars from yesteryear, they were on to the players from their Super Bowl championship teams in the late 1990s.

"I've had a lot of people mention that, you know, why aren't you there," Jones said. "But honestly, that type of stuff I haven't worried about very much. I think in the back of your mind it's there and you wonder about it. But I'm just not that connected with football."

Not connected? Soon after problems with his right knee forced him to retire early in the training camp of 1989, when he was 31 years old, Rulon Jones went off the grid.

Literally. A 6-foot-6, 260-pound defensive lineman who had more brains than brawn—and he had plenty of brawn—Jones is an introspective sort who loved football and the city of Denver so much as a player, he needed a new beginning when he stopped playing.

"We loved it there," Jones said. "For me, the emotional part of it—and I think a lot of football players go through some weird things—I loved Denver and was going to live there. But just being around football and being around Denver . . . Denver is so into the Broncos. It just didn't fit for me to stay there. I needed to get away from it. So, we moved back to Utah.

I had a ranch there. My son runs that ranch now, and then we eventually bought a ranch in Idaho and lived up there.

"But we loved Denver. Could have very easily stayed there, but especially right after I retired, it's hard to be amongst all that and not be part of it. I think you have this identity for so long and all the sudden it's over and it's not who you are anymore. It's a little weird. I know a lot of ballplayers struggle with that."

After covering professional sports for going on 30 years, I have concluded that the greatest thing a person can be on this earth is a professional athlete. And the toughest thing a person can be in this world is a former professional athlete.

There is nothing in the real world that can match the euphoria, the adrenaline rush, of performing in front of a sold-out stadium of fans. Nothing in life ever beats the thrill of victory. But once the cheering stops, the best times of one's life are finished. And the former athlete knows it.

"I agree," Jones said. "I remember [former NFL defensive tackle great] Merlin Olsen, who was a good friend of mine, kind of a mentor—he came from where my wife is from, Logan, Utah. So, we were really good friends and he said to me about a year after I retired, we sat down and he said, 'How you doing?' I was like, 'Great; what do you mean?' He said, 'No, I want to know how you're doing.'

"It really hadn't sunk in for me yet. The transition. For most players, it hits them a little sooner. But I later realized what he was talking about. It is a tough transition. Like you say, those highs and the lows. It's not easy explaining that. In life, you don't have the peaks and valleys. In one game, you can be on top of the world and three plays later, you're on the bottom. That sounds bad, but actually the highs and lows of emotion is pretty addictive. You just don't get that in life."

Jones found himself just fine. In fact, you'd have a difficult time finding a former major-league athlete who achieved greater post-playing career success, and a more quality lifestyle, than Rulon Jones.

He took his wife Kathy and their four children (they now have six) and moved back to his guided hunting ranch outside his hometown of Liberty, Utah. While keeping his Utah ranch, Jones later moved to Firth, Idaho, to open another self-powered ranch, and they later added a third ranch in Mexico, near Monterrey.

It's not easy keeping up with the Joneses, much less tracking them down. I happened to catch up with Jones while he was conducting business in Puerto Vallarta, where he could get cell-phone reception.

"In reality I'm off the grid," Jones said. "My ranch in Idaho, I'm totally off the grid. We produce our own power and I have a 10,000-acre ranch that's real close to the Teton Mountains, and I love that. Then we've got a new place down here in Mexico on the beach where we're building a new home now. It's about two hours from Puerto Vallarta. Now that our kids are raised and gone, we're kind of doing our own thing. Doing a little service for our church."

The life Jones leads was most likely the life he was born into. His father, Larry Jones, who recently passed away at 90, was a wildlife photographer and cinematographer.

"He did hunting movies where he would go all around the world. He was an archer," Rulon said. "He did archery hunting movies. He would go around to smaller high school communities and rent a high school gym or theater. He would give a little speech about his adventures out on the field and then he would play the movie. And he did really well with that. Traveled all over the world. Probably had a lot to do with my love of hunting and the outdoors."

As dad traveled, mom raised Rulon and his two brothers and sister in Liberty, Utah, a community so small that its kids go to elementary school and junior high in the town of Eden and attend Weber High School in Pleasant View.

There weren't any youth football leagues, so Jones didn't put on pads until his sophomore year in high school. Then he suffered a broken arm early that year, so he didn't get in the football groove until his junior year.

"Which I think was kind of good," Jones said. "I didn't wear down my body quite as fast. I was a skinny ranch kid."

He played enough to get a football scholarship to Utah State, where in a serendipitous moment he came across a graduate assistant coach.

"Got hooked up with an amazing coach by the name of Rod Marinelli," Jones said. "Rod was my defensive line coach and pretty much made me who I was. I had no coaching up until that point. I was just real skinny and he got me in the weight room and put some weight on me and gave me discipline. I was lucky. Then I got with Stan Jones there in Denver, and Stan was a great coach, too."

The NFL didn't officially start tracking sacks as an official stat until 1982. Unofficially, Jones had two of his better seasons in his rookie and second years. Thanks to the exhaustive research of John Turney, it was determined Jones had 11.5 sacks as a rookie in 1980 and 9 sacks in 1981.

"He was the most explosive player ever, just pure pass rusher," said Greg Boyd, who had 9.0 sacks while playing the opposite end of Jones in 1980.

The Broncos had just 19 sacks in 1979 as they struggled to generate a pass rush after trading away Lyle Alzado. But after drafting Jones in the second round and signing Boyd, the Broncos more than doubled their sack total in 1980, with 39.

Boyd remains one of Rulon's closest friends.

"He was a real outdoorsman, a Jeremiah Johnson type," Boyd said. "I was blessed to have been Rulon's roommate, and then we went nuts on the football field in 1980."

Jones's career suffered a setback in 1983 when he tore the posterior cruciate ligament in his right knee and missed the final four games. He bounced back to have 11 sacks in 1984, 10 sacks in 1985, and 13.5—for 152 yards in losses—in 1986.

And that doesn't include his 3.0 sacks in the 1986 postseason, including his sack safety of New England's Tony Eason, with 1:37 left in a back-and-forth, second-round AFC playoff game. The Broncos had just taken a 20–17 lead when Jones's safety made it 22–17, which held as the final score.

There are some longtime Broncos observers who swear Mile High Stadium never shook more from the rafters than during the moment of Jones's safety.

"It was hard to enjoy it because the second after it happened, my teammates tackled me," Jones said. "They had a big pile there in the end zone. It was fun. I went home—my kids weren't at the game, they were real young then. They put a big banner up on my garage and I think the score was 22–17 or whatever, and they had an arrow pointing to the 2 and saying that belonged to Dad. It was to the point where they were just starting to understand what was going on."

The 1986 season is also known as the year New York Giants' Lawrence Taylor changed the game as an outside linebacker. Taylor became the second defensive player in history (after Alan Page in 1971) to be named the NFL's MVP. But Jones was recognized by UPI as the AFC Defensive Player of the Year.

Jones was on top of the football world, but those highs and lows he was talking about? Just two years later, in 1988, he was coming off the bench as a third-down, pass-rush specialist. He had 7.0 sacks in 1987 and another 5.0 in 1988 to surpass Barney Chavous's team record in sacks (although later, Turney found a couple more sacks for Chavous, who is now third on the team's list with 75.0 sacks. Jones is tied with Von Miller for fourth, with 73.5).

"One of the best pass rushers I've ever been around," Chavous said in the spring of 2017. "A great person, too. Family guy. Rulon had heart."

Jones was struggling with his right knee in his final season of 1988, and he had it scoped in the off-season. He believes he overtrained during his rehab because the knee was still bothering him during the first week of training camp, to the point where he decided to retire.

"I went back to my ranch in Utah [in the off-season]. I was chasing some cows up a hill and I thought, I pushed it too hard," Jones said. "The stability in my leg was really bad, and I thought it was going to be a problem the rest of my life. But after I rested a couple months it came back and it felt great. I've had a few more scopes, but looking back, I think I attacked my rehab too hard. I should have rested a little more.

"But at that point, I had seen a lot of my teammates play a little longer, and I couldn't understand how they couldn't see they were losing a step. I could see how *I* was losing a step, so I pulled the plug at that point."

He was only 30 years old when he played his last game. Rulon's oldest son Garet now runs the Utah ranch. The 2002 Olympics brought the downhill and giant slalom events to the area, which in turn brought in more vacationers and tourists to the Ogden Valley. The Joneses found another desolate place in Firth, Idaho, for another ranch. Another son, Chase, runs that ranch.

Both places are called Broadmouth Canyon Ranch. It's known for its guided elk hunts. The ranch in Mexico features some sheep and mule deer hunts.

"Ninety percent of what we do is elk, because we can raise those animals," Jones said. "We have free-range hunting, too, but we also have the herds that we manage. I've kind of let my boys take those over."

The Joneses raised three other sons, Dalton, Hayden, and Parker. Their only daughter Lauren played college basketball. Their kids have given 13 grandchildren to Rulon and Kathy, who are planning on spending the next year or two in Mexico.

"We're just doing a little bit of a church mission down here, as well as trying to help out with our church," Jones said. "We'll be down here full-time a couple years, and then we'll be going back and forth. We're trying to learn the language better down here. Maybe I waited too long, because I'm not getting the language that good. But that's kind of the goal, to get a little better with the language."

He stays in occasional touch with a few of his former teammates, including Boyd, Chavous, Rubin Carter, Rick Parros, Dave Preston, and Karl Mecklenburg.

"I do miss a lot of the guys," Jones said. "But I've only been back to Denver, I think, once since I retired. We've been in contact with people, but we just never really get back."

Perhaps, the Broncos Ring of Fame committee can do something about that.

RULON JONES STATS			
YRS	G	S	TCK
9	129	73.5	713

26

RILEY ODOMS

Tight End, 1972–83

A simple check of the career numbers revealed a stunning comparison.

While compiling interviews for this project, I didn't have to conduct a formal survey to understand that Broncos players from the 1970s and '80s believe tight end Riley Odoms is the most glaring omission from the team's Ring of Fame.

I checked out Odoms's stat sheet, and while they were impressive, it was unfortunate that injuries and the 1982 players' strike robbed him of the chance to top off his numbers in his final two years.

"Then those numbers would have been something to look at," Odoms said.

But wait. While digging into Odoms's career, I accidentally came across the career stats of Dave Casper. Just about everybody agrees Casper was deserving of the Pro Football Hall of Fame. He was elected in 2002. Then I remembered Detroit's Charlie Sanders was elected as a senior candidate in 2007.

I remembered because I didn't think there was any way Sanders should have gone in when at least five or six Broncos deserved to go in first.

From 2000–17, only three tight ends had been elected into the Hall of Fame: Casper, Sanders, and Shannon Sharpe, who in 2011 became the fourth Bronco honored. Sharpe played in the 1990s, which was a more pass-happy period, a time when he could be used more as a receiver than a blocker.

Casper, Sanders, and Odoms had their best years in the 1970s, when they blocked at least 80 percent, if not 90 percent, of the time. Here's a comparative look at the stats compiled by those three tight ends during their careers:

> **Charlie Sanders:** 1968–77 (10 years): 336 catches,
> 4,817 yards, 31 touchdowns

> **Dave Casper:** 1974–84 (11 years): 378 catches, 5,216 yards, 52 touchdowns
> **Riley Odoms:** 1972–83 (12 years): 396 catches, 5,755 yards, 41 touchdowns

Odoms smoked Sanders in all three significant categories of catches, yards, and touchdowns. I was surprised to learn that Odoms also outproduced Casper in catches and yards. Odoms had 18 more catches and 539 more yards than Dave Casper? Casper and Sanders are in the Hall; Odoms is not.

Never mind whether Odoms should be elected into the Broncos Ring of Fame. That should have happened long ago. But look at those numbers again and ask why Odoms hasn't joined Casper and Sanders in Canton?

"The way I look at the Hall of Fame, or Ring of Fame, is, it's out of my control," Odoms said from his Houston home in February 2017. "There's nothing I can do about it, so I don't worry about it. But I played with so many great ballplayers."

And those great ballplayers from the Broncos' Orange Crush years all say that Odoms was their most underrated teammate.

"Riley was a fantastic athlete. He could crash down on the O-line," said Broncos receiver Haven Moses. "He was very instrumental in the run game and had the softest hands for a tight end I had ever seen. He ran great routes. That's what made us so successful, because when you have a tight end like that it puts a lot of pressure on the strong side of the defense. He should be in the Ring of Fame. To me he is the foundation of the tight end history here with the Broncos."

There's a story behind those soft hands. Raised in Corpus Christi, Texas, Odoms would return every summer to his grandmother's house and his birthplace of Luling, Texas. There he and his three brothers and five sisters—raised by their father, George, who worked as a hotel bellhop, and mom, Narcissus, a cafeteria cook—would help in the watermelon field.

"I was the second youngest of nine kids," Odoms said. "The youngest person there would be on the trailer, catching the watermelons. You could catch them and stack them all day long, but once you'd drop one and it'd burst, you'd have to get down off the wagon."

The wagon meant not walking or lifting. Just catching and stacking. The field meant walking miles on end, crouching, lifting, and hoisting.

"I did my best to never drop one," Odoms said. "We did that every summer."

There is also a story behind Odoms's athleticism. The description has been used frequently in this book. You don't become one of the 50 Greatest

Players in Broncos history without some form of superior athleticism. Odoms, though, was a 6-foot-4, 235-pound freak.

"He did something I had never seen a human do," said Broncos safety Billy Thompson.

It was after Super Bowl XII, and Broncos players were again competing against the Dallas Cowboys, only this time in a less-intense Superstars competition in Hawaii. Players on both sides were competing in an obstacle course race. It was fun until someone said "Go." Then the intensity of competition between these elite athletes raised to game-day Sunday levels.

"There was a high-jump pit," Thompson said. "Most guys would get to the high-jump pit and would just lag over. Riley Odoms hurdled it and came down on the other side in stride and kept running. I had never seen an individual that big do that. That's the kind of talent he had."

Odoms explained that instead of using the customary Western Roll technique in clearing the bar, he used the Eastern Cut, which features a scissors action with the legs, a maneuver more closely resembling the hurdle clear.

"I was a 6-10 high jumper in high school," Odoms said. "I did the Eastern Cut and I just went over it. And it was perfect. They were all saying, 'How did you do that?' It was natural."

Odoms played mostly receiver at West Oso High School in Corpus Christi, but because it was a smaller-classification school, he also played running back, quarterback, and middle linebacker. At the University of Houston, the Cougars ran a veer offense, but in his senior year, Odoms was one of three All American tight ends named after he had 45 catches for 730 yards and eight touchdowns in 12 games.

In the subsequent NFL Draft, Odoms became the highest pick in Broncos history when he was selected No. 5 overall in the first round. Since then, the Broncos have only had three players taken higher: Chris Hinton, at No. 4 overall in 1983; Mike Croel, at No. 4 overall in 1991; and Von Miller, who went No. 2 overall in 2011.

Odoms was a backup tight end and special teams player in his rookie year of 1972, then started all 14 games in his second season of 1973, breaking out with 43 catches for 629 yards and 7 touchdowns.

"There were times when Denver would flank Riley out at wide receiver," said Broncos receiver great Lionel Taylor, who was coaching the Pittsburgh Steelers receivers from 1970–76. "And throw that hitch to him or a slant and he'd scare the hell out of you. I know when I was coaching Pittsburgh, we'd go, 'Oh no.' Riley was big. He'd run over you."

Odoms was a first-team All Pro in 1974 and '75. He did not miss a game through his first seven seasons, then played with a broken arm in 1979 and dislocated shoulder in 1980.

" 'The Judge,' we used to call him," said Broncos defensive back Steve Foley. "There was a good reason. He was 260, and if Riley got the ball and the defensive back was coming, he would punish you. That's why we called him 'The Judge.' I mean, he's looking for you. He had an edge to him that was, 'Don't mess with Riley.' He was a mean—not a mean person, a great person—but on the field, he's got a meanness to him that I felt for the DBs who were coming up on him. You don't know what you're about to run into. You're 195 pounds? Watch this."

Odoms made the Pro Bowl team four times, but he was mostly over-shadowed in his era by the likes of Kellen Winslow, Ozzie Newsome, and Russ Francis. All played in the AFC.

"Just my opinion, Riley was the prototype tight end at that time," said Rick Upchurch, the Broncos returner and receiver from the mid-1970s until the mid-'80s. "He was just as good or better than Russ Francis or Casper, Ozzie Newsome, and all those tight ends. He was the total package. He could block. He could run. He could catch. He was a beast, man.

"And Riley was the type of guy who would pull you off to the side and say, 'This is how you catch the ball. This is what you have to do. This is what you ought to do. Because I know the type of potential you have.' "

The highlight of Odoms's 12-year career with the Broncos?

"You never forget the kinship we had with the Super Bowl team," he said.

He then recalled his favorite play, a 13-yard reception early in the third quarter of the AFC Championship Game that turned second-and-8 from the 15 into first-and-goal at the 2. (And on the next play, Raiders fans, Rob Lytle did *not* fumble!)

Odoms had 37 catches in that championship '77 season before having a career-best 54 receptions for 829 yards and six touchdowns in 1978.

"Our offense was never highly rated; it was just the Orange Crush defense that everybody recognized," Odoms said. "It wasn't until we crossed the 50 when they let us go. Even though we had Otis Armstrong and Haven Moses, our offense was set up so we would not make a mistake on this side of the 50, because we knew teams couldn't go 80 yards against our great defense. So we never wanted to leave our defense with a short field. But once we got across the 50-yard line we had a very explosive offense. Once we crossed the 50, then we'd start throwing the ball around a little bit.

"But I don't complain. Our era just started to throw to the tight end. I watched John Mackey growing up as a kid. And I would go, 'Whoa, this Mackey can catch the ball.' But then he'd go back to blocking."

The Broncos never could get their offense going in the Super Bowl against Dallas, but as Odoms recalls it, it could have been different if not for some bum luck early in the game.

"I remember running out there in the big old stadium for the Super Bowl," Odoms said, referring to the Louisiana Superdome in New Orleans. "And I remember one play. We knew that [linebacker Thomas] Henderson was going to bite up on that run on play-action. We called it. It was early in the first quarter. I'm at the Dallas 30- or 25-yard line cutting across the field. Wide open. And Too Tall Jones leaps up and knocks the ball down. Oh, my gosh. It was my time. Wide open."

Since his retirement as a player, Odoms has stayed busy while settling back in Houston. He was in the auto parts business for years, then worked for cable and communications companies. His left knee still bothers him from an injury suffered near the end of his career, as does the right ankle from his rookie year. His back is stiff most of the morning until it loosens up as the day goes on.

"You just deal with it," Odoms said. "I have quality of life. I just deal with the pain and go about my day. I walk better as I step. First thing in the morning I'm real stiff, but it's better than looking up at the roots in the ground."

Around Houston, Odoms still follows the Broncos closely.

"They don't call me 'Riley' here," he said. "They call me 'Omaha.' When Peyton would call out, 'Omaha, Omaha,' I'd walk into a bar here and they'd say, 'Here comes Omaha.'"

Maybe someday he'll walk into the Ring of Fame, if not through Canton's hallowed halls.

"If it happens, it'll be nice to go on back there and see the guys again," Odoms said.

RILEY ODOMS STATS					
YRS	G	REC	Y	Y/R	TD
12	153	396	5,755	14.5	41

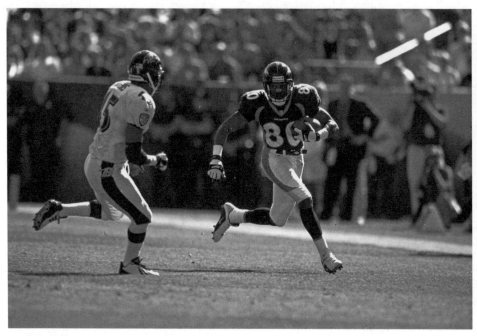

Rod Smith © *Eric Lars Bakke*

Terrell Davis © *Eric Lars Bakke*   Al Wilson © *Eric Lars Bakke*

Jake Plummer
© *Jamie Schwaberow*

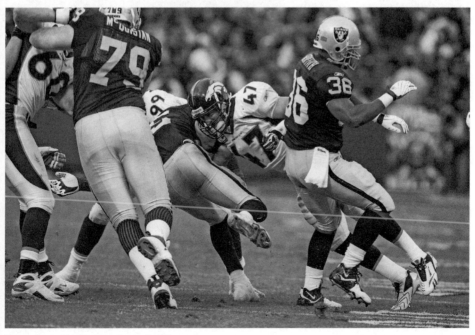

John Lynch © *Eric Lars Bakke*

Champ Bailey © *Eric Lars Bakke*

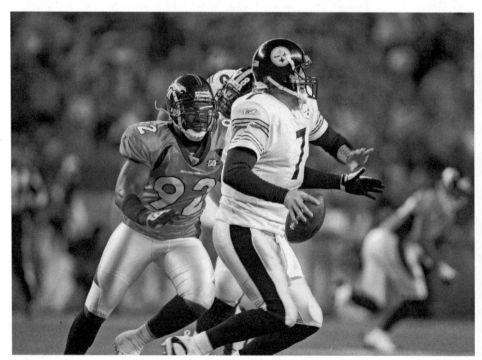

Elvis Dumervil © *Eric Lars Bakke*

Ryan Clady © *Eric Lars Bakke*

Demaryius Thomas © *Eric Lars Bakke*

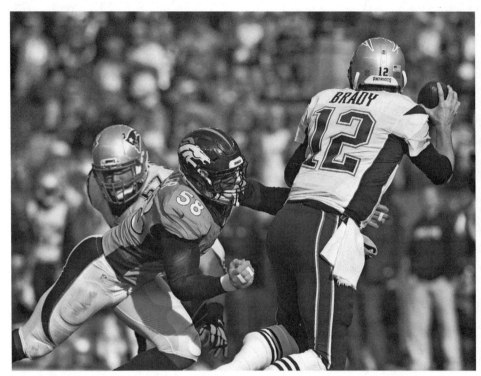

Von Miller © *Eric Lars Bakke*

Chris Harris Jr. © *Eric Lars Bakke*

 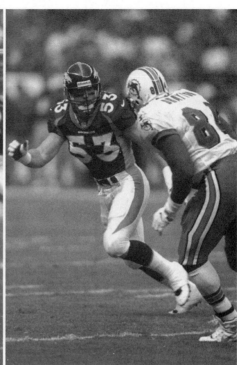

Shannon Sharpe © *Eric Lars Bakke*   Bill Romanowski © *Eric Lars Bakke*

Ed McCaffrey © *Eric Lars Bakke*

Tom Nalen © *Eric Lars Bakke*

Tyrone Braxton © *Eric Lars Bakke*

John Elway © *Eric Lars Bakke*

Jason Elam © *Eric Lars Bakke*

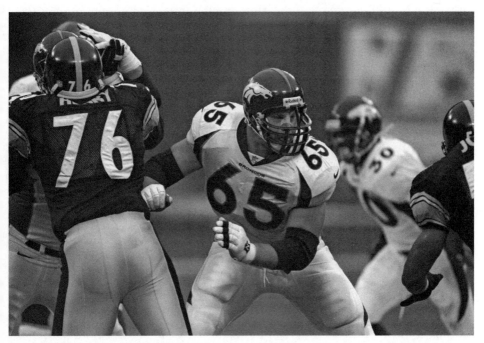

Gary Zimmerman © *David Gonzales*

Gene Mingo
© *Dick Burnell*

Trevor Pryce © *Ryan McKee*   Steve Atwater © *Eric Lars Bakke*

Peyton Manning © *Eric Lars Bakke*

Rulon Jones
© *Eric Lars Bakke*

Keith Bishop © *Eric Lars Bakke*

Sammy Winder © *Rod Hanna*

Haven Moses
© *Rod Hanna*

Craig Morton © *Rod Hanna*

Barney Chavous © *Barry Staver*

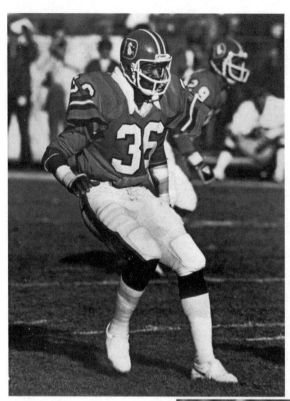

Billy Thompson
© *Rod Hanna*

Randy Gradishar
© *Rod Hanna*

Otis Armstrong
© *Dick Burnell*

Lyle Alzado
© *Rod Hanna*

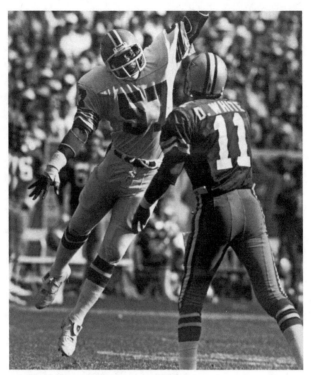

Tom Jackson *Photo credit unavailable*

Floyd Little © *Dick Burnell*

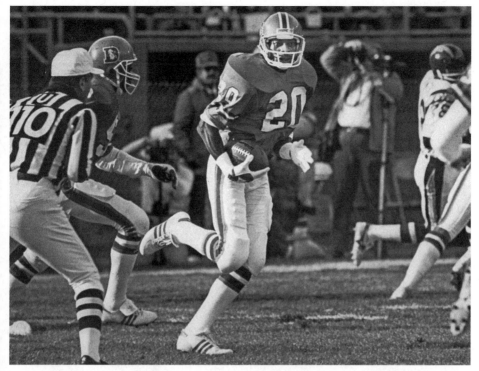

Louis Wright © *Rod Hanna*

Frank Tripucka © *Dick Burnell*   Paul Smith © *Dick Burnell*

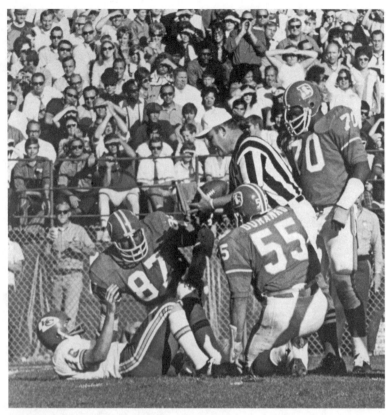

Rich "Tombstone" Jackson © *Dick Burnell*

Rick Upchurch © *Rod Hanna*

Steve Watson
© *Rod Hanna*

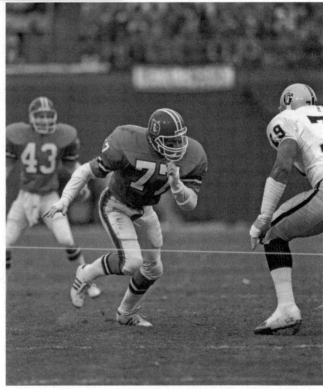

Karl
Mecklenburg
© *Rod Hanna*

Rubin Carter © *Barry Staver*

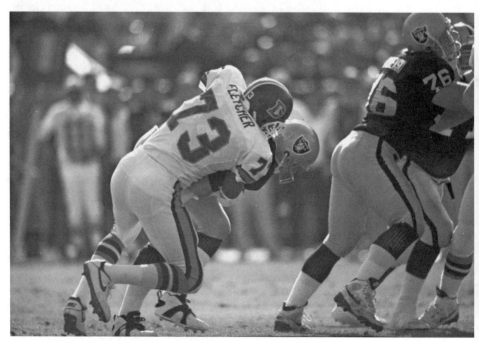

Simon Fletcher © *Eric Lars Bakke*

Steve Foley
© *Rod Hanna*

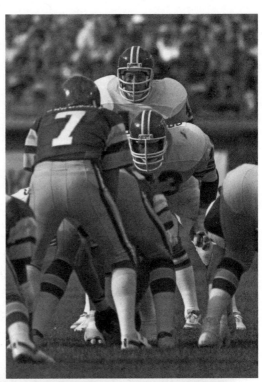

Ken Lanier © *Rod Hanna*

Riley Odoms © *Rod Hanna*

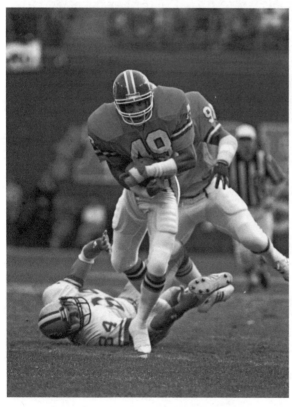

Dennis Smith
© *Rod Hanna*

Lionel Taylor © *Dick Burnell*

Austin "Goose" Gonsoulin © *Dick Burnell*

27

— **ED McCAFFREY** —

Receiver, 1995–2003

When some players, especially receivers, say all they care about is winning and trying to capture a Super Bowl, it's tempting to look behind their backs to see if their fingers are crossed.

I've seen several receivers, including a few Broncos over the years, pout after victory. We know why. Catches make them happy. Lack of catches can leave them disappointed, even in victory.

Ed McCaffrey was a receiver who not only said all he cared about was winning, he made an unprecedented sacrifice to prove it.

Selected by the New York Giants out of Stanford with the final pick in the third round of the 1991 NFL Draft, McCaffrey in his second season led his team with 49 receptions. But then Dan Reeves took over as Giants head coach in 1993, and he brought some of his favorite Denver Broncos with him, including Mark Jackson.

McCaffrey not only didn't get much action that year, he was released after that season. A free agent, McCaffrey had good offers from the Kansas City Chiefs to catch passes from Joe Montana in the quarterback's final season, and from Washington, which was breaking in a highly touted and highly drafted (No. 3 overall) rookie quarterback in Heath Shuler.

Instead, McCaffrey took less money to play behind Jerry Rice in San Francisco. That's right; McCaffrey took a smaller salary to back up the greatest receiver of all time.

"I had gone to Stanford and I really wanted to be part of a Super Bowl championship football team," McCaffrey said. "One, I was going back to the Bay Area and play in an offense I was familiar with. But the main thing was, I wanted to be part of a Super Bowl championship team. I knew if I could make the team—because they only took four wide receivers, and Jerry Rice and John Taylor were two of them—then I felt like I could be part of something special. They had lost to Dallas in the NFC Championship a couple years in a row, but I got there and fortunately I worked real hard and made the team backing up Jerry Rice.

"You can imagine I didn't get a ton of reps, but I did get in the Super Bowl when Jerry hurt his shoulder for a play and I got a catch. And I was part of a very special team. We became Super Bowl Twenty-Nine champs, beat San Diego. That was the first football championship I had ever been a part of."

McCaffrey had just 11 catches for the 49ers in 1994 (Rice had 112), yet he was one of the happiest players in the NFL. He also didn't get his Stanford education for nothing. McCaffrey's decision to play with the San Francisco 49ers as backup receiver in 1994 was shrewd, because on George Seifert's staff was offensive coordinator Mike Shanahan and quarterbacks coach Gary Kubiak.

When Shanahan moved on the next year to become the Broncos head coach in 1995, nabbing Kubiak as his offensive coordinator, they brought McCaffrey along with them.

"Even though they didn't say too many words to me during that year in San Francisco, I got the call from them after the season and they invited me to Denver," McCaffrey said. "And I was blessed to be part of those Broncos teams in the late '90s."

He didn't become the great receiver partner to Rod Smith right away. Check that. McCaffrey and Smith did instantly become the best receiver duo in Broncos history. Only no one outside the Broncos starting defense and the Monday-morning film room knew it.

The top two Broncos receivers in 1995 were Anthony Miller and Mike Pritchard. John Elway also threw a ton to a tight end named Shannon Sharpe and a rookie running back named Terrell Davis.

McCaffrey and Smith were scout team stars.

"When we first started getting into games, we'd have little side bets on who could have the most de-cleaters in the game," McCaffrey said. "Because they weren't throwing us the ball. John running was the second option in the progression before they would throw us the football. So how do we get on tape?"

Smith was undrafted out of Division II Missouri Southern and spent his rookie 1994 season on the Broncos practice squad. He had six catches for 152 yards and one memorable touchdown (a game-winner against Darrell Green) in 1995. McCaffrey wound up with 39 catches for 477 yards in his first year with the Broncos in 1995, although he got 9 of those catches and 99 of those yards in a final game victory against Oakland as the Broncos were wrapping up an 8-8 season.

"It was cool because he was in the same boat that I was," Smith said. "He was a little older, somewhat of a journeyman. We both knew inside we could play, but we respected the process and said we're going to work and we're going to get on the damn tape by doing stuff other receivers didn't want to do. Which was block."

Eventually, Smith and McCaffrey became only the second receiving duo in NFL history to each have 100 catches and 1,000 yards in the same season. It was the 2000 season when McCaffrey had 101 catches for 1,317 yards and 9 touchdowns, and Smith had 100 catches for 1,602 yards and 8 touchdowns.

And before that they had worked their way into becoming the two starting receivers for the Broncos' back-to-back Super Bowl championship teams in 1997 and 1998.

"For nine years I got to play for Rod, and I'd like to think we rooted for each other and we competed really hard against each other to push each other to get better," McCaffrey said. "That's one of those things you can't script."

McCaffrey and Smith may have been joined at Smith's good hip through long parts of each other's careers, but Eddie Mac's lifelong partner is the former Lisa Sime. They met at Stanford and later became parents of four football-playing sons.

"I knew of Lisa and had seen her around campus," McCaffrey said. "But we formally met at a friend's birthday party. I got up the courage to ask her out to a movie."

Julia Roberts's 1990 breakout movie, *Pretty Woman*, was the backdrop to the budding romance of football's first couple.

Ed and Lisa had much in common. Lisa was a terrific soccer player whose dad was an All-American baseball player at Duke who later became an Olympic silver medalist in the 100-meter sprint.

Ed was the oldest of five children born and raised Catholic by Edward and Elizabeth McCaffrey. Ed was born in Waynesboro, Virginia, but the family moved when he was four to Wilmington, North Carolina, where he played pickup basketball at Empie Park. Five years earlier, Empie Park was the same stomping grounds for a young hoops player named Michael Jordan.

McCaffrey's father was a systems analyst who got moved around, and he brought the McCaffreys to Allentown, Pennsylvania, when Ed was in the seventh grade. McCaffrey's favorite sport in North Carolina was baseball, and it was basketball in Pennsylvania.

"We had a pretty good basketball team; we won a couple of state championships," McCaffrey said of Allentown Central Catholic High School.

"Our football team went 0-11 my junior year and 2-9 my senior year. We were not good. We had fun. Great teammates. But we were not good.

"Most people were shocked when I wound up playing football in college. People who didn't follow high school football closely. They thought of me as a basketball player."

Somebody watched him, because he made the 1985 Parade All American high school team as a 6-foot-5, 238-pound tight end. (He lost weight to play receiver at Stanford.)

Ed's sister, Monica, was a four-year letterman basketball player at Georgetown (1988–91). His brother Bill played for Duke, where he was the Blue Devils' third-leading scorer on their national championship team that upset UNLV in the 1991 Final Four and Kansas in the championship game. Bill then transferred to Vanderbilt and became the co-SEC Player of the Year with Kentucky's Jamal Mashburn in 1993. Mike McCaffrey was a four-year basketball starter at NAIA Hasson College. Youngest sister Meghan was into dance.

Ed was unique as a football player. His formal college visits were Michigan, Notre Dame, Penn State, Purdue, and Stanford.

"Jack Elway was probably the biggest reason I chose Stanford," McCaffrey said of John Elway's dad. "I really liked him as a head football coach. Obviously, loved the Bay Area. The weather is phenomenal. And at the time they were rated number one in terms of academics by *U.S. News and World Report*. I thought I could get a great education, playing for a coach that I loved, in beautiful weather. And also, they were willing to let me play receiver."

Had he gone to Michigan, Penn State, or Notre Dame, he would have been a tight end. Back then, tight ends were blockers first, blockers second, and maybe mix in a catch third. McCaffrey would turn out to be one of the best blocking receivers in NFL history. But there's a difference in blocking cornerbacks and safeties downfield than as a sixth offensive linemen in a scrum against linebackers.

Stanford also told McCaffrey he could play for the Cardinal basketball team, but once he got there he realized football and the classroom left him with little time for any other sport.

During his time with the Broncos, McCaffrey was known for his fearlessness. A physical, possession-type receiver who could get deep if you fell asleep on him, McCaffrey also often made catches while getting walloped.

For all of his accomplishments—565 catches and 55 touchdowns, plus another 42 catches and 2 touchdowns in 14 postseason games—Broncos and NFL fans often link McCaffrey with the opening of Denver's new football stadium on September 10, 2001.

It was a Monday night and McCaffrey was having a terrific opener against his former Giants, catching six passes for 94 yards. On that sixth catch, McCaffrey snagged a 19-yard pass from Brian Griese and pivoted to run upfield when his lead leg kicked safety Shaun Williams. McCaffrey's leg hit Williams so hard, his leg snapped.

"It was a bad day. And an even worse tomorrow," he said.

Just after midnight of September 11, McCaffrey underwent surgery to repair his leg.

"I woke up and I was watching television and I was on a morphine drip and I was thinking about my career and the possibility that it was over," McCaffrey said. "And while I was watching television, I remember Bryant Gumbel was on the screen and standing in front of the Towers, and one of them was smoking.

"I thought it was a movie. I didn't realize it was the news. At the time, everybody thought it was some kind of accident—a plane accidentally flew into the tower, something happened. And then live I saw the second plane hit the second tower, and immediately everybody on the planet watching live realized this was no accident."

After terrorists had flown the first plane into the World Trade Center's North Tower, much of the nation was watching live when the second plane crashed into the South tower. The towers were hit 17 minutes apart.

McCaffrey immediately called Lisa, who was getting Max and Christian ready for school. Ed was lying on his hospital bed with his eyes stuck on the television screen, even if he was viewing through a semiconscious state.

"It felt like the world was coming to an end," he said. "The nurses were coming into my room and looking at the television screen, listening to the radio, and calling people they knew and loved. Along the East Coast the phone lines started going down. And then you hear a report of Pennsylvania and the Pentagon, and at the time it did really seem like the world was coming to an end. I didn't know if I was going to get out of the hospital the way things were unraveling.

"Then it was pretty amazing to watch those heroes risk their lives and give their lives to save others and spread love and support and help to all people who were in need and suffering. And that was a big motivating factor for me to get up out of bed and work hard to get better and appreciate my family and friends. There was no room to feel sorry for myself for breaking my leg after watching what unfolded the next day."

After months of pain, sweat, work, and intense rehab, McCaffrey returned for the 2002 season and had 69 catches for 903 yards. His first catch in his first game back was a 23-yard touchdown in the fourth quarter that beat St. Louis.

McCaffrey's final season of 2003 was slowed at the start by an off-season sports hernia operation, and then he suffered concussions in two of his final three games during the regular season. He didn't dress for the Broncos play-off game at Indianapolis, and McCaffrey formally retired on March 2 during a teary press conference in which he embraced owner Pat Bowlen.

Since then, McCaffrey hasn't exactly had trouble filling his days. He and Lisa have four sons—Max, Christian, Dylan, and Lucas. Let's look at what the year 2015 was like for the McCaffreys. They spent their weekends traveling cross-country to watch Max, who caught 52 passes for Duke, and Christian, who had 2,019 yards rushing, 645 yards receiving, 1,200 return yards, and 39 yards passing—3,903 yards and 17 touchdowns total—for Stanford to nearly win the Heisman Trophy.

Meanwhile, Dylan McCaffrey was a blue-chip quarterback and safety for football powerhouse Valor Christian High School on his way to Michigan, while Luke was a high school freshman who was collecting scholarship offers from Michigan and Colorado halfway through his sophomore season.

Max, Christian, Dylan, and Luke had helped Valor win seven of eight state football championships entering Luke's junior year.

If Ed and Lisa have been asked once, they've been asked hundreds of times. And the answer is, No, there is no secret to raising boys to become highly successful athletes.

"I wish there was one," Ed said. "I guess we're lucky that they're all inherently good kids. There's definitely no secret formula. Lisa is pretty amazing with our boys. I love my sons and try to be there for them as a father and give them love and support and guidance when possible, but in the end, they're their own kids. We're just here to do whatever we can as parents to help them, but they're hardworking, driven kids who have good heads on their shoulders. I guess we lucked out a little bit."

McCaffrey was still playing when he came up with a way to bond with his boys. In 2000, he started putting on a youth football camp that has now grown into unquestionably the biggest and best in the Rocky Mountain region.

"I love football," he said. "It's the greatest sport in the world. I've played it since I was eight, as early as you can play it as a kid. I love camps probably more than anything, because you can help everybody. You don't have to decide who's starting, who's backing up. You're helping to teach everybody and hopefully provide some life lessons on and off the field. I love bringing in former teammates of mine, other NFL stars, to talk to the kids and to coach them and to teach them about the game that I love.

"I guess it's one small way for someone like me to give back. My kids, they all played football from the beginning. Their buddies would come over and play in the backyard or in the park. A lot of people had asked me for advice when it came to the sport of football, and I thought, 'Hey, why don't we just formalize this and have a camp every year, a couple of camps. Get kids together and teach them about the game and bring in some wonderful speakers to talk with them and try to have some fun.' And that's how it started; it just got bigger and bigger and bigger over the years."

His camps led to an invitation to put on a Dare to Play Football Camp, which is for young men and women and kids with Down syndrome.

"And that's one of the biggest blessings of my life, because I didn't realize there weren't many opportunities for people with Down syndrome to participate in team sports and to play the sport of football," McCaffrey said. "The response I get from parents after our football camps and our Dare to Play camps is just phenomenal. Parents who love their kids, want to see them have fun and be part of something bigger than themselves. It's really the reason I started playing football to begin with, and it's a blessing to be able to give a little back."

Unquestionably, the McCaffrey boys benefited from their dad's strong character. Like many of the subjects I interviewed for this project, I asked McCaffrey what his most vivid flashback was from his nine seasons with the Broncos.

"It would be the Super Bowls. Super Bowl Thirty-Two, the win against the Packers, was my favorite game of all time. A moment I'll cherish forever," he said. "And then the win the next year against Atlanta. My two older boys were really young at the time, but they got to go to the game and ran around on the field after the game in the confetti. So, a really special moment in our lives."

Wait a minute. Super Bowl XXXII was about the Elway Helicopter spin and Terrell Davis running roughshod against Gilbert Brown and the Packers. McCaffrey had just two catches in that game, albeit for 45 yards.

He had a much bigger game in Super Bowl XXXIII with five catches for 72 yards.

"It depends on what you mean by bigger game," McCaffrey said. "I probably had more catches and yards [in the second Super Bowl]. The first one, it felt so unbelievably special to be part of the Denver Broncos' first Super Bowl championship. My favorite moment in football was lining up in the victory formation standing behind John Elway as he took the final knee of the game and seeing the expression on his face and then seeing all our teammates rush the field. The last second on the clock seemed like it took an eternity to tick. That moment for me is frozen in time. I'm really blessed I was part of a special team and had a great moment."

ED MCCAFFREY STATS

YRS	G	REC	Y	Y/R	TD
9	121	462	6,200	13.4	46

28

RICK UPCHURCH

Returner/Receiver, 1975–83

Rick Upchurch made it difficult to come up with an encore.

Selected in the fourth round of the 1975 NFL Draft out of Minnesota, where he was a running back and returner, Upchurch delivered the most impressive rookie debut in Broncos history.

It was the season opener against the Kansas City Chiefs at Mile High Stadium when Broncos fans immediately fell in love with their new speedy weapon. Upchurch had three catches for 153 yards—including a 90-yard touchdown strike from Charley Johnson—all in the second half as Upchurch filled in for Haven Moses, who was injured late in the first half. There was a 13-yard touchdown run on an end around that started the Broncos' comeback from a 10–0 deficit in the first half.

Upchurch also had a 30-yard punt return and a 38-yard kickoff return. Throw in two more kickoff returns and one game into his NFL career, Upchurch had 284 combined yards, which was not only the best rookie debut output by a Bronco, but the best opening act in NFL history. The Broncos won, 37–33.

"When people say I was a returner, they might not have seen my first game," Upchurch said. "I could play wide receiver. But they thought I was more valuable at returning kicks at that time because we had Haven and Jack Dolbin starting in front of me."

So what did Upchurch do for an encore? He had an 80-yard touchdown catch in his third game at Buffalo, plus another 110 yards on four returns. In Game 7 of his rookie year against Oakland, Upchurch had three catches for 76 yards, five rushes for 17 yards, four kickoff returns for 129 yards, and one punt return for 18 yards—another 240 yards in combined yardage.

And you should have seen Upchurch in 1976 when he became the first NFL player in history to return four punts for touchdowns.

"Tadpole," said Steve Foley, a Broncos defensive back and Upchurch's teammate. "His nickname was 'Tadpole' because he could run sideways, backways. He was so fast it was ridiculous what he could do with punt return and kickoff return—but punt return more than anything.

"That was the first time where I saw in a pro game where they stopped punting to a returner. That was the first time I had seen that. I think he had four touchdowns one year [in 1976], and they stopped punting to him."

Upchurch is one of the few NFL players who has made two All-Decade teams, as he was a first-team returner in the 1970s and second-team punt returner in the 1980s. His eight career touchdowns off punt returns held as an NFL record for 14 years after he retired.

His 3,008 yards off punt returns in nine seasons held as an NFL record for two years, until Billy "White Shoes" Johnson went past that number 13 years after he entered the league.

Upchurch was also an excellent kickoff returner his first three seasons before he gradually stopped handling that chore as he became a starting receiver. Is the key to returning running scared?

"No, I had been returning punts and kickoffs my whole life," Upchurch said. "That's all I did, and I took pride in it because that was something from the grass roots; the coaching I had back in Ohio taught us if you want to do something, you put your whole heart and all your ability into it so that you can make a difference.

"They used to always emphasize, there's three parts of the game: offense, defense, and special teams. Offense and defense are going to do their jobs, but where is special teams going to make the difference? And that always stuck with me. I was always back there on kickoff returns and punt returns, and I was always very comfortable with it. I knew I could run. I knew I was fast. I was a running back, so I could take some punishment. I used those skills to do a good job. But also it took the other 10 guys to have confidence in me that I was going to do the right thing."

Juanita Upchurch was just 20 years old when she delivered the best returner in Broncos history on May 20, 1952, in Toledo, Ohio.

"When I left the hospital as a baby, my grandfather took over and said he's coming home with me," Upchurch said in a February 2017 interview. "So I was raised basically by my grandparents."

The grandparents, Louis and Beatrice Lindsey, lived in Holland, Ohio, a rural town outside Toledo. No streetlights at the time.

"The only thing that lit us up out in the country was lightning bugs," Upchurch said.

Louis Lindsey played in the Negro Leagues in the 1920s, and his grandson spent most of his youth wanting to play Major League Baseball.

"Major League Baseball basically started in Toledo, Ohio," Upchurch said, and indeed, the city's baseball roots go back to 1883. "My grandfather taught me how to hit, how to throw the ball. I was a baseball player more than anything else. Matter of fact, everybody thought I was going to be a baseball player."

It was while in junior high that Upchurch's destiny changed course. The town's high school football coach, Julius Taormina, had seen Upchurch sprint in track and told the impressionable youngster baseball was for wimps and football was the sport he needed to play.

Upchurch played running back and then got his start outside Ohio through a junior college in Centerville, Iowa, called Indian Hills Community College. The baseball coach there was Pat Daugherty, who later became the top scout for the Colorado Rockies.

Daugherty had an eye for talent and tried to get Upchurch to go out for baseball, but to no avail. Upchurch was on his way to becoming a second-team All American running back as a freshman and first-team All American as a sophomore, which led to the University of Minnesota.

Lining up behind a quarterback named Tony Dungy, Upchurch led the Gophers as a senior in 1974 with 942 yards rushing in 11 games, and added 14 receptions for another 209 yards. Upchurch even completed 5 of 7 passes for 93 yards to post a 183.0 passer rating that would have ranked in the top three among NCAA passing leaders in 2016.

"I knew Rick; he was from Minnesota, and I played at Ohio State, so I played against Rick in college," said Broncos linebacker Randy Gradishar. "Him coming out to Denver, I think he was in a couple Pro Bowls, but his return ability—he had a sense for dodging guys, and of course with his speed and his size, he was able to do that."

The Broncos' terrific draft class of 1975 featured cornerback Louis Wright in the first round, Upchurch with the second of two picks in the fourth round, nose tackle Rubin Carter in the fifth, and Foley in the eighth.

Upchurch took off, literally, from there.

"He gave me a break as a returner," said Broncos safety Billy Thompson, who led the AFL in both punt and kickoff returns as a rookie in 1969. "He was definitely special. He was unbelievable. He had great hands. Great hands and speed. One of those guys who had a lot of heart."

Asked to name his favorite return, Upchurch first mentioned the 87-yard punt return for a touchdown that gave the Broncos a 14–0 lead in a regular-season game against the mighty Pittsburgh Steelers in 1977. The Broncos went on to win that game, 21–7, and later handled the Steelers in the playoffs on their way to Denver's first Super Bowl appearance.

Upchurch also had two touchdown punt returns in the same September 1976 game against Cleveland. The first was a 73-yard return score off a Don Cockroft punt following the opening Browns series that gave the Broncos a 7–0 lead. Midway through the third quarter, Upchurch returned a 47-yard punt off Cockroft, who prepped at Fountain–Fort Carson High School, for a touchdown and a 30–7 lead.

"That was a great day because they were broadcasting that game back home in Ohio," Upchurch said. "But my most memorable game was my very first game. People don't realize I had a concussion before I had to go back out there to take over Haven's spot at wide receiver."

Despite his breakout debut as a receiver, Upchurch had trouble convincing the Broncos coaching staff, first led by John Ralston, and then Red Miller, that he could become a bona fide receiver.

Upchurch had 18 catches as a rookie, 12 in 1976, 12 in '77, and 17 in 1978 before Miller finally gave him a chance in 1979. Upchurch responded by leading the Broncos with 64 catches for 937 yards and 7 touchdowns. A 33-year-old Moses was next, with 54 catches for 954 yards and 6 touchdowns. Upchurch had two more 40-catch seasons before calling it a career.

"I knew how to play the game, I just didn't have the opportunity to get out there and be a full-time player," Upchurch said. "But I was very happy to be a full-time returner on punts and kickoffs because I knew that was going to make a difference. Field position is everything."

Especially when he had the 1977 Orange Crush defense on his side.

"Certainly the most vivid memory I have was going to that very first Super Bowl," he said. "Denver never had the opportunity to go the playoffs, much less the Super Bowl. Back in '77 we lost coach Ralston and we brought in Red, and we didn't know our chances of going to the Super Bowl were that good. We couldn't see it. We knew we had a very good team. But the way we came together that year when Red came in and gave us that attitude that we can win, and we will win—it was probably the greatest moment in Broncos history."

Indeed, even though the Broncos have since won three Super Bowl titles, Broncomania was never more euphoric than during that 1977 season.

"That Western Division back when we were playing was awfully good," he said. "San Diego could score with anybody. Seattle could beat anybody on any given Sunday. The Kansas City Chiefs were world champions and

Oakland Raiders were world champions. So that division was awful, awful tough.

"And that year when we did win, we had to beat Oakland twice. Al Davis was, 'I'm going to get my boys out of work release; I don't care what it takes, we're going to win football games.' Al Davis was about winning. We had to beat them during the season, and then we had to beat them in that AFC Championship. And people don't realize how good Kansas City was in those days. Our division was strong."

Upchurch finished his career with 4,369 receiving yards on 267 catches, 349 rushing yards, 3,008 punt return yards, and 2,355 yards in kickoff return—10,081 yards total, the second most combined yardage in Broncos history at the time to Floyd Little's 12,173. (Rod Smith has since moved into the top spot, with 12,488 combined yardage.)

Following his retirement as a player, Upchurch for two years coached a then-downtrodden Pueblo East football program. He inherited a team that went 1-9 in 2004, and in his first year of 2005, Pueblo East went 0-10. That will humble a man. The next year they went 1-9 with an upset win against Widefield.

"It was rewarding in one sense in that even today I get letters from kids who played for me," Upchurch said. "Back then the east side was the rough side of town. We had gang members, you had the single-parent homes. You had dysfunction, and for me to walk into that situation, that first year I was like, 'This is going to be a tough one.'

"But the thing about it was the teams we played, Pueblo South and Rampart, top teams in the state, we would only get beat by two touchdowns or one touchdown or a field goal. We made improvement. The kids were starting to believe, the school was starting to believe. We were dealing with kids with their grades and kids with their problems at home. They had a lot on their plates to deal with."

So why did Upchurch hang up coaching?

"In the last game of our second year against Centennial, my kids went hunting on me," he said. "It was the opening day of hunting season. The seniors went hunting on me. I told them we don't have the numbers as it is, and you're going hunting on me? I said that's enough for me."

Pueblo East is now a football powerhouse, having won the state championship three times in the past decade.

In 2011, Upchurch was diagnosed with leukemia. He didn't publicly reveal his battle until he announced one of the Broncos' selections in the 2015 NFL Draft in Chicago.

"I go back every three months for my blood test and my doctors have kept me in remission," he said in early 2017. "I still take chemo pills three times a day to keep that under control."

He's been married to Donna for 21 years. They have five children.

In 2014, Upchurch was inducted into the Broncos Ring of Fame.

				RICK UPCHURCH STATS					
YRS	G	REC	Y	Y/R	TD	PR	Y	AVG	TD
9	119	267	4,369	16.4	24	248	3,008	12.1	8

29
CHRIS HARRIS JR.
Cornerback, 2011–present

The pro football version of the Chris Harris Jr. story begins with the 2011 NFL Draft he was snubbed from.

Although he was a four-year starting defensive back for the University of Kansas—including as a true freshman for the 12-1, Orange Bowl–winning Jayhawks—Harris fell through the scouting grid when he was moved from cornerback to safety as a senior.

"I wasn't getting any action at corner," Harris said. "We thought it would be good to show scouts I could play anywhere on the field. It ended up backfiring on me. I was rated higher at corner than at safety, and they had me listed at safety. That's what messed me up."

The Denver Broncos, though, were coming out of the 2011 NFL lockout with a new front office headed by John Elway, a new coaching staff headed by John Fox, and an aging secondary in need of some fresh legs.

The first hour after the seventh round of every NFL Draft is a free-for-all, with coaches, scouts, and personnel executives of every team scurrying to call agents who represented the best of the rest. Remember, the NFL Draft went 17 rounds from 1967–76, 12 rounds from 1977–92. There are still good players available after the seventh round. The Broncos got Karl Mecklenburg and Tyrone Braxton in the 12th rounds, Paul Smith in the 9th, and Steve Foley in the 8th, to name four of the top 50 Broncos players of all time.

Then again, more players are drafted in each round in the modern era, so there's no excuse for the NFL's 31 other scouting departments: They whiffed on Harris.

Richard Sherman out of Stanford was ranked as the 23rd best corner by Walter Football. Chris Harris was ranked 48th, even though he ran the 40 in 4.49 seconds. There were 33 corners drafted. At safety, NFLDraft Scout.com had Harris ranked as the 30th best. Rahim Moore and Quinton Carter were 1-2.

The Broncos almost missed on Harris, too. At draft's end, Dave Ziegler, the Broncos player personnel assistant and an area scout, was rushed a printout with a list of 20 corners on it. He started with the top 10.

"And Chris might have been, like, 12," Ziegler said. "Those 10 top guys started signing with other teams, so Chris started moving up the board. We looked at it and he had played corner and safety, so the guy had some versatility. We started to get more interested."

The Broncos had already signed one undrafted cornerback, Brandon Bing of Rutgers, to a $3,000 signing bonus, but they wanted one more to fill out their camp roster.

"Finally at the end of the day, there were two cornerbacks available," Ziegler said. "It was Chris and one other kid."

Harris wasn't slow, but the other corner was a speedster. Ziegler tracked down Coach Fox, who was talking about another player in the office of special teams coordinator Jeff Rodgers.

"I said, 'Foxy, I've got a guy that's real fast, and dumb,'" Ziegler said. "'And I've got a guy that's not as fast, and smart. Who do you want?' He said, 'Let's go with the smart guy.'"

Ziegler had been talking to Fred Lyles, Harris's agent, a couple times during the hour after the draft. This time, Ziegler called to close the deal.

"I said, 'Okay, Fred, I've got 2,000 dollars,'" Ziegler said. "He said, 'Let's do it.'"

Ziegler moved on to the New England Patriots, where they found their own Chris Harris in Malcolm Butler, an undrafted free agent from West Alabama.

"They both jumped off the practice tape from day one," Ziegler said. "Right away, they started making plays. In Chris's case, like you said, Coach Fox threw the right dart."

By the second week of the abbreviated Broncos training camp in 2011, Fox gave Marlon McCree an assignment. McCree was fresh off a nine-year NFL career as a safety for the San Diego Chargers and Broncos, among others, and he had hooked up with the Broncos as a training camp coaching intern. McCree spent most of his camp as Harris's personal coach.

"One thing I took away from him was, he told me to be feisty," Harris said. "And also, never to have mental errors. That's one of the first things they told me, no MEs and they'll keep you here."

Look at him now. Harris is one of only three active players to become one of the 50 Greatest Broncos, joining Von Miller (No. 6) and Demaryius Thomas (No. 18). Harris, who has at least two interceptions in his first five seasons as a starter, and was named to the Pro Bowl team in three consecutive seasons of 2014–16, comes in at No. 29.

"As long as he stays healthy, he'll move up," said Champ Bailey, whose last three seasons with the Broncos overlapped with Harris's first three. "There's nobody with a bigger heart than Chris. He's unbelievable in the way he prepares and how hard he goes in practice. He's one of the best competitors I've been around. He's kind of got some Rod Smith in him."

Smith was also an undrafted player who went on to become the Broncos' all-time leading receiver in every significant category. Like Smith, Harris is a relentless competitor. Almost every athlete is described as a competitor. But there is an edginess in the way Harris competes.

"It comes from being slighted so much my whole life," Harris said. "Starting in high school. I was killing people in high school. Touchdowns, interceptions, taking them in for a score. I was an underdog, still. Nobody was wanting me. No schools. Then I get to KU and it was kind of the same thing. The only person they knew was Aqib [Talib], and I'm the underdog as a true freshman starting at the other corner opposite of Aqib. So, I always had that uphill battle my whole life."

Chris Harris Jr. was born June 18, 1989, in Tulsa, Oklahoma, to Chris Sr. and Lisa Harris (now Goff). His parents split up when he was young and he lived with his mom outside Tulsa, in Bixby. She kept him active in sports. Dad was always there to watch his son's games.

"I was always basketball, though," Harris said. "I was never really football. I played tackle football when I was five years old, but I never really loved it. I quit off and on. I was just more about basketball. I didn't get my first football offer until late in my basketball season my senior year. I didn't know I was going to play football."

He had some basketball offers from Oklahoma State, Texas A&M–Corpus Christi, some other small schools. But one of his assistant coaches at Bixby High School, D. J. Howell, had a fateful talk with Harris one day.

"He sat me down and said, 'Hey, you're better at football than basketball,'" Harris recalled. "And I listened to him."

Problem was, the 5-foot-10 Harris had trouble generating interest from college football programs. He started at both safety and receiver at Bixby, returned kickoffs and punts. But the football offers didn't come.

"Everybody kept saying I was small," Harris said. "My teammate had 50 to 60 offers. Jerry Glover. So, it wasn't like we weren't having big-time schools come watch us."

Finally, as Harris was playing point guard for the Bixby basketball team, Kansas coach Mark Mangino saw enough in Harris to offer him a scholarship. The Jayhawks were Harris's only offer. He took it.

Talib was there as a redshirt junior cornerback, who had such a fabulous season, with five interceptions, including two he returned for touchdowns, he became a consensus first-team All American. Harris was the other guy.

"Aqib was on the left, I was on the right, just like it is now," Harris said in December 2016.

Harris had two interceptions as a freshman, but just one more in his final three seasons. Although he was a sure tackler, there apparently weren't enough "wow" plays on tape to catch the attention of NFL scouts.

Even after he signed with the Broncos, he wasn't always sure he would make it.

"I was always scared because we started out with, like, 11 corners that year," Harris said. "The whole training camp, the whole preseason, I was like, number 11. And I didn't play the first preseason game, either. So I was really on edge.

"I would say it wasn't until the last preseason game that I figured I had a shot, because I started on all the special teams. I thought I had a shot to make it on special teams."

He played special teams for the Broncos through the first four games, and then in Game 5 at Green Bay, quarterback Aaron Rodgers was shredding the Denver secondary.

"We were getting killed," Harris said. "Champ didn't play that game. We were getting killed, and Coach Fox was, like, just let him play. And I got in there and they let me play the whole fourth quarter."

Harris was the Broncos nickelback the rest of the season. His breakout moment came the next year, in 2012. He was still the Broncos nickelback, or number-three corner, behind Bailey and Tracy Porter. Even with new free-agent quarterback Peyton Manning, the Broncos were 2-3 heading to San Diego.

"And then Tracy got sick out of nowhere," Harris said. "He practiced the whole week. And then Sunday we were flying to San Diego and we were about to leave and he got sick out of nowhere. And they told me: 'Chris, you're starting.'"

The Monday-night game was not going well, as the Broncos were down 24–0 at halftime. In his first start at right corner, Harris intercepted Philip Rivers twice, including one he returned 46 yards for a touchdown that finished off a remarkable rally for a 35–24 win.

The Broncos went on to win their final 11 regular-season games.

"I would say that game is my most memorable as far as individually," Harris said. "Us being down so much, and me getting my first start on the road, Monday night. That kind of let me know I belonged in the league."

He's been the Broncos starting right cornerback ever since.

Whenever the Broncos go to their nickel package—which is about 60 percent of the time—Bradley Roby comes in to play the right outside corner spot, as Harris moves inside to the slot.

Why? Because Harris is the best inside defensive back in the league.

"It's not just being tough and playing good man coverage," Bailey said. "The guy is a technician. And he's smart. I see him on the field and see things and he's trying to tell everybody else. When you see him gesturing before the snap, it's because he knows what's coming. Not a lot of guys sitting in the slot can do that."

Generally speaking, the outside corners get paid the most, because shutting down the opponents' top receivers is highly valued. But Harris is more football player than he is cornerback, which is why the inside position suits him. There's more tackling involved inside. It requires more instincts on how the play develops.

"Playing the slot makes it where I can communicate with everybody," Harris said. "Deep linebackers, safeties. Being able to be a coach in the middle of the field. If I'm outside at corner, I can't really talk to guys. I'm pretty much on my own. If I'm in the slot, I can turn and say to the guys, 'Hey, this is what's coming.' Bam. This is what happened. We need to do this and this. There are a lot of things with our defense that I have to check. That's what having me in the slot does for our defense."

Football intelligence is one reason the slot is suited for Harris. So are his tenacious cover skills. Watch Harris cover a slot receiver—or any receiver, for that matter—and you can see a point guard on the court hounding the opposing team's dribbler.

"Basketball definitely helped me," Harris said "Change of direction, my press technique, how I play guys—that's all basketball. Being able to play the nickel. That's exactly what that is. That's basketball."

Late in the 2014 season, Harris had a choice of waiting until season's end for free agency, where he might have commanded a $10 million a year contract, or accept a "team discount" contract proposal. When Lyles deftly negotiated that team discount up to $8.5 million per year, with a large percentage paid up front, Harris stayed with the Broncos.

His wife Leah liked Denver. Leah and Chris were friends at KU, but it would be wrong to call them college sweethearts. Her best friend was dating his best friend, Darrell Stuckey, who plays for the San Diego Chargers.

"We never dated at all, but then when I got here in the NFL, I just called her up to see how she was doing," Harris said. "And we just started dating."

Chris and Leah have two daughters, Aria and Avianna.

"I loved it here," he said. "I wanted to win. A lot of the teams that were looking at me weren't winning teams. I wasn't ready to leave this atmosphere yet."

CHRIS HARRIS JR. STATS

YRS	G	I	Y	TD	TCK
6	95	14	342	3	367

30

PAUL SMITH

Defensive Lineman, 1968–78

Of all the great Denver Broncos players, history may have recorded less about the life of Paul Smith than any other.

He was just 54 years old when he died alone in his Aurora, Colorado, home from complications of pancreatic cancer. There were more than 20 former teammates who attended his funeral.

"This was a life that demanded notice," former Broncos safety Billy Thompson said following the service.

It would not be difficult to prove that Smith's career deserved more attention. Look at the 1971 season, for instance. The merger had occurred the year before, so the Broncos were very much part of the NFL. That season, Minnesota Vikings defensive tackle Alan Page became the first defensive player to win the NFL's MVP award. Page had 9.0 sacks that season.

Smith, meanwhile, had 12.0 sacks from his defensive tackle position. Smith's honors that year were nothing more than honorable mention all-AFC.

Yes, Page also had two safeties, but he received MVP as the symbol to the terrific Vikings defense that posted three shutouts and an 11-3 record. The Broncos in 1971 fired coach Lou Saban after nine games and finished 4-9-1.

And so it goes with so many of the great Broncos players before they won back-to-back Super Bowls in the late 1990s.

"He was a guy who couldn't do any of the agility drills, but could he play," said Rich "Tombstone" Jackson, Smith's defensive line mate from 1968–72. "We used to joke with him when he had those drills where you had to run through those ropes. But once we got rid of those drills, boy, could he play."

Paul Edward Smith was born August 13, 1945, and raised in Roswell, New Mexico. In high school, he played football, center for the basketball team, and threw the shot put and discus for the track team.

He was a three-year starter for the New Mexico Lobos, and led his team in tackles each year, with 83 in 1965, when he was named first-team Western Athletic Conference defensive tackle, 81 in 1966, and 95 in 1967.

He should have received more attention from NFL scouts, but the Lobos were 3-7, 2-8, and 1-9 in his three playing seasons. Credit Saban for finding a gem when he selected Smith in the ninth round of the 1968 draft.

The Broncos media relations department, with the help of John Turney's *Pro Football Journal*, did an outstanding job of digging up Smith's impressive sack totals in the four-year period from 1970–73—well before NFL statisticians began acknowledging sacks in 1982.

In those four years, Smith had 11.5 sacks in 1970, 12.0 sacks in 1971, 10.5 sacks in 1972, and 11.0 sacks in 1973. That's 45.0 sacks in four years—and from the inside pass rush.

Smith was considered large in those days at 6-foot-3, 256 pounds, and for a guy who struggled with the rope ladders, he had incredible, get-off quickness. Those four terrific seasons—which included Pro Bowl berths in 1972 and '73—plus the fact he became the first 10-year player with the club, is why Smith was part of the third class in 1986 to be inducted into the Broncos Ring of Fame.

At one time, Broncos head coach John Ralston called Smith "the finest defensive tackle in football." Which was saying something, when NFL defensive tackles of that era included Page, "Bubba" Smith, "Mean" Joe Greene, Bob Lilly, and Merlin Olsen.

Later, Broncos defensive linemen like Lyle Alzado, Rubin Carter, and Barney Chavous were extremely loyal to Smith. After a ruptured Achilles in the second game of the 1974 season put a crimp on Smith's terrific career, he still managed to contribute in the following seasons of 1975 (4.5 sacks) and '76 (3.0 sacks).

In 1977, when Broncos defensive coordinator Joe Collier went full-time with the 3-4 system, he alternated a second-string front three of Smith, John Grant, and Brison Manor every third series. The starting three of Chavous, Carter, and Alzado played two out of three series.

Alzado became increasingly displeased with the arrangement, but Chavous and Carter would defer without complaint in large part because of their affection for Smith.

"One of the most wonderful influences for me was Paul Smith," Chavous said. "When I came in as a rookie, Paul was a [second-team] All Pro defensive tackle. Paul made me feel so comfortable. He gave me confidence. Everyone on the team felt confident when he was around."

Smith gave back to the younger players, just as Tombstone Jackson gave to him.

"An All-American guy," Jackson said. "Very humble. He paid attention to details. He had all the tools to play and he was eager to learn. You could see when he came in he paid attention. You could tell that. Sometimes you try to help guys, but you can see they're not coachable. But Paul, you didn't have to tell him more than once. He just took off. We got to the point where we told each other: 'Let's develop our thing where we'll have our meeting at the quarterback.' "

Ralston once revealed that during the 1972 season, Smith was so good, Oakland Raiders owner Al Davis offered to trade his backup quarterback straight up for the Broncos defensive tackle. That backup QB was named Kenny Stabler. Ralston declined, and while hindsight says the Broncos should have taken a Pro Football Hall of Fame quarterback in exchange for a Ring of Fame defensive tackle, at the time it would have been considered a lopsided trade in the Raiders' favor.

Remember, Smith may have gone down as one of the best defensive tackles in NFL history if not for his torn Achilles early in 1974.

"I did call Ken Stabler's college coach at Alabama, Paul Bryant, and he was adamant that Ken would be a great player," Ralston said in an interview with the *Denver Post.* "He said, 'If you can get him for any cost, do it.' But it wasn't worth it. I also had polled all of our coaches who had been with the Broncos, and I even called Lou Saban. They said you never give up a Paul Smith.

"Of course, everybody will say I should have listened to 'Bear' more than the NFL people. But I felt that strongly about Paul. He was an amazing player. He could overpower you or run right by you."

After his 11th season with the Broncos—a franchise record in service time—Smith played two more years with Washington before retiring. He was credited with 55.5 sacks with the Broncos—which still ranks 9th on the team's all-time list entering the 2017 season—and 57.0 in his career.

Paul Smith had a son, Paul Smith Jr., and three grandchildren. At his funeral, held at New Hope Baptist Church in Denver in April 2000, former Broncos head coach Red Miller said of Smith: "A lot of guys you have to talk into playing football. He would have played in the parking lot. It didn't take much to start his engine. His engine was going."

PAUL SMITH STATS

YRS	G	S
11	164	55.5

31

SIMON FLETCHER

Outside Linebacker, 1985–95

It wasn't only that Simon Fletcher showed up every day, impressive as that was. It was also that he was there all day. To the very last play.

The Denver Broncos' all-time sack leader with 97.5, Fletcher never missed one of the 172 regular-season games the Denver Broncos played (not including the three replacement player games in 1987) during his 11-year career, from 1985–95. There were another 12 consecutive games played in the postseason, including three Super Bowls.

"I wanted to be able to hold my head up when I went to collect my paycheck," Fletcher said in November 2016.

He played on despite broken fingers, broken thumbs, a staph infection he received during a post-Raider game cleanup of a scar. There were sore ankles, bruised ribs, a pulled latissimus dorsi muscle behind his ribs.

"Ever try to breathe with a pulled lat muscle?" Fletcher said. "Honestly, the toughest thing for me was leaving the birth of one of my daughters an hour after her delivery to shoot out to the airport to go to Minnesota and leave mother and baby shortly after they were introduced to each other personally. That was tougher than any injury."

Of course, no player gets to play in all those games without performing in them. Fletcher's wife Pinkie delivered the youngest of their six daughters, Rasheedah, on November 3, 1990. The next day, Fletcher had the best individual sack game of his career, bringing down Vikings quarterback Rich Gannon four times.

"Simon was basically the Von Miller of his day," said Karl Mecklenburg, Fletcher's pass-rushing teammate. "He was just faster around the corner than the tackle could get back. He would come around the corner and just beat guys.

"The other thing about him was, he was so consistent with it. Everyone else would wear down at the end of the game, and that's when he would make his plays. Everyone would wear down at the end of the season—I mean, if you looked back at his statistics, I would guess two-thirds of his sacks were in the last third of the season. He was still going full blast while everyone else was nicked up from the season. That's why he didn't make any Pro Bowls. He was kind of middle of the pack in sacks until the end of the year when he would blow by everybody, but it was too late for the Pro Bowl voting."

It was preposterous Fletcher didn't make any Pro Bowls from 1989–93, when he posted, in succession, 12.0, 11.0, 13.5, 16.0, and 13.5 sacks. The likes of Derrick Thomas, Howie Long, and Rufus Porter got the AFC nod in 1989, even though each had fewer sacks than Fletcher. Greg Townsend, Neil Smith, and Greg Lloyd were chosen ahead of the sack-superior Fletcher in 1991.

In Fletcher's 16.0-sack season of 1992 that held as a Broncos record—until Elvis Dumervil picked up 17.0 in 2009—all but Leslie O'Neal among AFC linebackers and defensive ends had fewer sacks.

That would have never happened today, as sacks have become increasingly valued with the NFL altering its rules to enhance the passing game. That's just it about Fletcher's sack totals: He compiled them in a time when it was still a run-first league.

Fletcher's 97.5 sacks are a whopping 18.5 better than Mecklenburg's runner-up total of 79.0, and it's a team record that has held up through the 22 years since he retired.

Mecklenburg was right, by the way. In Fletcher's three-best sack seasons from 1991–93, 33 of his 43 sacks came in the second half of the season. Fletcher posted an incredible 12.5 sacks in his final seven games of 1992, then added 3.0 more in his first three games of 1993. Fletcher's 10-game sack streak set an NFL record that has never been broken, although DeMarcus Ware tied the mark in 2007–08 when the Broncos outside linebacker was playing with the Dallas Cowboys.

And while no pass rusher will pass up the chance to chalk one up to cement a decisive victory, Fletcher was hardly a garbage-time sack collector. In the three-year period from 1990–92, Fletcher amassed 30 of his 36.5 sacks in games decided by 7 points or less.

"When it's crunch time you've got to get your stinger out and try to hold on if your offense put you in position to win a game or you're close behind," Fletcher said. "I think in those moments you have to dig to find any extra that you can."

Even if the Pro Bowl honor eluded him, Fletcher wound up with better. He is a member of the Broncos Ring of Fame after being inducted along with safety John Lynch and kicker Jason Elam on October 23, 2016.

"From the time that I sat on that stage, my eyes were focused on my mother," Fletcher said, following the ceremony to unveil his pillar that is now among the 32 in the Broncos Ring of Fame Plaza. "Some of the [nice] things that they said about me, she may have heard them before, but to hear somebody say it in this form, she was filled with joy.

"I'm also feeling gracious and gratitude to the guys that I was blessed to play with. If your DBs aren't covering, if your front three aren't getting a push, then you'll never get a quarterback sack. The guys opposite of you, whether it's Rulon Jones, Barney Chavous, Karl Mecklenburg, if they're not containing, you never get one sack because the guy just runs out of the pocket. They were talking about Simon Fletcher, John, and Jason, but the three of us know that there are literally hundreds of guys who had to contribute to our being here this evening."

Fletcher's work ethic was passed on from his parents. His father, Elijah, started out as a laborer, went back to school, and became a pipe fitter for the remainder of his working days. His mother, Ethel, was a stay-at-home mom until she and Elijah split up when Simon was nine years old.

At that point, Ethel Fletcher went to work for a year, then realized she needed to make a better living for her four children. She went to nursing school, making a 130-mile commute from Bay City, Texas, to Corpus Christi, to become what is now called an LPN, or licensed practical nurse.

It wasn't long before Simon was helping out.

"I tried to wake up before the sun heated the house and became unbearable," Fletcher said when asked about his typical summer day as a kid. "I'd fixed something to eat for my little brothers and then between 12 and 13 years old, I got a job cutting lawns."

Fletcher never played football until his junior year. His varsity coach, the legendary Marshall Brown, had tried convincing Fletcher to go out for football prior to Simon's freshman, sophomore, and junior years. Finally, with two games left in the season during Fletcher's junior year, Brown had himself a pass rusher. Fletcher immediately had success against some all-district offensive tackles.

"We got to the playoffs and then I think we lost in the second round," Fletcher said. "I went back to my life. And just prior to the start of my senior year, Coach Brown came out to my job—I was still working for the same guy who was home building, cutting lawns. I ran track the previous year. I trusted [Coach Marshall], so I went out and gave it a shot."

Not before he got the required blessing from his mom.

"Part of the deal I made with my mother when she let me play football my senior year in high school, I promised her I'd get a scholarship and I'd play 10 years in the NFL," Fletcher said.

Promise kept. In track, Fletcher threw the shot put and discus and anchored the 4-by-100-meter relay. Brown nicknamed him "Tree." (When Coach Brown passed away in August 2016, Fletcher was one of three who officiated at his funeral.) Fletcher had such a fine senior football season for Bay City, every school in the Southwest Conference recruited him.

"I was a native Texan; I wanted to stay close to my family," Fletcher said.

Lou Holtz did bring Fletcher in for a visit to Arkansas. But Houston's Bill Yeoman was the only coach who met personally, one-on-one, with the young recruit.

"He actually came to track practice my senior year," Fletcher said. "I was practicing discus. Yeoman said to me: 'Young man, all I need from you is a verbal commitment that you will come to the University of Houston the next fall. If you break your ankle or your knee throwing that Frisbee'—that's what he called the discus, a Frisbee—he said, 'based on your verbal commitment, I'll give you a scholarship.' I thought he was joking."

Yeoman started to leave without Fletcher's commitment. He'd almost left when Fletcher turned and yelled at him: "Hey, Coach—I'd like to attend the University of Houston in the fall."

He started in the final three seasons of his five years there, a stint that included a redshirt season. The 6-foot-6, 245-pound prospect was taken by the Broncos with the second of their two, second-round picks, No. 54 overall, in the 1985 NFL Draft. The team had taken receiver Vance Johnson earlier in the second round, making it the most productive second-round draft in Broncos history.

Fletcher broke in gradually with the Broncos, playing special teams and getting part-time duty along the defensive line in all 16 games in each of his first two seasons. He had three spot starts in his first two years, including one at defensive tackle.

He then started at left outside linebacker in the season opener of 1987 against Seattle, and never left the starting lineup again until he retired following the 1995 season.

"He had these big, long arms where he could distance himself from the O-line," said Elam, whose first three seasons with the Broncos were Fletcher's last three. "He was fast. He was instinctive. Just knew how to make plays, and he did it all the time.

"And then Simon's personality was a lot of fun. I think the Broncos have always been very successful in having guys on the team—and maybe this was intentional—but having guys who brought a lot of fun to the locker room, without going too far overboard. But they bring a lot of levity to a sport and a business that can really weigh on you. The Simon Fletchers and Shannon Sharpes, those kinds of guys are so valuable to a locker room. It was always fun playing with Simon."

The Broncos only had two losing seasons during Fletcher's 11 years, which were offset by five, 10-win-or-better seasons and five playoff appearances.

Following his playing days, Fletcher stayed in the Denver area, where he has been in the restaurant and construction business. During his playing career, he had three hot-dog houses before moving into his specialty of barbecue.

Any physical effects from his 11 years of banging bodies during the pass rush?

"I have some, but nothing worth complaining about," Fletcher said. "I get up every day and look at what I need to do and I go do it. I don't have to take any type of painkiller. It's just like warming up the engine on an old car. Once I get it going, she'll run for 12 or 14 hours."

In the next five years, Fletcher said he'd like to move on from the structural restaurant business and go mobile with his barbecue throughout the state of Colorado, tying it in with Broncos' game-day weekends. However, it turns out, Fletcher has already lived an extraordinary life for a kid who didn't commit full-time to competitive football until his senior season in high school.

And once Simon Fletcher committed, he was all in, all the way. For every game. Until the final play.

"Clearly, the fact that I played in every game, that I never had to close my eyes and put on a blindfold and go to the pay window," Fletcher said, when asked about his proudest moment as a Bronco. "I was paid to play in a set number of games. I showed up to every single one. Being from where I grew up, my grandparents right in the area around me, that is who they are, and . . . they tried to instill the right values in me. It was my job to be there every play."

SIMON FLETCHER STATS

YRS	G	S	FF	FR	TCK
11	172	97.5	21	10	851

32

STEVE FOLEY

Cornerback/Safety, 1976–86

Think about what an interception is. If it were basketball they'd call the turnover a "steal." Baseball prefers the term "rob," as in, 'The center fielder robs so-and-so of a hit.'

An interception, then, is stealing a pass, robbing the passer of a completion.

To rob from a quarterback, the thief is helped if he first cases his victim's intentions. A quarterback may develop tendencies before throwing certain passes. They have repeated patterns of behavior, where they look before throwing, habits that can be read.

Any coincidence Steve Foley became the Denver Broncos' all-time interceptions leader, with 44, after he first grew up playing quarterback in the streets, in high school, and all the way through college, before his pro team decided to move him to defensive back?

It is not.

"It was definitely an advantage," Foley said in November 2016. "There were times when I saw a quarterback's pump fake—I did it a thousand times—and that's when you take off to the opposite side of the field for the deep route.

"It definitely helped. And being a quarterback, I knew the blitzes, and when we're coming with a big blitz, small blitz, and I'd know that quarterback has one second and he's going to feel the pressure, and if he's a young quarterback, he's looking right where he's going to go. It was all anticipation.

"I don't care how fast you are, if you don't have anticipation skills, you'll never be around the ball."

Steve Foley grew up in a big Catholic family in uptown New Orleans. How big was it? It was so big, the Foleys lived in a Catholic convent. That big.

Ivan McIvor Foley, a good Irishman and certified public accountant, and his wife, the former Jane Mestayer of French descent, raised 13 children—eight sons and five daughters.

Steve was born smack-dab in the middle as the seventh child. Six older siblings, six younger. A convent? Where else were the Foleys going to live?

"My father bought a Catholic convent when I was in fourth grade," Foley said. "The school had burned down; it was right across the street from us. They rebuilt it—it was right next to a Catholic church—and they had a house, an old Victorian house that was a convent. My father bought that. It was big enough for us to live in. It was uptown, 10 blocks from Tulane.

"We went to a Jesuit high school and us brothers worked our way through. Served meals, which was a bonus for us. We worked at a cafeteria, serving meals. That was the best job in the world, because you got a bunch of food."

All those kids kept the Foleys young. Dad passed away in 2002 at 87. Mom lived till she was 95.

Foley made two significant position changes in his football career. The first was the most dramatic, as he was shifted from quarterback to defensive back in his first professional season of 1975, with the Jacksonville Express of the World Football League. It was a position move he initially resisted.

At Jesuit High School, Foley was not only a two-year starting quarterback, he was also a fine long jumper, high jumper, and javelin thrower in track. At Tulane, Foley was the Green Wave's starting quarterback for three years. Although he ran a pro-style offense, Foley had the option-like statistics of 72 yards passing and 44 yards rushing a game in his three college seasons.

If that doesn't sound like much, consider the early-1970s era in college football. Ohio State, in back-to-back classics against Michigan in 1973–74, got 1 of 4 passing for 4 yards from quarterback Greg Hare in a 10–10 tie, and the next year Cornelius Greene of the Buckeyes was 3 of 6 for 58 yards in a 12–10 win.

Make no mistake: Foley was a two-way athletic threat. As a junior, he led Tulane to a 14–0 win against No. 8–ranked LSU, a 9-2 record, and a trip to the Bluebonnet Bowl.

He was selected by the Broncos in the eighth round, pick No. 199 overall, as a quarterback / defensive back in the 1975 NFL Draft. (Twenty-five years later, with that identical No. 199 selection, the New England Patriots would take another quarterback, Tom Brady.) But in that same 1975 draft, the Broncos in the third round took a 6-foot-3, 220-pound quarterback out of Central Michigan named Mike Franckowiak.

"The Broncos wanted big pocket passers and not mobile quarterbacks," Foley said. "We were a pro-style offense (at Tulane) and we threw a lot, but I ran a lot, too. I loved running. I loved running track, which was kind of odd for a quarterback. Most quarterbacks don't like to run. But I used to just love training. They drafted me because I could run. They drafted me as a possible quarterback/DB.

"But it was clear to me, I didn't even get to warm up at quarterback. I was like, 'Gee, what's up?' Not having played any defense—I played it a tiny bit in high school, maybe my junior year I played some safety—but when I was drafted they thought I would be a good safety. They didn't know. They didn't know if I could hit or not. But I was pretty aggressive coming from a family of 13."

After one season in the WFL, Foley returned to the Broncos in 1976 and started to play cornerback. He came off the bench in the first eight games of the season, but replaced the injured Calvin Jones as the starting right cornerback for the final six games. Foley never left the starting lineup again, except for injury and his retirement after the 1986 season.

"One of the greatest guys, ever," said Tom Jackson, a starting outside linebacker all 11 seasons of Foley's career. "And an anchor for what we did. One of the most fun and beloved guys in that locker room. We still, to this day, we love each other. To this day. We all feel it when we're together. I know when you talk to them that's what you feel. We love each other."

It was halfway through the 1980 season that Broncos defensive coordinator Joe Collier shifted Foley from right corner to free safety. A few years earlier, Collier had made the same move with Billy Thompson. And a few years later, Collier arranged the cornerback shift with Mike Harden and Tyrone Braxton.

Foley got his first interception as a safety in his third game at the position against San Diego's Dan Fouts, returning it 30 yards. He got another the next week against the Jets' Richard Todd, returning it 18 yards.

That was the thing about that Orange Crush defense in the late 1970s, early 1980s: They didn't just force turnovers, they did something with them. Foley had 622 return yards with his 44 interceptions, including a 40-yard touchdown return against Seattle's Dave Krieg in the final game of the 1984 season.

Earlier that year, in a memorable mid-October game against the Green Bay Packers played in an incredible blizzard at Mile High Stadium, Foley on the first play of the game returned a fumble 22 yards for a touchdown. On the second play of the game, Broncos cornerback Louie Wright returned a fumble 27 yards for a touchdown.

The Broncos were up, 14–0, with 37 seconds gone in the game, and wound up winning, 17–14.

"That had to be the most fun game I had ever played in," Foley said. "It was the closest thing to a Little League, sandlot game that you ever played in. You were falling all over. I remember hitting a 235-pound tight end and he felt like he weighed 180 pounds. I said, 'This is great.'"

Foley had 21 interceptions in his four and a half seasons at cornerback, 23 in five and a half seasons at safety. (He missed all but one and a half quarters in 1982 because of a broken arm suffered in the opener.)

"He had great hands. Great hands," said Billy Thompson, who played six seasons in the same backfield with Foley, two as a safety tandem.

"Steve was smart, and he was fast enough and athletic enough to make plays," said Broncos receiver Steve Watson. "And he knew what was going to happen. He was the beneficiary of Joe Collier and that [3-4] system. And they always talk about [the Chicago Bears safeties] Doug Plank and Gary Fencik, and how those guys hit. Well, I'm telling you, Foley was the same kind of hitter."

As a cornerback, Foley averaged 62 tackles a year in his four full years at cornerback. But it was after Thompson retired following the 1981 season that Foley really came on as a run enforcer. He was third on the team with 124 tackles in 1983, compiled a career-best 167 stops in 1984, and 92 in his final season of 1986.

In all, Foley had 877 tackles in his 11 NFL seasons. Take away his injured 1982 season, and that's 87 tackles a year. Not bad for a defensive back who was listed as 6-foot-2, 190 pounds.

"I remember one time we were playing the Houston Oilers and Earl Campbell," Thompson said. "Our game plan was one guy couldn't get Earl Campbell, we all have to gang-tackle him. I remember Steve hit him—and that was one thing about Foley, he was not afraid. He would hit and that's what set him apart. And one time he hit Earl Campbell and Earl knocked him out. I went over to him—he was lying on the field—and I said, 'Steve, are you all right?' And he said, 'How are the fans taking it?'"

It was Foley's ball-hawking skills, though, that made him unique among Broncos defenders. Unlike Goose Gonsoulin, who had been the Broncos' interception leader from the first game in franchise history in 1960 and got his picks in bunches, Foley got his interceptions at a steady pace.

Gonsoulin had 43 interceptions though his, and the Broncos', first six seasons, an average of better than seven a year. Foley never had more than six interceptions in a season, but he had six picks three times, five interceptions twice, four picks twice, and two, three-interception years.

That left him with 42 picks, one shy of Gonsoulin's team record, heading into his final season of 1986.

"I remember around game 10, 11 every year, you'd get injuries," Foley said. "Once you'd get injuries that hobble you—you're playing with a sprained ankle, you can't make good plays—it would limit you. And you knew the guy was going to have to throw the ball right to me [to get an interception]. I'm not at that full speed I was in the first half of the year. There were a few years where you're just playing injured the last half of the season. You're not making as many plays as you were in the beginning."

Foley tied Goose's career record in Game 2 of 1986, intercepting Pittsburgh's Mark Malone with 48 seconds remaining—and returning it 24 yards, of course—to clinch a 21–10 victory.

The record breaker came in Game 4 against New England, and was probably the key play in the Broncos' rally for a 27–20 victory. It didn't look that way at the two-minute warning of the first half. The Pats were up 10–3, and had first down at the Broncos' 11.

New England tried tricking the Broncos by having Steve James throw a halfback pass. Foley intercepted it at the 3-yard line. And yes, he returned it 15 yards to the 18.

"I was watching the linemen and they were pass-blocking when they pitched it to him," Foley said. "I'm like, 'This is going down.' I just took off and . . . yeah."

For the first time in 36 years, Austin "Goose" Gonsoulin was No. 2 on the Broncos' all-time interceptions list.

Franckowiak, by the way, never threw an NFL pass. He became a 6-foot-3 running back and kick returner, if you can imagine that, and played part-time for four NFL seasons.

Foley admitted he was better off playing defense, anyway. After starting in Super Bowl XXI against the New York Giants, Foley notified coach Dan Reeves he would be hanging them up. All his Orange Crush teammates were going, too. Barney Chavous had retired the year before. Rubin Carter got hurt in Game 5 of the 1986 season and didn't play again. Jackson and Wright also played their last game in Super Bowl XXI, a 39–20 loss.

They were the last of the Orange Crush players.

"It was a special time in Denver's history," Foley said. "It was the Orange Crush defense and it was the coming of age of the Denver franchise. And getting to play Pittsburgh and Oakland [in the 1977 season playoffs], who were in the midst of their Super Bowl years. Domination years. Pittsburgh was in the midst of their four Super Bowls, and we caught them in the middle there.

"As long as we had home-field advantage and beat them and Oakland to go to that first Super Bowl, that was a special, special time. We had some special defenses. Pittsburgh had the Steel Curtain. Joe Collier was the architect of the Orange Crush. Everybody loved Joe Collier. We were just excited to be playing in Joe Collier's defense, knowing we could play with anybody in any game."

Foley never made a Pro Bowl, although it was a joke he didn't make it in 1984. He is not in the Broncos Ring of Fame, although that may change after Simon Fletcher, who also never made a Pro Bowl but is the team's all-time sack leader, was inducted into the elite club in 2016.

Foley's lack of recognition can no doubt be blamed on all those great defenders who played next to him and often hogged the honors, players like Randy Gradishar, Lyle Alzado, Wright, Jackson, Thompson, and later, Rulon Jones and Dennis Smith.

Not that Foley has a single gripe. The shattered forearm he suffered in the 1982 opener while breaking up a pass against Wes Chandler in the end zone? He suffered no lingering effects. The hit he took from Earl Campbell? Shook it off.

"As a matter of fact, I never had a knee surgery," Foley said. "I still run. I'm fine in my hips, shoulders. I really feel blessed. I don't wake up aching. I have full spacing in my knees, which I can't believe. It's just a blessing."

After his playing days, Foley paid the bills through real-estate development, and more recently he's been in the oil and gas business. He and Cindy, his wife of 37 years at the time of this writing, raised two children, David and Natalie. They each had four kids.

Which means Steve and Cindy have eight grandkids. How about that. Foley has a large family again.

STEVE FOLEY STATS					
YRS	G	I	Y	TD	TCK
11	150	44	622	1	877

33

AL WILSON

Middle Linebacker, 1999–2006

In the great history of the Denver Broncos, only seven players earned six or more Pro Bowls.

Al Wilson had five.

And five Pro Bowls were no small feat considering Wilson played the same middle linebacker position as Baltimore Ravens superstar Ray Lewis.

There was something about Al. Everyone liked the guy. Fans loved him. The media appreciated him. Pro Bowl balloters voted for him. His teammates played for him.

"The fans loved him and his teammates loved him, because there was never any question you were going to get 100 percent effort from Al," said Broncos safety John Lynch. "He's what you would call the modern-day inside linebacker, because he could do it all. He could fill and play with the big boys inside, but he also had the athleticism where he could cover. And he had great natural leadership instincts."

Wilson's impact on the Broncos was perhaps best exemplified through the final, career-killing moment in his career. Wilson was having a fantastic season in 2006, one in which he would be named to his fifth Pro Bowl and earn second-team All Pro.

But with the Broncos 7–4 and leading the Seattle Seahawks, 13–7, early in the fourth quarter of Game 12, Broncos second-year cornerback Darrent Williams fumbled away a punt return.

Broncos defensive lineman Gerard Warren dove for the ball, only to inadvertently nail a teammate. Wilson's head snapped back.

Wilson was strapped onto a stretcher, his head immobilized. When he was carted off the field and immediately placed in an ambulance, his condition looked grim to those who didn't see him move his extremities on the field.

Williams recovered the ball, but the Broncos didn't recover from losing Wilson, the defensive captain and team's emotional leader. Before Wilson's injury, the Broncos defense had not allowed a point through the first three quarters and one drive into the fourth. Seattle's touchdown came on an interception thrown by Denver quarterback Jay Cutler, who was making his NFL starting debut.

After Wilson left, Seattle scored on its next four possessions—a short touchdown run by Shaun Alexander, and three Josh Brown field goals, including a 50-yard game-winner, with five seconds remaining.

Incredibly—and ludicrously—Wilson was back playing the next week at San Diego. Wilson had six tackles, but the Denver defense fell apart against Chargers running back LaDainian Tomlinson, who broke the NFL's single-season touchdown record in a 48–20 rout of the Broncos.

The stinger in Wilson's neck became increasingly excruciating, to the point where he appeared to all but avoid contact in the Broncos' Game 15 win against Cincinnati. All the Broncos needed was to win the final home game against 6-9 San Francisco, and they would have made the playoffs. But Shanahan benched Wilson, and the Broncos lost to begin a skid of five consecutive seasons without a playoff berth.

It was no coincidence.

At 6-foot, 240 pounds, Wilson was a tad small as middle linebackers go. Yet, in 2002, he was credited with 199 tackles. His best all-around season was 2000, his second year in the league, when he had 104 tackles, 5.0 sacks, and three interceptions.

Look around the NFL today. There is no such thing as an inside linebacker who records 100 tackles, 5 sacks, and 3 interceptions in a season.

"Al Wilson is not as publicized as [Brian] Urlacher and [Ray] Lewis," longtime Dallas Cowboys scout Gil Brandt said in 2005. "But I believe Al Wilson is just as good as those two guys."

Wilson was a first-team All Pro in 2005 when he anchored a Denver defense that ranked third in the NFL with 16.1 points allowed per game, and No. 2 with 85.2 rushing yards per game. That great Broncos defense of 2015 that was chiefly responsible for winning Super Bowl 50 allowed 18.5 points and 83.6 rushing yards per game.

"Intense. I remember him being incredibly intense," Broncos place-kicker Jason Elam said of Wilson. "Phenomenal, natural leader. Guys wanted to be around him, they wanted to follow him. And he wasn't trying, he was just a natural leader. A great teammate. I loved watching him play. He was kind of an undersized guy. But he never played undersized. He was intimidating. He was all over the field."

By now you've caught on. Wilson's teammates don't remember him as a terrific middle linebacker. They remember him as a terrific player and extraordinary leader. Rarely was a story written about Wilson that didn't mention his leadership qualities. He was the Broncos defensive captain the final five years of his eight-year career.

"I always appreciated him because he was kind of the leader on the defense when myself and Champ arrived," Lynch said. "And right away, rather than be threatened, he welcomed us because he knew we could help him get to where he wanted to get. I'm sure that wasn't easy. He had to defer a little bit, but he did it willingly."

Said Broncos cornerback Champ Bailey: "My first two or three years in Denver I wasn't a captain. For much of my career I wasn't a captain because of Al and John Lynch. I didn't deserve it at that time. These guys were born leaders. The way Al prepared and the way he went about his business—he was a knucklehead as a rookie, and then to see him turn that corner and become a leader vocally on and off the field—it was impressive."

Let's go back to Wilson's rookie year of 1999. He had just helped the University of Tennessee Volunteers to a 13-0 record and the 1998 national championship, and he became a first-round draft pick of the Broncos, who had just won back-to-back Super Bowl titles.

It was a championship mix that never quite materialized. Wilson became the Broncos middle linebacker from the time John Mobley suffered a torn ACL in the first quarter of the second game of Wilson's rookie 1999 season.

A captain of the Tennessee Vols' national championship team, Wilson became caught up in the nightlife early in his Broncos career. That changed during his third season of 2001 when Wilson was summoned to head coach Mike Shanahan's office for an intervention with several of the team's leaders.

What Wilson did off the field wasn't necessarily the problem. The problem was, it was causing Wilson to show up late for work.

In Shanahan's office were Rod Smith, Shannon Sharpe, Ed McCaffrey, Tom Nalen, John Mobley, Brian Griese, and Dan Neil.

"When Al started becoming a leader, we had to tell him," Smith said. "He was doing a lot of wild stuff when he was young, being late. We vets sat him down and said: 'Look, man, you're a leader of this football team. We know this is only your third year, but we love the way you're playing, we love the way you perform; you can't be late anymore.'"

Wilson took the talk to heart.

"That changed my life," Wilson told the *Denver Post*. "At the time, I felt like if I was doing my job on Sunday, that's all I had to do and that's all that mattered. But in truth, it was way more than that. There were guys watching me and depending on me.

"It hurt me to hear that I was letting them down. They all were talking. It was an eye-opener. I needed it, because I was definitely going down the wrong path."

By the time Jake Plummer showed up to become the Broncos quarterback in 2003, Wilson was a consummate professional.

"He loved his teammates, number one," Plummer said. "He loved the game and worked his ass off. He didn't skimp on having fun, either. Football was big and it was important and he took care of business, but when it came time to have some fun, he had fun. This day and age, guys get portrayed as uncommitted to the cause and bad teammates when they're out living their life. Al Wilson brought that to the locker room, he brought that to the field, that love of life, that energy."

Wilson's pregame speeches were legendary, if a little too vulgar for print.

"My mother told me one time she didn't know who I was on Sundays," Wilson said. "Which is good. That means I'm getting in the mind frame I need to be in. I don't put any thought into a speech. I don't rehearse them. It's a feeling, it's an emotion. Guys know when you're true. These are grown men. They know when it comes from your heart or if you just practiced your speech."

Wilson was raised by his mom in Jackson, Tennessee, the same town near Memphis that raised former Dallas Cowboys great Ed "Too Tall" Jones.

"To stay out of trouble, stay off the streets, I played sports," Wilson said. "I played basketball, football, baseball, boxing, soccer. I did it all, man. It was my way of staying out of trouble. When I left one sport, I went to another."

Mom worked hard as a secretary, but the money wasn't great. Once her son got a few NFL paychecks, Wilson's mom got a nice home in Jackson.

Wilson brought his mom's work ethic to the football field. In his eight seasons with the Broncos he missed just three games. The first was because of a dislocated shoulder suffered in the opener of 2000. He missed Game 2, then came back earlier than most would have to play in Game 3.

The second missed game was the regular-season finale of 2005. Wilson suffered a broken thumb in the Broncos' AFC West–clinching Game 15 victory against Oakland. He had surgery two days later and with the final game meaningless to the Broncos' playoff implications, Wilson sat out.

Playing the postseason with a cast, Wilson had 9 tackles in a 27–13, second-round win against New England and six tackles in a disappointing home loss to Pittsburgh in the AFC Championship Game.

Wilson's willingness to play hurt, though, became detrimental to his career. He later admitted he should have taken at least one game off after he was backboarded off the field against Seattle. After that 2006 season, Shanahan traded Wilson to the New York Giants. But it fell through when Wilson's neck caused the Giants' doctors to flunk his physical.

Wilson never played again. He did have a chance to play for near vet-minimum salaries in 2008, but decided against it. He sued the Broncos, claiming they improperly treated his neck injury, but lost his case.

It would appear some ill feelings on both sides remain.

"It was sad to see him leave the game the way he did, because he had so much football left in him," Bailey said.

In his eight seasons with the Broncos, Wilson was credited with 731 unassisted tackles, 228 assisted tackles, and 959 total tackles. He had 21.5 sacks, 8 forced fumbles, and 7 fumble recoveries.

There are 13 Broncos players who earned at least five Pro Bowls: John Elway (9), Champ Bailey (8), Steve Atwater (8), Shannon Sharpe (7), Randy Gradishar (7), Karl Mecklenburg (6), Dennis Smith (6), Von Miller (5), Louis Wright (5), Austin "Goose" Gonsoulin (5), Tom Nalen (5), Floyd Little (5), and Wilson.

Ten are in the Ring of Fame. Bailey isn't eligible until 2019. Miller is still playing. Wilson awaits.

AL WILSON STATS

YRS	G	S	I	TCK
8	125	21.5	5	959

34

RYAN CLADY

Left Tackle, 2008–15

At his best, there was no one better. Not as a blind-side pass protector, there wasn't.

Ryan Clady was never nicknamed "Dancing Bear," which is too bad, because it would have been an apt moniker. Had he stayed healthy for 10 seasons, Clady may well have gone down as one of the five best pass-protecting left tackles in NFL history.

He had ideal size at 6-foot-6, 309 pounds, extremely long arms and twinkle-toes agility.

"Really long arms," said DeMarcus Ware, who was one of the best pass rushers in NFL history. "That's what made him tough was those long arms. You think you have him beat and—hey now!—he'd reach out and get you."

Clady's arms are 36.75 inches long. By comparison, Cleveland's Joe Thomas, who is widely considered the best left tackle of the 21st century, had 32.5-inch arms—more than 4 inches shorter than Clady's reach.

Arm length, though, was only one reason why Broncos boss Mike Shanahan selected Clady out of Boise State with the 12th overall pick in the 2008 NFL Draft—making Clady the highest-drafted Broncos offensive lineman since Chris Hinton went No. 4 in 1983.

"The thing that impresses you is his feet," Shanahan said at the time. "I haven't been around a tackle that has that type of feet. He's got the longest arms in the draft."

Long arms, quick feet, big body, superior agility. Not a bad combination for stepping in to play in the Broncos' highly regarded zone-blocking system.

There wasn't much question Clady belonged among the 50 Greatest Broncos Players. It wasn't so easy determining where to rank him.

He is tied with Marv Montgomery as the highest-drafted Broncos offensive lineman who played with the team. Montgomery was a No. 12 overall choice in 1971. He played five and a half seasons with the Broncos, only two and a half as a starter.

Hinton never played for the Broncos. He was traded six days after the 1983 draft in the deal that brought the No. 1 player on our list, John Elway, to Denver.

Clady and center Tom Nalen are the only Broncos offensive linemen who were twice selected to the NFL's first-team All Pro team. And only Nalen, with five, had more Pro Bowl appearances than Clady's four among Broncos blockers.

Clady should have made five Pro Bowls. He was robbed during his rookie year of 2008 when he allowed just a half sack in 16 games and was named second-team All Pro. Yet his AFC Pro Bowl berth went to fellow rookie Jake Long, who wasn't named first- or second-team All Pro. Long benefited, perhaps, from the publicity of being the No. 1 overall pick in the 2008 draft by Miami.

So, if Clady is a shade behind Nalen in terms of league honors, and Nalen is the top-rated offensive lineman in this book, at No. 14, why is Clady 20 spots behind, at No. 34?

Because Clady only had six healthy seasons for the Broncos. He played in all 16 games in those six seasons. And really, Clady only had two healthy seasons—his first two in 2008 and 2009—before he began suffering the misfortune of devastating injuries.

Still, given some of the hardship he had growing up, Clady can't complain about his NFL career. He was raised along with a younger brother, and two younger sisters, by Ross and Sharon Clady in the Los Angeles area.

Ryan didn't play much youth football because of those inconvenient weight restrictions in the Pop Warner Leagues.

"Every week I had to cut weight," Clady said. "I finally had enough of that."

He quit playing football at 10 with the idea of playing again once he got to Eisenhower High School in Rialto, California.

That was the plan. What wasn't planned was his mom dying suddenly of a heart attack at 53 years young. Ryan, the oldest of four, was 13 years old and in eighth grade at the time.

"When Mom died, it was such a shock," he said. "I was kind of quiet and reserved before she died, and then I was even quieter after that. I hardly spoke to anybody. It took me, I would say, at least two years to get over it. I was sad, I guess, is how you would put it."

The next year as a high school freshman, Clady started playing football again, although he primarily played defensive end.

He only had two scholarship offers to play college, and both programs thought he projected as an offensive tackle. He picked Boise State, which was then coached by Dan Hawkins.

"We just thought he was a big guy who had great feet," Hawkins said.

After starting three years at left tackle for the Boise State Broncos, Clady opened his Denver Broncos career with 20 consecutive games before he gave up his first full sack—the NFL's best career-starting run among offensive tackles since at least 1994. He was named first-team All Pro in his second season of 2009, even though new coach Josh McDaniels switched from a zone-blocking to gap-power running scheme.

Clady was never a great run blocker, although in fairness, his skill set was built for the zone scheme. Only in his rookie season did he get a chance to play in the zone system.

In April 2010, as McDaniels was finishing up his second draft with the Broncos that produced Demaryius Thomas and Tim Tebow in the first round, Clady tore the patellar tendon in his knee while playing basketball.

Although surgery and rehab forced him to miss the entire off-season and preseason, Clady played all 16 games in the regular season. By his own admission, Clady played at about 75 percent effectiveness.

He bounced back to play well as a run blocker for Tebow and Willis McGahee in 2011, when the Broncos led the NFL in rushing. Clady then had another terrific pass-blocking year in 2012 while protecting the blind side of newly signed quarterback Peyton Manning.

In a memorable play in the Broncos' season-opening win against Pittsburgh before a nationally televised audience on *Sunday Night Football*, Manning threw a screen pass to Demaryius Thomas out wide to the left side of scrimmage. Clady sprinted out from his left tackle position to throw a block 20 yards downfield.

His remarkable size and agility were on display. Thomas was sprung for a 71-yard catch-run touchdown.

"It's fun to get out in space," Clady said. "You kind of have all eyes on you, so if you blow it, everyone knows it. But it's fun having that clean-up block that helps spring for big yards."

As bum luck would have it, Clady started 90 consecutive games, plus 3 more in the playoffs, through his first five seasons while playing on his five-year rookie contract. It was after the Broncos signed him to a five-year, $52.5 million extension prior to the 2013 season that Clady started suffering season-ending injuries.

The two season-ending injuries that struck Clady happened to be in the two years the Broncos played in the Super Bowl. Late in the second game of the 2013 season against the New York Giants at MetLife Stadium, Clady suffered a Lisfranc injury in his left foot.

Manning set all the single-season passing records that season and the Broncos won the AFC Championship before getting crushed in Super Bowl 48 at MetLife Stadium—where Clady's season ended back in week two.

He returned in 2014, played all 16 regular-season games, then a playoff game, but before he had a chance to play in the zone system favored by new head coach Gary Kubiak in 2015, Clady suffered a torn ACL in his left knee on the first day of organized team activities [OTAs].

After paying $33 million to Clady in the first three years of his contract and getting just one playing season in return, the Broncos traded him to the New York Jets prior to the 2016 season.

RYAN CLADY STATS	
YRS	G
7	98

35

JASON ELAM

Kicker, 1993–2007

Since he finished his 17-year career as an NFL kicker, including 15 with the Denver Broncos, Jason Elam has lived in Alaska; was featured with his wife, Tammy, a former Denver Broncos cheerleader, on a Discovery Channel home-buying program; added two more children to their brood of six; made several volunteer trips to the Middle East; piloted his plane; finished the third and fourth books in his four-book Christian novel series; spent a year in Oxford, England, getting an incomparable advanced degree in theology before settling, if he's capable of such a thing, in Charlotte, North Carolina.

All this adventure began with a power line at the end of his driveway.

Elam grew up in the suburbs of Atlanta, Georgia, playing soccer while competing in swimming and track. As of Jason's freshman year at Brookwood High School in Snellville, Georgia, he had yet to play football. And then one day he made a fateful decision to support his school.

"I went to a high school varsity game and the kicker was really struggling," Elam said. "And I thought: I can do that. So I went out in my driveway and there was a power line at the other end, and I would kick over that power line. That's how I first started. I didn't even really have a football. I was using one of my brother's really old footballs, and then I'd have to go chase it. And then my dad bought me a few footballs and we went out to the actual football field and I would punt. It was easier to go chase the ball down from punting. So I started doing that more than anything."

From that unusual start came the most accomplished kicker in Broncos history. When he finished with the Broncos following the 2007 season, Elam had set franchise records with 395 field goals and 1,786 points, marks that won't be broken anytime soon, if they're surpassed at all. He added a 51-yard field goal in the Broncos' first-ever Super Bowl championship, a 31–24 win against the heavily favored Green Bay Packers in XXXII, and two more field goals in an easier Super Bowl XXXIII victory against the Atlanta Falcons.

"A Renaissance man," said Jake Plummer, a former Broncos quarter-back who held for Elam from 2003–06. "A guy who travels the world, flies. He had a strong faith but he was also consistent in his faith. It's not something he did to gain attention or gain favor. He truly believes deeply in his beliefs.

"Jason was like a ghost. You hardly saw him until it was time to kick field goals, and there he was from however far he wanted. He won a lot of games for the Broncos. I think he was one of the greatest kickers. He wasn't fancy or anything; he had his methodology and he did it. He had ice in his veins, which is what you want as a kicker."

Elam owes much of his success to his father, Ralph, a World War II veteran who went through France, Germany, and Austria. After the war, Ralph had a lengthy career in law enforcement, including a stint as chief of police in Fort Walton Beach, Florida, where Jason was born.

"I'm kind of the black sheep," Elam said. "I'm the only one in generations that wasn't a policeman. My brother, my dad, my grandpa—everybody was in law enforcement."

Kids during the Great Depression, Ralph was 45 and his wife Evelyn was 41 when they had Jason. It wasn't until his sophomore year in high school that Jason wound up on the football field. He played some receiver as a junior, when the Brookwood Broncos posted a 1-9 record that forced a coaching change to Dave Hunter.

"The first day of practice we had a special teams practice, and I kicked a few field goals and the coach came up to me and said, 'You need to go sit down on the bench,'" Elam said. "I didn't know what I'd done. He came over about 10 minutes later and he said, 'Son, you're going to get your college education paid for, and I'm going to make sure it happens.'"

Hunter came along at the right time for Elam. Not only did he transform Brookwood from 1-9 to 10-2 in his first year to begin a remarkable coaching career, but he also helped Elam earn a scholarship to the University of Hawaii.

"It was really hard going thousands of miles away from your family," Elam said. "We have a very tight family. That was difficult the first year. But I'm so glad I stuck it out there. I have friends all over the world. And it probably shaped me a little bit as to why I love to travel. Why I love being exposed and meeting new cultures. I just love that stuff. I think that's a lot of it."

Elam was so good at Hawaii, Denver Broncos head coach Wade Phillips made the unusual move of using his third-round pick in the 1993 draft on the kicker. What Broncos fans came to appreciate about Elam was not just his consistency—that goes without saying when a player kicks for 17 NFL seasons. It was his ability to shake off a miss. He would miss every now and then; all kickers do. Rarely, though, did Elam miss a second time, or for a prolonged time, or during clutch time.

"My mentality was, I'm going to go through slumps if you want to call it that," Elam said. "Just keep on swinging. It's like a golf swing. Early on I heard Jack Nicklaus say one time that three out of four of his shots are mishits. No one really knows it, because my mishits stay in the fairway."

Elam credits a chance meeting with Morten Andersen following the 1988 NFL season Pro Bowl with finding his consistent leg swing. Actually, it wasn't by chance. One of the advantages of kicking for Hawaii was the opportunity to watch the NFL's best players make an annual trip to your backyard. Elam didn't wait for chance—he seized the opportunity. Andersen was practicing with the NFC Pro Bowl team at Aloha Stadium when he was approached by the resourceful Elam.

The ice-breaker was the new kicking rule in college. After the 1988 season, college kickers were no longer allowed to kick field goals or extra points off a kicker's tee, which was more like an elevated block. Elam kicked his freshman year at Hawaii with the block, but starting with his following sophomore season, he would have to kick with the ball placed on the ground.

Andersen was obviously impressed by the young college kicker who had the courage to ask for advice.

"I went up to him and said, 'Mr. Andersen, I'm the kicker here at UH, and I was just wondering if you had any tips for me for kicking off the ground,'" Elam said. "He kind of looked around and said, 'You've got your cleats with you?'"

Right here in the locker room.

"He said, 'Tell you what; go get 'em and I'll just catch a cab,'" Elam said. "So he stayed after. He didn't know me from Adam. It was pretty cool of him. He stayed out there and watched me for a little while. And he gave me a couple recommendations that is the same thing that Nicklaus was saying. I used to come in at a real big angle and I would kill it. I could hit it a long way, but I didn't know exactly where it was going. Morten basically got me to—instead of a driver, hit a seven iron. That's basically what his message was. A 35-yard field goal doesn't have to go 60 yards. It has to go 36 yards. Be controlled, hit everything like at 90 percent, real easy with a fluid swing. Once I mastered that, my accuracy went way up."

The sophomore Elam nailed 20 of 22 field-goal attempts and was good on all 46 extra point attempts. He kept swinging those seven iron–type kicks until no other Bronco—not even John Elway—played in more games than Elam's 236. Elway played 234. For his feats, Elam was inducted into the Broncos Ring of Fame on October 23, 2016, the night before Denver spanked the Houston Texans, 27–9, on *Monday Night Football.*

Elam's fondest memory during his 15 seasons with the Broncos can be summed up in two words: Toro! Toro!

Most people would think Elam's top moment would have been his 63-yard field goal in an October 25, 1998, game that at the time tied Tom Dempsey's long-standing NFL record. That was sweet, but that boot to end the half stretched a 24–10 lead to 27–10.

The Toro! Toro! kick from 42 yards away at Buffalo to open the 2007 season turned defeat into stunning victory at the gun.

"Yeah, that would probably be even above the 63," Elam said prior to his Ring of Fame induction Sunday. "Because that was for a win. The 63-yarder was more an individual thing. We were winning at the time and that was just a fun kick. But the Toro! Toro! thing, that was awesome. Just the way the whole thing went down. The season opener, on the road, everything about it was just a fun kick."

The Buffalo Bills, behind the rookie debut of running back Marshawn Lynch, had mostly outplayed the Broncos, but were trying to protect a 14–12 lead with 1:08 left when Denver coach Mike Shanahan was forced to take his final time-out with the ball on the visiting side of the 50.

Broncos quarterback Jay Cutler eventually threw an 11-yard completion to Javon Walker with 18 seconds left, moving the ball to the Buffalo 24.

Toro! Toro! was the call from the Broncos' sideline, which meant fire drill. The field-goal team had to run onto the field and set up for Elam's kick while the offensive team sprinted off the field. The clock was ticking.

"The fans were counting it down." Elam said. "They were loud. Ten, nine, eight . . ."

What the fans didn't realize is that their countdown helped the Broncos field-goal team. They knew how much they had to hurry, and how much they didn't.

"They didn't think for a second we were going to be able to get that kick off," Elam said.

There was one second left when Elam struck the ball. The gun went off as the ball carried beyond the crossbar. Shocked Bills fans went silent. It was one of 24 game-winning or game-saving field goals Elam kicked for the Broncos. He added another 15 field goals in the postseason.

"He was just money as a kicker," said John Lynch, a Broncos safety who was inducted into the team's Ring of Fame along with Elam and pass rusher Simon Fletcher. "Throughout my career, I played with some really good kickers. Down in Tampa, Martin Gramática comes to mind, but it was always exciting. You always watched. I hate to say it, but with Jason, you took him for granted. You just turn your head and go back about your business—the kickoff team gets ready, regardless of where he was kicking from. That's how much faith we had in him."

Elam's contract expired after the 2007 season, and while he wanted to finish his career with the Broncos, his hometown Atlanta Falcons offered a longer and more lucrative contract. He had the best individual season of his career with the Falcons in 2008, when he made 29 of 31 field goals and went 42 of 42 in extra points.

Elam suffered through injuries, though, in 2009, and called it a career. Life was just beginning. And he wasn't about to kill grass with the bottom of his shoes. Off he went.

"You never know how long the NFL is going to last, so I was trying to figure out, 'How can I make a contribution to people in the best, possible way?'" Elam said. "So we had kind of fallen in love with Alaska. The people there, there were a lot of cool things I could do with some of the villages and natives as far as my Christian faith. I'm a pilot as well, so it all seemed to come together. So in a nutshell, that's why I went up there. I was able to combine a lot of things I love to do, and I'm very passionate about. I could do all of them in Alaska."

His work in the Middle East caused him to start gravitating toward the East Coast. And beyond. For years, Elam was volunteering his time as the director of Israel for a group called e3 partners, which shares Christianity with Jews and Muslims. The group offers medical, dental, and vision care, along with humanitarian aid.

"But it's all centered around trying to get the genuine Christian message to them," Elam said. "I decided if I'm going to continue to do all that in the Middle East, it's too hard to do it from Alaska. We kind of had to choose. I felt like I needed to be back on the East Coast. And then this England thing, and Oxford popped up. It was a one-year study program in theology. They were going to move my whole family over there, I'd study and complete that program, and then come back here to Charlotte where I'm working on continuing my education. I just love doing it."

His work in the Middle East, his faith, his work with the Broncos—they all came together in his four-book series, *Monday Night Jihad,* an action-adventure tale about football and an attempt to stop a terrorist plot.

Book projects are all-consuming. By now, it's been established that Elam doesn't exactly lead a sedentary life. How did he write two full books while he was playing, and most of a third?

"You remember how the kicker schedule with Broncos was different than everyone else's?" Elam said. "Once we had our special teams meeting, I had, like, three or four hours before anything else. So instead of sitting around and watching ESPN, Troy Smith, the head grounds guy there, he made me a little desk where the grounds crew was. That's where I did a lot of those books. I would be typing away on the team flights. Whenever I felt like writing, I'd grab my laptop and write.

"Before you knew it, I had a book. It was just going to be a one-book thing. The publisher really liked it. I hate to put out a spoiler alert here, but I killed the main character at the end. And they said, You can't do that! I said, Why can't I? They said, Well, then you can't have a book two. And I said, Well, I'm not going to have a book two. They said, You've got to have a book two.

"So I thought, Well, okay, I guess I can keep him alive and write book two. And then they said, Well, you can't have him die at the end of book two. So, we went through the whole thing and finally ended it with book four. I wanted to model Jesus, model what it meant to lay down his life for a friend. So, that's why I felt like I needed to have him die at the end."

Jason said his plan for the next five years is to be the best husband he can be to Tammy, and best father to his six children, who at the time of this writing were aged 2 to 19.

"He was the best kicker I ever played with," said Broncos cornerback Champ Bailey, who shared the same agent, Atlanta-based Jack Reale, with Elam. "The reason I say that is this dude, you never knew how he felt. He was always even-keel. He would come to work, get the job done, and go home to his family. That's how I remember Jason Elam. Show up, do his work, go home to his family. I just had a lot of respect for that."

JASON ELAM STATS						
YRS	G	FGM-FGA	PCT	EXPA-EXPM	PCT	PTS
15	236	395-490	80.6	601-604	99.5	1,786

36 (TIE)
— RUBIN CARTER —
Nose Tackle, 1975–86

Rubin Carter didn't get many accolades. He didn't make one Pro Bowl.

All he did was make history.

"I always tell people to this day, when we got Rubin Carter, we became the Orange Crush defense," said Tom Jackson, the Denver Broncos star outside linebacker in the 1970s and '80s.

Rubin "Hurricane" Carter (the football player, not the boxer) was drafted out of the University of Miami in 1975 as a defensive tackle. He played defensive tackle as a part-time, rookie starter. Then as a starting defensive tackle in 1976, Carter could only watch as the guy next to him, Lyle Alzado, suffered a season-ending knee injury in the Broncos' opening game against the Cincinnati Bengals.

Alzado's injury was the impetus to stirring the defensive genius of Joe Collier into devising the 3-4. The key to the 3-4 was moving Carter directly over the center and telling him to take on the center, and cover the gaps between the center and right guard, and center and left guard. It all starts there.

"Lyle got hurt, and then Joe Collier and [linebackers coach] Myrel Moore and [defensive line coach] Stan Jones, those guys in preparation for the [New York] Jets, sometimes you have to make drastic changes," Carter said in March 2017. "I guess we didn't have a whole lot of defensive linemen, but we had a lot of good linebackers, a lot of them were playing special teams. We kind of transitioned to it."

The 3-4 system was what made the Orange Crush. And the nose tackle is what made the 3-4. At first, Collier only experimented with the 3-4, but started the game with the 4-3. John Grant replaced Alzado at defensive tackle.

The first time the Broncos started a game with three defensive linemen and four linebackers—the birth of the Orange Crush—was naturally against the Oakland Raiders on October 17, 1976, the sixth game of the year. Grant was out and Bob Swenson was in as the fourth starting linebacker.

The Broncos' front three, from left to right, was Barney Chavous, Carter, and Paul Smith.

The Broncos lost that day, 17–10. But a defense was born, if not quite ready to sprout. Collier went back to the 4-3 the following week against Kansas City, then switched fronts from game to game. The Broncos were 7-4 and needing to win out to make the playoffs when they used a 4-3 in Game 12 while getting shellacked at New England, 38–14. It was this loss that caused the Dirty Dozen mutiny against head coach John Ralston. (Carter and Chavous, by the way, were not among the 12 players who pleaded with owner Gerald Phipps to fire Ralston.)

With the Broncos officially eliminated from the postseason with their 7-5 record, and many players grumbling about their head coach, Collier went exclusively with the 3-4 for the final two games—a 17–16 win against the Chiefs and a season-ending 28–14 win against the Bears at Chicago's Soldier Field.

Kansas City was held to 59 yards rushing on 29 carries, or a meager 2.0 yards per carry. Chicago quarterback Bob Avellini completed 2 of 17 passes. That's right, 2 of 17. Carter had three tackles and an assist in each game.

The 3-4 alignment could stop the run, and thwart the pass. The 3-4 was here to stay.

"We became the Orange Crush—this gets a little bit technical—there is nothing more important than the nose," Jackson said. "Because you have to stop the run with limited people up front."

One after another, the testimonials came in. Rubin Carter was seldom honored by anyone but every single one of his teammates.

"Rubin Carter was the anchor," said Broncos receiver Haven Moses. "He was the anchor of the Orange Crush. I remember getting him from Miami. When he came in he said he was 6-foot, but I think he was shorter than that. But boy, there was no one tougher. They had to double-team him. Which really made Lyle more than anybody. Because Rubin and Barney would tie up the offensive lines and Lyle would pretty much freelance.

"And then Rubin really helped make our linebackers. We had it up front, we had it in the middle, and we had it in the back. But Rubin Carter was the key to making that defense."

"He was the noseguard of the decade, Rubin Carter," said Broncos cornerback Steve Foley. "Rubin, you could not move him. He was 6-foot, 260. Could stretch like a ballerina, was the softest-spoken player, but we had the best run defense in the league for a few years running. And Rubin and Barney, you could not move.

"He may not have made as many plays, but he allowed everyone else to make them. Because you had to double-team him. That was the whole essence of our defense, to let the linebackers come free and they can handle their gaps. We were a gap-control defense, and we were excellent at it. You didn't see holes."

Carter was underappreciated in many respects, but he had the respect and admiration of his peers. What else is there?

"I've always said a nose tackle is like a manhole cover: You don't miss them till they're gone," Carter said.

Ask 21 of the 22 other starters on a football team what's the position they'd least prefer to play, and nose tackle may be top on everyone's list. But from what Carter saw and lived through as a youth, playing the nose position in the 3-4 was easy money.

His parents, Charlie and Susie Carter, were migrant workers. They worked up and down the Eastern Seaboard, picking fruits and vegetables, riding a bus from town to town. Rubin was the eighth of their eight children. He was born in Pompano Beach, Florida, only because that's where the migrant workers' bus had stopped as Susie Carter was ready to deliver.

"I was born in Pompano Beach, but we wound up all the way up in Salisbury, Maryland," Carter said. "And they were touring the bus and that's the way we traveled, so I learned hard work early in my life. Because as a migrant worker, what you pick is what you're paid for. If you don't produce, you don't get paid."

He played basketball, not football, in his youth. That changed in eighth grade.

"I started to develop and get a little bit bigger and stronger and started to grow, and started fouling out in the first quarter of basketball games," Carter said, laughing at the memory. "One of the football coaches saw me and said, 'Hey, you know what, you need to start playing football. I don't think you're going to make it in basketball; you're always sitting on the bench.' "

Rubin was mature and respected his mother enough to make sure the coach cleared the game of football with her.

"Mom said as long as you take care of him, he can go out there and see if he likes it," Carter said. "And I went out there and found out I loved it. The best thing that happened to me in my life was going into football."

Another person who had a tremendous impact on Carter was his high school track coach, Jack Erkie. Figuring that Carter was put together like those who had had some success in the shot put, Coach Erkie had Carter try the event for the first time as a sophomore.

"He made me throw it every day," Carter said. "He made me lift weights every day. My junior year, he said, You can be a champion if you work hard and you can stay focused. I didn't believe it. I didn't know I could, but sure enough, by my senior year, I was able to become a state champion in the state of Florida in the shot put. That developed a lot of confidence in a young man. And that strength and explosion you need in throwing the shot put really helped me as a football player."

At Miami, Carter noticed the walls at the Hurricanes' football office had a void.

"There were no black All Americans at the University of Miami when I got there," he said. "No blacks on the wall at the University. I walked in and I was a snot-nosed kid and I told the secretary I wanted my picture to hang right there on the wall."

He became a UPI All American defensive tackle in 1974. That empty spot on the wall was filled with his picture.

Speaking of pictures, Carter did not always toil in obscurity. On October 17, 1977—exactly one year after the 3-4 Orange Crush offense was born—a close-up of the helmet-wearing Carter filled the cover of *Sports Illustrated*. It wasn't a menacing look Carter was wearing, but a serious, businesslike, snap-the-ball-let's-go stare.

The accompanying article was entitled, "Say Hello to the Fearsome Threesome." It was Carter's face that was picked to represent the Orange Crush.

"I was shocked that they wanted me on the cover," he said 40 years later. "I told them, 'Are you sure you've got the right guy? Tommy's making a lot of plays, and Randy's making a lot.' And they said, 'Well, you cause those guys to be free. You're clogging up things in the middle.'

"It was quite an honor. Going on the cover of *Sports Illustrated* was one of the better things that happened to me. It was recognition from people throughout the league and also from opponents I was playing against. That's the highest form of flattery as a nose tackle."

The flattery was nice. The *Sports Illustrated* jinx was frightening. The *SI* jinx has lost considerable power over the years, but at its peak in the 1970s, it was no urban legend. It seemed real.

"I was cognizant of the *Sports Illustrated* jinx," Carter said. "You heard of the jinx of guys or teams on the cover and all the sudden their performance goes down," Carter said. "I wanted to avoid that, so I tried to take my game to another level."

Perhaps one reason why Carter didn't earn any Pro Bowls is a 3-4 nose tackle wasn't up for the vote. It was always two defensive ends and two defensive tackles on the ballot. Defensive tackle is not the same as nose tackle.

Carter had more than 1,036 tackles in his 12-year career with the Broncos, and 33 sacks—unheard-of statistics for modern-era nose tackles. Had the NFL appreciated the position like it does today, Carter's 6.0 sacks in 1977 and 6.5 sacks in 1978 from the nose-tackle position would have been worth a contract between $10 million and $15 million per year.

He wasn't the first NFL noseguard. That distinction belonged to Curly Culp, who was the Broncos' first player taken in the 1968 draft, but who was discarded before playing his first game by coach Lou Saban.

Culp wound up becoming a Pro Football Hall of Fame defensive lineman for the Kansas City Chiefs.

"Growing up, I watched him a lot when he was with Kansas City and I was in high school," Carter said. "I would notice some of the action he had, and certainly he was the strength of that defense because he would get double- and triple-teamed. He had the strength and ability to play with natural leverage, and just the quickness he had to be able to beat blocks, and pursue down the line of scrimmage and make plays. I tried to implement a lot of that, what he'd done, into my game."

Carter was a quick study. He wound up playing more games at nose tackle (152) than any other player in NFL history. For the longest time, the journey to Super Bowl XII was the highlight of the Broncos franchise. The game was a drag, although Carter shone with six tackles and two sacks.

"Rubin was very . . . he was good. He was very good," said Chavous, Carter's longtime defensive line mate and friend. "He was the epitome of a nose tackle. No one center could block Rubin. He was very physical. That's something we took pride in. Rubin was very good at getting people off him to get to the ball. People had to double-team Rubin because they couldn't leave the nose one-on-one with the center. When they put two on him, that meant the linebackers would be free."

While finishing his playing career on injured reserve in 1986, Carter served as an unofficial player-coach to the likes of Greg Kragen, Andre Townsend, and Rulon Jones.

He was so good at it, Carter coached football the next 29 years. He coached for the college programs of Howard, San Jose State, Maryland, Temple, Florida A&M (where he was head coach), New Mexico, Towson, and Purdue. He coached in the NFL for Washington and the New York Jets. He coached at a Miami high school, and he is still a volunteer coach for high school kids in the Tallahassee, Florida, area, where he and his wife Karen have otherwise retired.

Carter's son, Andre Carter, had a nice 13-year NFL career, registering 80.5 sacks. Better believe Andre played 13 seasons because Dad played 12.

"I told him your dad was a Sherman tank," Carter said. "You're on the outside, you're a jet fighter. I passed the baton to Andre. And now he's coaching."

Andre Carter began the 2017 season as an assistant defensive line coach for Adam Gase's Miami Dolphins. Football coaching is in Andre Carter's blood, just like playing football was in his blood.

One thing Andre never did that Pops did: score a touchdown. In a 45–10 whipping of New England in a 1979 game, Rubin Carter started the romp by returning a fumble 2 yards for a touchdown. It wasn't the most athletic play, perhaps, but it counted.

"Tom Jackson hit the quarterback, the ball came out, I picked up the ball, and when I picked it up, I stumbled and fell and I kind of rolled a little bit," Carter said. "And then Barney Chavous comes and picks me up and rolls me in like a ball and we scored a touchdown. That was the only touchdown of my career, and it was because Barney rolled me in."

It wasn't the last time Carter and Chavous were linked. Notice how the two are next to each other on the list of 50 Greatest Broncos.

RUBIN CARTER STATS			
YRS	G	S	TCK
12	166	33.0	1,036

BARNEY CHAVOUS

Defensive End, 1973–85

Barney Chavous was 16 years old, driving a school bus before and after school.

He got his sunup to sundown driver's license at 14, then two years later drove a school bus for one job, and added some financial stability by working at his uncle's automatic transmission shop.

During vocational school at Schofield High School, Chavous and two other students in his group won a state auto mechanic contest. His group diagnosed an engine's problem in record time.

It's how it was growing up in the 1960s in Aiken, South Carolina.

"I only played one year of high school football," Chavous said in March 2017. "I wasn't even thinking football growing up. I'm a certified mechanic. I got my certification when I was at vocational school in high school. And then for a while in high school I drove a school bus. I quit driving a school bus when my high school coach told me if I come play football, I'll get you a scholarship. When he told me that, a light went on in my head. So, I quit the auto mechanic business, quit driving the school bus. I played that season."

Chavous's high school football coach? William Clyburn, who is now a 12-term member of the South Carolina House of Representatives.

Turns out, the best training for football isn't necessarily playing football. The best training for football is good, old-fashioned hard work. Chavous brought that lunch-pail mentality to the Denver Broncos for 13 seasons.

When he was nudged into retirement following the training camp of 1986, no Bronco had played more than 13 seasons with the team. His 182 games played were the most by a Broncos player at the time of his retirement. And his 177 games started was one off the team record set by safety Billy Thompson.

Chavous still ranks tied for fourth in seasons played, tied for fourth in starts, and ranks eighth in games played. One key to his durability will not surprise you. Another key will interest you.

"Hard work," Chavous said. "Preparation all season. In 1976, [defensive line coach] Stan Jones came over from Buffalo. Stan was one of the first players to lift weights. He was playing for the Chicago Bears for George Halas when Stan was one of the first to lift weights.

"So when he got to Denver in 1976, Rubin [Carter], myself, Billy Thompson, Lyle [Alzado], and some other guys, we started working out in the off-season. And then in 1977 we took it to another level. The whole team started lifting weights during the off-season. That's how we got to the Super Bowl. That's a little bit of the history of our '77 team. No one expected us to do anything, but we were in such great shape. We were stronger than other people. That's why we wound up in the Super Bowl. Stan initiated that."

Chavous was never flashy as the strong-side defensive end in the Broncos' famed 3-4 defense. He never made the Pro Bowl, primarily because it was always the 4-3, pass-rushing defensive ends who drew the honors.

None of those Pro Bowl defensive ends in the Chavous era, though, were tougher against the run. And none of those run-stopping defensive ends could rush the passer like Chavous. He retired as the all-time Broncos leader, with 75.0 sacks, a mark he held until Karl Mecklenburg passed him eight years later.

"Barney is s-o-o-o underrated," said Broncos cornerback Louis Wright, who played on the same left side of Denver's famed Orange Crush defense from the mid-1970s to the early 1980s. "To me, Barney was one of the best in the league because he never got beat, one-on-one. People don't appreciate that. Unless you jump up and down and make a lot of noise, like Lyle did on the other side. But Barney was like the solid rock. The guy who held it together."

Said Broncos nose tackle Rubin Carter, who was Chavous's roommate during training camp and road games: "Barney was a two-dimensional player. He could play against the run, and he could play against the pass. He was a complete, four-down player. You didn't have to take him off the field.

"Never got his due, making Pro Bowls and things of that caliber, but he was just a tremendous, solid, consistent player all the time. And one of the best demeanors off the field as anybody you'd want to meet. The way he carried himself. A classy man. Loved his wife, loved his family, loved his kids. Loved to hunt. He was a hunter. Just a down-to-earth guy."

There are Broncos, and there is Barney Chavous. In the first 40 seasons of the Broncos franchise, Chavous was employed for 25 of them—13 as a player, 12 as a coach. That's 62.5 percent Chavous through the Broncos' first 40 years.

"I was very blessed to be with the Denver Broncos," he said. "It's a great organization. I didn't have to move my family, my kids got to keep the same friends. We all lived there in the off-season. All the players stayed in Denver. And that made a big difference in our relationships as players, and made us close as a unit."

Chavous could have returned for a 14th season in 1986, but he would have ridden the bench alongside his defensive line mate Carter, as coach Dan Reeves wanted to go with the younger Andre Townsend and Greg Kragen up front.

Instead, Chavous went back home to South Carolina with his wife of now 44 years, Odessa, and their three children. He sat out the 1987 season, then called Reeves up and asked for a job. Reeves gave him an intern coaching position in 1988, and Chavous got a full-time gig as an assistant strength and conditioning coach and assistant defensive line coach in 1989.

Chavous stayed through 1999, becoming the only assistant to serve on the coaching staffs of Reeves, Wade Phillips, and Mike Shanahan. That's an even 25 years with the Broncos as a player and coach. Consider that John Elway was entering his 23rd (combined) season with the Broncos as a quarterback and general manager in 2017.

"It's hard to pick just one highlight, but I can give you two: the Super Bowls, when we played in them as a player and won as a coach," Chavous said. "That first Super Bowl that we won [against Green Bay, to cap the 1997 season], that's your dream and goal as a player and a coach.

"And then when we went to the Super Bowl in '77, that was a highlight from the standpoint that when I first came to Denver, they had never had a winning season. And then our first winning season in '73 was my rookie year. I started that year. It was great to be a part of that. The Broncos tradition started then, and it's been going on ever since."

Growing up in Aiken, South Carolina, Barney Lewis Chavous was greatly influenced by his father, Barney Oscar Chavous, and his mother, Mary Bell.

"My mom's family came from slavery," Chavous said. "My dad's family was a free family. So, it was a good balance for us growing up. We understood both sides.

"My dad, he was so special. He used to lay brick, he built houses. He was an auto mechanic. I got bits of pieces of him. Anything he could put his mind to do, he could do it. He was very gifted, especially with his hands."

A four-year letterman and three-year starting defensive end at South Carolina State, Chavous was the second-round pick in the Broncos' terrific 1973 draft class that also included running back Otis Armstrong in the first round, guard Paul Howard in the third, linebacker Tom Jackson in the fourth, and defensive end John Grant in the seventh. Chavous started all 14 games a rookie, and was named by the NFL Players Association as the NFL Defensive Rookie of the Year.

It was during the 1976 season that Broncos defensive coordinator Joe Collier began to flirt with the 3-4 front that placed Chavous at left defensive end, and he was a force there during the famed 1977 season of the Orange Crush.

Chavous tied Alzado with a team-most 8 sacks that year, as Denver allowed just 148 points in 14 games—a 10.6-points-per-game average that remains a franchise record, unlikely to ever be broken. That great 2015 Denver defense? It allowed 296 points in 16 games, or 18.5 points per game. Not even close.

"Barney was our anchor on the strong-side run," Jackson said. "Barney was someone beloved by everybody on that team, but also a tremendous pass rusher, also a tremendous player."

In that day, sacks were not the be-all to measuring a defensive lineman, as they are today. The NFL didn't even acknowledge the sack as a statistic until 1982. Broncos statisticians, though, went back and were able to document sacks going back to 1970.

"When I came along, what you wanted to be was a complete football player," Chavous said. "You wanted to be able to stop the run, which was first, and then be able to get to the quarterback as well. Now, you have guys [who] specialize in getting to the quarterback. Our first priority then was to stop the run, because more people ran then than they do now."

After his final season as a Broncos assistant coach in 1999, Chavous and Odessa went back to Aiken, where they live on Chavous Road.

"Our family has owned land in this area going back eight generations," Chavous said.

He commuted across the Savannah River to Augusta, Georgia, where he coached 11 years at T. W. Josey High School before retiring. He said at least 20 Josey High School players earned college scholarships during his time there, including nose tackle Lawrence Marsh, who played with Tim Tebow for the Florida Gators.

"I wanted to help kids through the same life experience my high school coach gave me," Chavous said.

He and Odessa are now retired.

"I'm working with my son, raising Black Angus cattle," Chavous said. "Trying to do some things my father passed on to me, with him."

BARNEY CHAVOUS STATS

YRS	G	S	TCK
13	182	75.0	1,105

38

— BILL ROMANOWSKI —

Linebacker, 1996–2001

My expanding fanaticism for taking care of my body was matched
only by my intensity to hurt others.

— *Romo: My Life on the Edge*

There would be two NFL stops in Bill Romanowski's career before he
arrived in Denver. The first was a six-year stay in San Francisco, then two
more years with the Philadelphia Eagles.

In his autobiography that was published two years after his retirement,
Romanowski made the above statement in context with his final season of
1995 with Philadelphia.

By the time he became a Broncos linebacker by way of free agency in
1996, Romanowski's obsession with supplements, workouts, and nutrition
off the field, and full-out, bone-crushing rage on the field, had reached its
crescendo.

To Romo goes the victory. Nearly 20 years after the Broncos won their
first two Super Bowls in the back-to-back seasons of 1997–98, the lion's
share of credit has gone to, in order, Terrell Davis, John Elway, and Mike
Shanahan.

It is no coincidence, though, that Romanowski played in five com-
bined Super Bowls with three teams, winning four. Make no mistake: The
Broncos would not have been world champions twice in the late 1990s had
Romanowski decided to sign with the San Diego Chargers and not Denver.

"When I think of Bill, I think of the word *intense*," said Broncos kicker
Jason Elam. "I remember pregame just before we ran on the field, just him
walking around with a crazy look in his eyes. And how important it was
for him to be the best. I remember the great lengths he would go to with
nutrition and hiring the support squad he did, to work on his body. It was

his life. He was going to give it everything that he had. And that spilled over to the guys. Everybody was: I've got to do more; this guy is going the extra mile. He had an impact on so many people, whether they know it or not."

Yes, there were times when Romanowski crossed the line, both in terms of sportsmanship and once in seeking pharmaceutical aid. His deep-seated desire to not just hit, but punish the opponent took a physical toll on his mind and body. But a man cannot possibly know how far he can go until he goes too far.

"I always looked at it this way: There's an intensity line, and I never, ever wanted to be below that 100 percent," Romanowski said, when interviewed for this project in February 2017. "And if you're toeing that line on a daily basis, playing linebacker in the NFL, it's going to be hard not to step over that line at times."

Romanowski's extreme desire for greatness was inherent but not necessarily genetic. His father, Bill, and mom, Donna, were loving parents who, like most Americans in the 1960s and '70s, worked hard while struggling with finances. They raised five children in Vernon, Connecticut, and while sports were big in the Romanowski household, only young Bill was over the top in his quest to make it.

Romanowski was an impressionable 14-year-old when he read a *Sports Illustrated* profile on how University of Georgia running back Herschel Walker did all these push-ups, sit-ups, and sprints.

The single-minded aspirations inside every fiber of Romanowski were triggered. He never let up.

"That drive I had came from fear," Romanowski said. "Ultimately that fear is about not being good enough. The intensity around that, and doing something that I loved to do and wanting to be the absolute best I could be, to package that together and realize the harder I practiced, the more I prepared, the better I played on Sunday. There was a direct correlation, and no different than how I prepared in the weight room. How I'd eat, how I supplemented. Not drinking and partying—doing the right things is what it took for me."

Romanowski played football, basketball, and baseball at Rockville High School in Vernon, then played with Doug Flutie at Boston College. It was 1984 when Flutie threw his famous Hail Mary pass to Gerald Phelan the day after Thanksgiving to stun Bernie Kosar and the Miami Hurricanes, and two games later, Romanowski was the MVP of the Cotton Bowl on New Year's Day.

A third-round draft pick by the San Francisco 49ers in 1988, Romanowski immediately began a streak of 243 consecutive games played in the

NFL—all 16 games in his first 15 seasons, and the first three in his 16th, plus 28 more playoff games—when consecutive concussions essentially ended his career in 2003.

Among non-kickers, only Brett Favre (323) and Jim Marshall (301) had longer streaks than Romanowski's combined regular-season/playoff run of 271 games.

Romanowski played 6 seasons and 96 consecutive games, plus 9 more playoff games for the 49ers, winning back-to-back Super Bowls in the 1988 and '89 seasons. And he played 6 seasons and 96 consecutive games, plus 9 more playoff games for the Broncos, winning back-to-back Super Bowls in the 1997 and '98 seasons.

Marv Fleming (Green Bay and Miami) and Charles Haley (San Francisco, Dallas) were the only other players in NFL history to win back-to-back Super Bowls with two different teams.

"I wouldn't say we were as talented as the 49ers teams, but we were a closer team, and I think we were a better team," Romanowski said of the Broncos. "But the 49ers teams had a lot of talent."

Those 49er teams had four first-ballot Hall of Famers, two at quarterback in Joe Montana and Steve Young, plus receiver Jerry Rice and safety Ronnie Lott. The only first-ballot Hall of Famer from the Broncos' back-to-back championship teams was John Elway, although Gary Zimmerman, Shannon Sharpe, and Terrell Davis eventually had their busts bronzed.

"Now hearing you say that, hey, we were damn good, and we were really close," Romanowski said. "We truly loved one another. And we played hard for one another."

Between San Francisco and Denver, Romanowski played two seasons for the Philadelphia Eagles. His workout regime and various new vitamins, along with his supplemental intake, reached new levels of intensity when he became a free agent following the 1995 season and picked the Broncos over the Chargers.

"The Denver Broncos were great on offense," Romanowski said, explaining his decision. "They needed a leader on defense and they didn't have it. I don't mean this in an egotistical way, but I just knew what I could bring, and felt like if I went there, I really believed we would win a Super Bowl.

"I truly believed Mike Shanahan, coming from the 49ers, he was going to bring coaching-wise what it takes to win a Super Bowl. And I thought I could bring the leadership on defense. They had what they needed on offense and we could get this done. Sure enough, I made the right decision."

Not immediately. With Romanowski playing strong-side linebacker, the Broncos started 12-1 in 1996, clinching the No. 1 AFC playoff seed and first-round playoff bye with three games remaining in the regular season.

But in a second-round playoff game, the Broncos were stunned by the upstart Jacksonville Jaguars. We'll never know because they didn't finish, but many Broncos observers claim the 1996 team was better than those that won back-to-back Super Bowls the next two years.

"That was a damn good team," Romanowski said of the '96 Broncos. "One of the problems was we clinched a little too early. And by doing that, I felt like we let our guard down a little bit. We still practiced hard. We prepared hard. We just lost our edge a little bit."

A couple days after that devastating loss, Romanowski—who has publicly said he played one of the worst games of his career against Mark Brunell and the Jaguars—met with Shanahan and told the coach he must accept part of the blame.

Shanahan, it seems, had stated in the team's season-opening meeting that the goal would be to win the division, get the No. 1 playoff seed, and the rest would take care of itself.

"Not to win the Super Bowl," Romanowski said. "You have to say exactly what your goal is. Me knowing what I know about goal-setting, which is a big part of my career and how I was able to have success, you have to define it. I just felt like that was a piece.

"Hey, at the end of the day there are little things that add up when you're trying to win a Super Bowl. And I felt that was a piece. You could ask guys on the team and they would probably beg to differ. In my mind, when I was in San Francisco, our goal was to win the Super Bowl. Nothing less was acceptable to the organization. The next year, when we got into minicamp or training camp, our goal was to win the Super Bowl. Not to win our division. Not to get home-field advantage in the playoffs. It was to win the Super Bowl. And that's what we did."

Romanowski wasn't just an inspirational leader for the Broncos. He was also a play-making, tackling machine, registering career bests with 128 stops and 12 pass deflections in 1996, while adding 3 interceptions and 3 sacks to earn his first Pro Bowl trip. In 1998, he had 95 tackles with a career-best 7.5 sacks with two picks, 3 forced fumbles, and 3 fumble recoveries to make his second Pro Bowl team.

His stellar period with the Broncos was also remembered for spitting on J. J. Stokes and breaking the jaw of Carolina quarterback Kerry Collins while coming in on a blitz. Regrets?

"Of course," Romanowski said. "I hold myself accountable for all my actions. But, yeah, I would do some things differently."

Romanowski also became a one-man marketing liaison between the Broncos and Golden-based EAS fitness products. Romo had two lockers—one filled with EAS products that he distributed at no cost to his teammates upon request.

He estimates that he spent $1 million on supplements, training machines, personal trainers, and therapists during his career, for himself and his teams.

Today, Romanowski remains maniacal about taking care of himself, spending hundreds of thousands on rest periods in a hyperbaric chamber in hopes of staving off possible harmful effects from the 20 or so concussions he suffered. More recently, he has been using a sauna / cold tub alternating technique that he says has been a game-changer.

What does he remember most from his six Broncos seasons?

"The people," he said. "The fans. I love the fans in Denver. Have a lot of great friends in Denver. Pat and Annabel Bowlen. Pat showed me Hawaii. He had been going over there for years. His family and my family had a lot of great times. I really truly cared about him and his family. He wanted to win Super Bowls. And he was going to give Mike Shanahan everything he needed to do that."

BILL ROMANOWSKI STATS

YRS	G	S	I	TCK
6	96	23.0	11	671

39

JAKE PLUMMER

Quarterback, 2003–06

Asked to come up with one game from his four seasons with the Denver Broncos he remembers most, Jake Plummer made a surprise choice.

As he was considering, I suggested his Halloween Day game in 2004 against the Atlanta Falcons. Although the Broncos lost, Plummer was terrific. He threw for 499 yards that day, a team record even Peyton Manning couldn't break during his wildly prolific, record-setting season of 2013.

Plummer threw two touchdown passes against Atlanta in the first quarter to give the Broncos a 14–3 lead. When Denver's defense couldn't stop the sensational Michael Vick that day, Plummer threw two more touchdown passes in the fourth quarter in an attempt to catch up.

"How many yards?" Plummer asked during an interview in late November of 2016.

That would be 499.

"Wow. We didn't win the game?" he said.

Um, no. Lost, 41–28. Too much Michael Vick.

"I don't remember that game very well then," he said. "Not till you just mentioned it. Michael Vick, that guy was sick, I do remember that."

And then Plummer's memory started to jog.

"One of the best games I remember I had here was when we beat Miami," he said.

Wait, Miami? The Miami game late in the 2004 season at then-named Invesco Field at Mile High? A surprising choice, because it was hardly Plummer's best game. He threw two interceptions without a touchdown pass. Surprising, because that was the game Plummer, while sitting on the bench and wearing a ball cap following a first-quarter interception, delivered a behind-the-head middle finger to a heckling fan.

The gesture became watercooler fodder for a couple weeks as the CBS telecast happened to point a live camera on Plummer as he flipped the bird. So why would this game, above all other games, be etched in Plummer's memory all these years later?

Because despite his struggles, his Broncos nevertheless won the game. Here's how Plummer recalled that game during a late-November 2016 interview:

"Miami had one of the best defenses in the league, and I ended up flipping off a fan. I had a non-stat-worthy game, but we won. I was able to make plays when it mattered and we needed them. That's what I was focused on. Today's QBs, they all put up stats. Every one of them. It's just the nature of the game. But did you make the plays that mattered when you needed to make them?"

Jake the Snake was 100 percent accurate. In his four Broncos seasons, Plummer didn't tear it up statistically, although he wasn't bad. He averaged 2,908 passing yards and 18 touchdown passes against 12 interceptions a season. Call it above-average stats for the times.

Yet, Plummer was also 39-15 in his four seasons in Denver: 9-2 in 2003, 10-6 in 2004, 13-3 in his career-best season of 2005, and he was 7-2 in 2006 when coach Mike Shanahan started plotting to replace him with first-round rookie Jay Cutler. Plummer and the Broncos lost his next two starts, and suddenly, and shockingly, his career was virtually finished.

Even if it was never going to end with pomp and circumstance for the fiery Plummer, he was one of the first guys I thought of when I received this project from my publishers. Plummer received plenty of publicity during his NFL career, but few honors. He was a polarizing figure even by quarterback standards to the Broncos fan base and media, but no one could deny he was a tremendous athlete who, despite his average arm strength relative to the NFL level, was an incomparable winner.

His 39-15 record with the Broncos was third best among NFL quarterbacks who played in that four-year period, trailing only Tom Brady and Peyton Manning. That's it. Brady and Manning.

In my view, Plummer was the fourth-best quarterback in Broncos history, trailing only John Elway, Manning, and Craig Morton. Among the Broncos quarterbacks Plummer eclipsed were Frank Tripucka, Charley Johnson, Brian Griese, and the guy who eventually replaced him, Cutler.

"I'm glad you included Jake, because all he did was win," said Broncos Ring of Fame safety John Lynch. "You look at that winning percentage. And I will tell you this about Jake: He could have different political views or different views on life, but guys loved playing with him. He brought a kid-in-the-sandlot passion to the game.

"That's sometimes what would drive a head coach mad, throwing left-handed and stuff, but he was kind of like when you played against Brett Favre. You always just appreciated that he was having so much fun playing the game. Same thing with Jake as a teammate. The guy loved playing football for all the right reasons. And then his record spoke for itself in terms of what he meant to the team."

Plummer grew up in Boise, Idaho, the youngest of three sons raised by Steve Plummer, a lumberman, and Marilyn, an elementary and junior high teacher. In the house across the street lived his maternal grandparents, Elwood and Hazel.

Elwood wound up suffering from Alzheimer's disease, which became a major cause for Jake's charitable foundation. Grandma Hazel was the type who never judged anyone by their appearance.

Fame and fortune could not penetrate Plummer's Idaho spirit, or the piece of Grandma Hazel lodged in his soul. Rather than carry himself with the type of stately airs common among most successful NFL quarterbacks, Plummer in 2005 took on the nonconformist look of long hair and an untrimmed, full beard while leading the Broncos to a 13-3 regular season record and second-round playoff victory against Brady and the New England Patriots.

Part of his unkempt appearance was to honor his former Arizona State and Arizona Cardinals teammate Pat Tillman, who often sported long hair and facial hair during his playing days, but gave up his football career to join the US Army after 9/11. Tillman was killed in April 2004 by a "friendly fire" incident in Afghanistan that was initially covered up by the army.

It wasn't just a tribute to Tillman or in defiance to society's expectations that brought on Plummer's look, although maybe a little. It was also about the casual, take-me-as-I-am approach he believed in.

"My grandma would take me into her house if I was a complete stranger looking like this," Plummer told me then. "She was a big influence on all of us."

Plummer, too, was extremely generous. During the final game of the 2005 season at San Diego, Plummer bought every player on the team a double-double meal from In-N-Out Burger. This was after he'd bought every offensive player dinner for two at Morton's The Steakhouse and cowboy boots for each of his offensive linemen.

"George Foster just tweeted out that he came across his gift certificate just this spring," Plummer said 11 years later. "He called and got his free cowboy boots."

Talk about a gift of a lifetime. Another year he gave his offensive linemen remote-control cars. He got creative one year, sending them each a questionnaire asking if they liked red wine, hard alcohol, or beer. What does your wife drink? Have you ever seen the movie, *The Jericho Mile*?

He'd then buy a gift bag and stuff it with movie tickets, a bottle of the finest red wine or bourbon for the guys, and throw in a bottle of white wine for the wives.

"Just showing them how much I loved them," Plummer said.

He captured the nation's imagination in his senior season at Arizona State, leading the Sun Devils to an 11-0 record in 1996 and a Rose Bowl appearance, thanks to his swashbuckling play. Plummer led Arizona State to a clutch touchdown drive for a 17–14 lead against Ohio State with 1:47 remaining in the Rose Bowl, but the Buckeyes scored on their final drive to pull it out and deny the Sun Devils a co-national championship.

Plummer finished third in the Heisman Trophy balloting to Florida quarterback Danny Wuerffel and Iowa State running back Troy Davis, neither of whom had near the NFL career Plummer had.

Selected in the second round of the 1997 draft by his college hometown team, Plummer in his second season of 1998 led the Arizona Cardinals to their first postseason appearance since the franchise had moved from St. Louis ten years earlier. When Plummer then guided Arizona past the Dallas Cowboys in the first round of the 1998 season, it was the Cardinals' first postseason win since 1947, when they were the Chicago Cardinals.

It was on his birthday, December 19th, of that 1998 season that Plummer received a contract extension that in new money made him the richest player in NFL history—four years and $35 million, with $15 million fully guaranteed.

But Plummer could only temporarily interrupt the Cardinals' half-century of futility, and prior to the 2003 season, he was happy to reach free agency. His suitors came down to the Chicago Bears, where one-year wonder Jim Miller was a full year removed from his wondrous 2001 season, and the Broncos, who were ready to move on from Brian Griese.

"My agent's advice was to eliminate any external enticements like the city of Chicago may have been," Plummer said of David Dunn. "Denver was in my wheelhouse coming from Idaho, and mountain areas and trees. Chicago—I was very intrigued by what that city had to offer outside of football. I was intrigued with going to a dive bar and listening to some blues. I never felt a city like that. That was the one thing I was leaning on for Chicago. And then once I took that out of it, it was Denver.

"My agent reminded me, 'This is football. Go where you think you have the best chance to win a championship.' Although the Bears had won and would win again, I looked at what the Broncos had in place and ultimately took less money to go to Denver. It was about $1 million less to come here and play."

He led them to the playoffs his first three seasons, the Broncos' first such streak since the final three years of John Elway's playing career in 1996–98.

"He became one of my favorite quarterbacks," said Broncos cornerback Champ Bailey, who intercepted Plummer five times before they became teammates. "He's a hard-nosed guy. One thing I liked about Jake, he enjoyed the game. He was great to be around. Very team-oriented. Always caring about you. You go to his house, have a party, Jake was one of those guys people gravitate toward because he was a fun-loving guy. He also loved to play football. The guy was a winner, man. Some of the plays he made, not a lot of quarterbacks can make."

Broncos kicker Jason Elam was a polished, All American–type guy, nothing if not consistent both on and off the field. But Elam was also a Renaissance man who traveled, flew his own planes, and wrote books. He struck up a kindred friendship with the unique-thinking Plummer.

"I sat next to him on all of our flights on road games," Elam said. "We had some great conversations. He was spectacular one-on-one with people. His teammates, everybody loved him. If you didn't know him, he could come across abrasive sometimes. But I know he treated the O-linemen phenomenally. He appreciated them. He was very affirming. He would build people up. After you left a conversation with him you were ready to go on the field. You could feel the eagerness to get out there."

It should have been four postseason appearances in four Broncos seasons for Plummer. And it should have been another year or two after that. But it all fell apart when the Broncos were 7-2 in 2006 and leading San Diego, 24–7, midway through the third quarter of Game 10.

At that point the Denver defense collapsed and the Chargers rallied for a 35–27 win behind first-year starting quarterback Philip Rivers and running back LaDainian Tomlinson, who was in the midst of his career-best season. Shanahan then made plans to replace Plummer with first-round rookie Jay Cutler after the Broncos' next game on Thanksgiving night at Kansas City.

Although he was a dead quarterback walking, Plummer competed to the end, nearly rallying the Broncos late but losing, 19–10. It was the final meaningful game of his career.

The switch was made, and the Broncos finished 2-3 under Cutler to miss the playoffs. For a while Plummer was embittered, even retiring at 32 years old rather than going along with an off-season trade to Tampa Bay. He has since let go of those sore feelings.

"A couple things happened," he said. "One, coming back and living here. Visiting the facility and sitting across from Mr. Bowlen for, I think it was about an hour, give or take. I came back to Boulder in 2012, Peyton's first year. I went and saw Mr. B and he was doing good at the time. We had a great conversation. I let him know what he meant to me and he told me what I meant to him, and I thanked him for everything. We shed some tears and had some great laughs. He gave me some great advice. He basically said you are welcome here whenever you want. You're a Bronco for life.

"It made him feel good that I was back. And that's when I realized I had the privilege to play for an organization that doesn't just talk about taking care of their own and creating a family atmosphere. He meant it."

Bowlen invited Plummer to join him in his suite for Manning's first game with the Broncos, September 9, 2012, against Pittsburgh. Plummer didn't even last until the National Anthem. He had to get out of the enclosed box and walk around. This led to a second moment when Plummer let go of any misgivings he felt toward Shanahan.

"I start meandering through the stadium, I get behind the bench, and I'm standing by a tunnel so I could be sheltered a little bit," Plummer said. "And it struck me that these fans used to stand up and cheer for me just like they did one of the greatest players ever in Peyton. It did hit me I had nothing to be ashamed of, or mad about, or hold on to, because, man, I did it. I achieved so much. I played in the league 10 years.

"And that's when it dawned on me that I had something to do with that benching, too. I wasn't an innocent kid that got benched. I see fans all the time at the stadium, and they say, 'Man, that's so messed up what they did, that Shanahan blah, blah. And I'm like, Yo, man, you've got to stop. I don't feel that way. I'm over it. And it happened to me. It didn't happen to you, so you need to get over it. Let's go get a beer. Negative feelings do nothing good for the organization the Broncos have been, and are trying to continue to be."

After his career, Plummer went back to his Idaho roots and started playing competitive handball. He married Kollette Klassen, a Fort Morgan native and former Broncos cheerleader in 2007, and they moved back to Colorado and settled in Boulder. They have three children, Roland, Winston, and Laverne. He has worked as a color and studio analyst for the Pac-12 Network, and has been an advocate of medical marijuana as treatment for the pain football players endure each week.

Grandma Hazel would approve. As Plummer looks back on the Broncos portion of his career, his greatest source of pride comes not from the 39-15 record he earned, but the testimonies you read and heard from the likes of Lynch, Bailey, and Elam.

"I hang it on the stories you'll get from my teammates and the feeling they had toward me as their quarterback, a guy they went to battle with, to go out and fight to win," Plummer said. "That's what I really hang my hat on. When I'm on my deathbed, that'll be more than the win-loss record I had with Denver.

"*But* . . . as an athlete, as a competitor, I always said this: I never cared about the stats. Of course, I would have loved to have been leading the league in touchdown passes and all that, but that wasn't my game. My game was scrappin' and fighting and clawing, trying to win however I could do it.

"So, yeah, when I came here and suffered through what I did in Arizona, a couple of 3-13 seasons and then to bounce back and go 13-3 and be a part of how successful that [2005 Broncos] team was, I do take pride in knowing I won a whole lot of ball games in four years, and I wonder what would have happened had I played my whole career here. How many games would I have won? How many more opportunities would I have had to go to the Super Bowl? That one year, though, I think did prove I could win games, and wasn't just a run-of-the-mill quarterback."

JAKE PLUMMER STATS

YRS	G	A	C	PCT	Y	TD	I	RTG	W-L
4	59	1,596	944	59.1	11,631	71	47	84.3	29-15

40

— KEITH BISHOP —

Guard, 1980–89

Keith Bishop twirled his glass of water as he pondered the question.

What was the most vivid memory, or proudest moment, of your 10-year NFL career with the Broncos? Bishop understood this was a reference to his *playing* time in Denver. He's in his second stint with the company, as his post-playing days' work in law enforcement led him to his current job of heading the Broncos security department.

Bishop, a few months shy of his 60th birthday, was sitting in the concierge lounge of the team's hotel outside New Orleans in mid-November 2016, considering the inquiry for nearly 20 seconds, nudging his water glass round and round, when a possibility was interjected.

We all know what you're most famous for, Keith . . .

"Yeah, but that's press BS," Bishop said dismissively. Finally, he settled. "It would be, I played 10 years and I never graded below 90."

Whose grading scale?

"It wasn't mine," he growled.

No, it was the toughest blocking critics in football: The Broncos offensive line coaches. Bishop was one of only five offensive linemen included in this project of 50 Greatest Broncos Players, and the only guard. He made the cut because he was a Pro Bowler in 1986 and '87—the franchise's first-ever offensive lineman to earn such a distinction. He made it not only because he was a seven-year starter from 1983–89, but also a co-offensive captain and deep snapper each of those seven years.

And he made it because in the first huddle of the famous "Drive"—the most iconic moment in Denver sports history (meaning no disrespect to the Broncos' three Super Bowl championships and Colorado Avalanche's Stanley Cups)—Bishop uttered the most memorable line in franchise history.

With the ball at the 2-yard line and 98 yards to go, with the Broncos needing a touchdown and extra point to tie the Cleveland Browns in the 1986-season AFC Championship Game, with only 5 minutes, 32 seconds remaining in regulation on a frigid afternoon, and with chewed-up pavement serving as the playing surface of Cleveland Stadium, Bishop defiantly told his gathered teammates, "We got 'em right where we want 'em!"

Only that wasn't the exact wording.

"Obviously, it was a hard-fought game," Bishop said while recalling the moment nearly 30 years later. "But we're down there and we're in the huddle, and I don't think John was in there. In fact, I know he wasn't, because he comes back in the huddle and everyone is laughing their asses off and he's like, 'What? What?'

"So we're in the huddle, we're waiting and we're looking at the Browns. And several of the Browns were good friends of mine. They're all standing in their defensive huddle and they're all laughing. And I said, '[Bleep] them [bleep, bleeps], we've got those [bleeps] right where we want them.'"

Sorry, we can't print the exact wording of a famous quote in a book we hope is read by adults and kids alike.

"They left some words out of it," Bishop said about the press. "And if we hadn't driven and scored, nobody would have heard anything about it.

"Then you go back and watch that damn thing, and you watch some of the throws he made. And the toughness. The hits he would take. I mean it was cold, you're tired, and he takes hits like that and he keeps on keeping on."

The "he" and "John" to whom Bishop refers is John Elway. As Bishop speaks, the admiration he has for his former quarterback is palpable. Following a 16-year career as the Broncos quarterback that was stamped with two Super Bowl titles and a bronze bust in Canton, Ohio, Elway is now on a remarkably successful run as the team's general manager.

Elway is still the boss, and Bishop as head of security still protects him.

"John and I hit it off," Bishop said. "We were, and always have been, very close. I got to see for my seven years I played with him the stuff he had to put up with."

"The Drive" was Elway's signature moment. Until then, he was a quarterback of sensational potential. "The Drive" was the moment when his potential was realized. And it all began with the impromptu motivational speech of the Broncos left guard.

"It's kind of like the John Candy story of Joe Montana, when they were playing the Bengals [in Super Bowl XXIII]," said Broncos receiver Steve Watson, who was present for Bishop's huddle speech. "You just go, 'Huh?'"

Bishop grew up in Midland, Texas, the son of George and Wanda Bishop. Dad had his own residential home construction company. Mom sold real estate. Few people alive loved their parents more than Keith did.

He worked from the time he was in third or fourth grade as a paper boy, then got a job as a roustabout, or roughneck, in the oil fields. Out of high school, Bishop got a scholarship to play football at Nebraska, but he left after two years to go back home. He wasn't playing much for the Cornhuskers, and then when he learned his mom was sick, that was it.

"I went home and I wasn't going to play football anymore," Bishop said. "I was going to go to work with my dad in his construction company. I go back there and they were like, 'No. You've got an opportunity for a free college education; you're going back to school.'"

Baylor had recruited him hard before he decided on Nebraska. The old Bears offensive line coach was still there, and so the transfer was arranged.

Bishop started every game at center as a junior, and even though he suffered a season-ending knee injury in the opener of his senior season, the Broncos selected him in the sixth round of the 1980 draft.

As a rookie, Bishop played quite a bit on special teams and as a backup right guard and center. He might have been good enough to start, but his old-school offensive line coach, Whitey Dovell, didn't believe in starting rookies.

The next year, serious injury struck Bishop again, this time in the pre-season opener. A ruptured tendon in the bottom of his right foot ended his second season of 1981 before it began.

He returned as a left guard in 1982.

"Which I enjoyed more. For a right-handed quarterback it's the blind side, a little more responsibility for doing things," Bishop said. "So it made the position a little more fun."

He became a full-time starter to start the 1983 season—Elway's rookie year—and Bishop stayed there until injuries forced him to part-time duty late in his final season of 1989.

"I played against a lot of great defensive linemen," Bishop said.

He was prodded to go through the list. Howie Long, Reggie White, Bruce Smith, Dan Hampton, Randy White, Kevin Fagan, Keith Millard, Carl Hairston. Gary "Big Hands" Johnson, Fred Dean. Louie Kelcher, Bill Maas, Art Still, Mike Bell. Reggie Kinlaw, Lyle Alzado, Bill Pickel, Sean Jones, Greg Townsend, Bob Golic, John Matuszak, Charles Mann, Dexter Manley, Jim Burt, George Martin, Leonard Marshall.

Imagine knocking shoulder pads and helmets with that group of Hall of Famers and Pro Bowlers week in and week out.

The 1986 season may have been Bishop's best season professionally—his first Pro Bowl and the Broncos' first Super Bowl appearance of the Elway era—but it was also one of his most difficult years, personally.

He lost both of his parents that year, two months apart.

"That's when all my hair went gray and started falling out," Bishop said. "John really helped me through that."

Bishop's teammates had the same affection for him as he had for Elway.

"I'll tell you what, on the field? You talk about the enforcer, that was Bish," Watson said. "I remember one time I was supposed to crack back on Clay Matthews. The older Clay Matthews. And I was going up to him and he turned his back at the last minute and I hit his back and he turned around like he was going to whack me. And then I remember him disappearing and rolling up on their sideline because Bish had come rolling through and just pounded him. Bish was the enforcer."

"Yeah, I took up for my teammates," Bishop said. "But I wasn't dirty. I didn't talk [crap]. I wasn't everybody's buddy. After a game, if I saw you and I knew you, I'd shake the guy's hand and say, How you doing? But I didn't go around glad-handing before and doing all that kind of [stuff]."

After the Broncos reached their third Super Bowl in four years, Bishop knew his body couldn't hold up anymore. Not for football, anyway. But chasing down drug lords as a field agent for the Drug Enforcement Administration? Bishop wasn't about to sit still.

His father's influence was a major factor in Bishop post-playing career. Which started on Monday nights and Tuesday days *during* his playing career.

"Back then, we had to do three community appearances a year," Bishop said. "You could do appearances to make money, but you had to do three freebies for Colorado groups. So they'd come to you and say this school wants somebody, this YMCA, whatever."

Bishop loved volunteering, especially if it meant speaking to groups. His teammates knew it, too.

"If a teammate didn't feel like doing it, it was, 'Hey, Bish, can you take my YMCA?' 'Yeah.' As long as they checked it off, you were good," Bishop said. "Everybody knew I liked talking to kids, so I got a whole bunch of them.

"The guys in our security, Dave Abrams, they were Denver SWAT guys, and off-seasons that's who I hung out with. I'd go to barbecues and I'd go ride with them. Tuesdays was a day off. So Monday nights I'd go ride around with them. When I started to do [public] speaking, I'd take one of them with me.

"Sometimes, they'd insist on paying you. I'd say write the check to one of the security guys. They'd get 50 bucks, 100 bucks from a school, whatever it was."

His interest in fighting drugs stemmed from Dad.

"When I was growing up, he used to tell me, 'Son, do whatever you want to do, just don't do drugs,'" Bishop said. "That was a big thing. And then when he got sick and passed away, that was a motivational thing for me. What can I do? DEA."

Bishop started speaking for, and to, DEA groups. Bishop developed an "in" with the drug agency.

"And then when I left football, I was either going to go into coaching or go into law enforcement," he said. "If I went into law enforcement I wanted to be federal. If it was going to be federal, I wanted it to be DEA. Because of my dad. Don't do dope. And the other thing was, get your degree."

To become a DEA agent, a four-year degree was required. And because he'd left his final semester at Baylor to go play for the Broncos, Bishop was a few classes short of his diploma.

"I can't remember if it was 12 or 14 hours needed to graduate when I was drafted and left Baylor," Bishop said. "Ten years later that turned to 27 hours, because a lot of that [stuff] didn't count anymore."

The Monday after the Broncos got drubbed by the San Francisco 49ers in the Super Bowl in New Orleans, Bishop was sitting in class at Baylor University. What a sight he must have been.

"I had to pay for it, but I did the spring semester and then the first session of summer school, and I was able to graduate," Bishop said. "Got in the 27 hours, BS in education. I wish I'd applied myself when I was a kid like I did when I was 33. I was like, [shoot], this is easy. And all the classes I needed to graduate were the hardest classes I had in college. Because I put them off while I was playing.

"At Baylor, religion, which is a required course, was the most flunked course. And I had the hardest professor, Dr. Christian. Ironic name. She was the hardest teacher of religion. And that's who I got.

"But I never missed a class. I sat right in front of the class. This old guy, I was 32, 33 years old, sitting in the front of the class. Had a blast."

He stayed in good physical condition so he could pass the rigorous DEA training program. He became a street agent out of the Dallas branch for eight and a half years, then became a supervisor and manager. He was involved in some major drug busts, from Newark to Los Angeles.

His specialty was wiretap. He pioneered a bunch of wiretap methods that are still used by the DEA today.

A few years ago, Bishop retired from his second career and started a third: as vice president of security for the Broncos. On game days, his assignment is Elway.

KEITH BISHOP STATS

YRS	G
10	129

41
STEVE WATSON
Receiver, 1979–87

It was the holiday break of Steve Watson's senior year at Temple and he was on the Gulf Coast side of Florida, hanging out with his college buddies.

Why wouldn't he be?

His college career at Temple had finished up three weeks earlier, and Watson was going to have one more big time before he would have to get on with life. Football was still a hope, but far from a guarantee.

Unexpectedly, and not for the first time, his Temple football coach would issue an order that spoiled his fun. That coach, Wayne Hardin, has since been inducted into the College Football Hall of Fame. Prior to Temple, Hardin coached at Navy where he was a major influence on an assistant coach's kid named Bill Belichick, and helped Joe Bellino and Roger Staubach win Heismans.

After guiding the senior Watson and the Temple Owls to a 7-3-1 record in 1978, Hardin was helping Maryland's Jerry Claiborne coach the East All Star college squad for the East–West Shrine Game that would be played January 6, 1979, at Stanford Stadium.

"Jerry Butler, the wide receiver from Clemson, I think he wound up as the number-5 pick [in the 1979 draft], he couldn't play in the game, and my coach calls me, he finds me in Florida," Watson said. "I mean, we were having a party time down there. And he said, 'I'm here in the East–West Shrine Game, one of the guys didn't show up, I got you his spot. Get here fast.' Those were his words."

One does not get from Punta Gorda, Florida, to Palo Alto, California, very fast but Watson got there. His equipment, however, had no chance. Not with the Temple campus locked up for Christmas break. The next problem Watson encountered had to do with his atypical football frame, at 6-foot-4, 190 pounds. Forced to borrow equipment from a community college where the East team was practicing, Watson wound up with a mismatched look that would not have passed today's game-day uniform inspection.

"My helmet was too small, my shoulder pads were too big," Watson recalled in October of 2016. "It was a comedy of errors, but it was fun."

He not only took Butler's spot on the team, he also took his bed in the dorm room shared by highly touted Clemson quarterback Steve Fuller.

"You can imagine at an All Star game like that where scouts have contact with you," Watson said. "The phone rang, like, every minute for Steve Fuller. I'd pick the phone up and say, 'Hello, this is Steve. . . . Oh, that Steve.' I quickly became his answering service."

Watson was happy to play a subservient role. He knew one guy with the right connection was the only reason why he was getting the experience.

"Was I deserving of playing in the East–West game?" he said. "Probably not. I wasn't anywhere in line across the country as far as being the number-1, -2, -3, or -30 receiver. But I think the only reason anybody in the NFL showed any interest in me was because I was able to play in the East–West Shrine Classic."

Yes and no. Watson had a nondescript game. Everybody had a nondescript performance next to a Michigan running back named Russell Davis, who stole the show with 200 rushing yards and six touchdowns in a 56–17 East rout.

But the East–West game was a first step that led to a second step that led to Watson joining the Denver Broncos. Not as a draft pick, mind you. But as an undrafted invitee.

"I remember asking Fran Polsfoot, my receivers coach in Denver," Watson said during an interview in the fall of 2016. "My first year after I made the team, I said, 'Hey, Coach Polsfoot, what did you think of me in the East–West Shrine Game?' Because I had always kind of wondered. He goes, 'Stevie, you stunk the joint up. You were so bad you couldn't catch a cold.' He said, 'You were falling all over yourself. I thought you had something wrong with you.'"

By now, you should have a pretty good idea of Watson's pleasant, down-to-earth, aw-shucks demeanor. Continuing on with his Polsfoot conversation that wasn't going very well.

"And I said, 'Well, how did I make it here?' And he said, 'Babe Parilli.' He said, 'Babe Parilli stood up on the table for you, and none of us could figure out why.'"

Parilli was a former American Football League All Star quarterback with the Boston Patriots who in 1979 was the Broncos quarterbacks coach. After the Shrine Game, he went back to Temple to work out Watson.

It was raining, so Parilli had Watson run a couple 40s in a hallway, then had him run routes on a basketball court. Watson could run. At St. Mark's

High School in Newark, Delaware, Watson long-jumped 22 feet, 4 inches, and triple-jumped 43 feet, 6 inches. He once participated in a triangular track meet at Temple, finishing fourth in the triple jump.

Those were the pre-combine days, but Watson had the resourcefulness to train with Edwin Roberts, a sprint coach at Temple, who won bronze medals in the 200 meters and 4-by-400-meter relay for Trinidad in the 1964 Olympics.

With Roberts's help, Watson became faster than he looked.

"And Fran says to me, 'Babe came back after working you out and said, He's different.'"

He was different all right. Thanks to his track background, Watson ran a 4.5-second, 40-yard dash in the Broncos rookie camp in May, the fastest among the Broncos' 38 undrafted rookies and first-year players—a class that included the likes of linebacker Jim Ryan, offensive tackle Dave Studdard, and a Clemson nose tackle named Rich Tuten.

Ten years later, Ryan, Studdard, and Watson held a joint farewell press conference after they failed to make the Broncos' 1989 opening-day roster. Tuten never made his first cut, but he must have made a strong impression, as he later became the Broncos strength and conditioning coach for 17 years.

Watson made an immediate impression, and not only because of his surprising speed. It was while catching a seam route on a pass thrown by Craig Morton in his rookie training camp of 1979 that Broncos coach Red Miller, marveling at his young receiver's slender build, started calling Watson, "Blade."

"When he was a rookie and Fran Polsfoot was the receivers coach, I'd be throwing to Steve and I'd see him run and see how tall he was—it was an anomaly then; you didn't see a lot of tall receivers like him," Morton said. "Haven was pretty tall, but Steve was a little taller—and I said to Fran, You cannot cut this guy. He's going to be a great player. You've got to keep him.

"Of course, Steve worked to become what he was, and it was the end of my career, but it was certainly a lot of fun because he made some great plays consistently."

After catching 6 passes in his rookie year of 1979 and again in 1980, Watson exploded to have an All Pro season in 1981 when he led the NFL with 13 receiving touchdowns, and ranked third with 1,244 receiving yards, all off 60 catches.

Watson had made the incredible journey from underdog to top dog.

"I never would have seen the field. It was opening game of the season at Mile High against the Raiders," Watson said. "Rick Upchurch had a nice return by the sideline, but got hurt.

"There wasn't any choice. Dan Reeves turns around, and I remember him looking over one shoulder and over the other shoulder. And then [he looked at me] and I could hear with his voice of disappointment and disgust, 'Get in there.'"

He had one catch for 28 yards in the Broncos' season-opening win against Oakland—Watson was always making his catches count—and 2 catches for 36 yards in a loss at Seattle. And then came the moment when Watson arrived.

The moment occurred with back-to-back games for the ages in weeks 3 and 4.

In a 28–10 win against the Baltimore Colts, Watson had 7 catches for 143 yards and 3 touchdowns. He followed that up the next week with 8 catches for 178 yards and 2 touchdowns in a 42–24 win against the San Diego Chargers.

His two-game totals: 15 catches, 321 yards, 5 touchdowns, 2 wins.

"Craig would be in the huddle and he would just say, 'Hey, I'm coming up,'" Watson said.

Meaning, Morton was throwing a jump ball of sorts and letting Watson outmaneuver the defensive back. It was Watson's forte, playing the lofted pass better than the defensive back, and having the sticky fingers to finish.

All receivers work on "high pointing" the ball now. Watson was one of the first to master it.

"No question," Morton said.

Watson's stellar 1981 season, in which he averaged a remarkable 20.7 yards per catch, started a prolific five-year run in which his 5,017 receiving yards were the league's third-most in that span. Only future Hall of Famers James Lofton (5,804 yards) and Steve Largent (5,242) had more.

Among the receivers who Watson outproduced from 1981–85 were future Hall of Famers Art Monk (4,685 yards) and John Stallworth (3,970).

"What made him great is if you threw the ball up to him, he's coming down with it," said Broncos cornerback and safety Steve Foley. "One thing I remembered about Fred Biletnikoff, he wasn't fast at all. But he knew how to get open. He'd get open in the seams and he would never drop a pass. Steve, you could count on him. He was money. I don't remember seeing Steve drop a pass."

Morton was Watson's quarterback in 1981, Steve DeBerg and Morton during the strike season of 1982, DeBerg and a rookie named John Elway in 1983, and Elway from 1984–87.

Watson added 45 catches for 699 yards in 1986—plus another 6 catches for 130 yards in three postseason games—but then injuries and the Three Amigos started to move him to the sidelines. In the infamous replacement player season of 1987, Watson was one player who crossed the picket lines—almost all of them did eventually, including the likes of Joe Montana, Randy White, Mark Gastineau, Doug Flutie, and Steve Largent.

Watson didn't run into any kind of interference, but he did suffer six broken ribs and a punctured lung in a replacement game against Oakland.

"The reason I went back in was because I had a fully guaranteed contract from Pat Bowlen," Watson said of the Broncos owner. "It was unusual. You didn't get guarantees like that, not in that day. But it was a personal guarantee from Pat. So I had this great contract, although most of my numbers were probably what the rookies get as a minimum today.

"I crossed the line because, first of all, I didn't really believe what we were arguing about. But first and foremost was that Pat Bowlen had given me a personal guarantee. Well, a man does that for you, you don't turn your back on him."

Watson had just 11 catches for 167 yards in 1987, and, little did he know at the time, he had made the final catches of his career. In the 1988 preseason opener against the Los Angeles Rams in Anaheim, Watson ran a seam route. Backup quarterback Gary Kubiak threw the ball a tad high and Watson was high-lowed. He suffered a fractured neck vertebra that ended his final season before it started.

Watson went to training camp in 1989, but so did his heir apparent, Michael Young. The day after the Broncos' final cuts, Watson, Ryan, and Studdard held their joint press gathering. Watson was the only one who wore a suit and tie. They all were hoping to play one more year with another team, but it turned out to be a retirement press conference for all three of them.

Watson retired as the Broncos second-leading receiver to Lionel Taylor with 353 catches (Watson now ranks eighth) and 6,112 yards (now sixth). His career 17.3 yards per catch remains second to Haven Moses's 18.0 among Broncos with at least 100 catches.

The fans liked Watson and he gave back to the community. His annual golf tournament in Breckenridge raised money for numerous children's charities. He and his wife Pam were married in August 1985, and together they put in countless hours for abused and neglected children, the American Cancer Foundation, and other causes.

Steve and Pam raised three children together—Brittany, Stephen Jr., and Rachel—in the Denver area. Steve Jr. played for Mullen High School and the University of Michigan. He went there as a tight end for Lloyd Carr. Rich Rodriguez moved him to defense. Brady Hoke moved the younger Watson back to offense. He wound up playing five positions for the Wolverines.

When Steve Sr. was asked about his most vivid memories from his 10-year career with the Broncos, he first mentioned "The Drive" game, and the realization that the team was going to the Super Bowl. There are die-hard Broncos fans who can recite every play of "The Drive." The less obsessed may not realize that the 98-yard march only tied the game, 20–20.

In overtime, Elway completed a third-and-12 pass to Watson for 28 yards that moved the ball from the 50 to the Cleveland 22. Four plays later, Rich Karlis kicked a 33-yard field goal for the AFC Championship.

"And the other [memory] was, we were over at the Mart, the intern came over and banged on the doors and got us in the lobby at the Mart to walk over to the practice field," Watson said of the old Broncos practice facility. "They lined us up that day. We had a six-week camp or something, and I just remember lining us up over there at the Merchandise Mart and we walked single file down the street to the practice facility, which was only about a block away. And we walked down there and the door was open and [scout and future general manager] John Beake and [director of player personnel] Carroll Hardy were standing there inside the doorway, and I just remember both of them reaching their hands out, saying, 'Welcome to the NFL.'"

An undrafted underdog would have his run as top dog.

STEVE WATSON STATS

YRS	G	REC	Y	Y/R	TD
9	126	353	6,112	17.3	36

42

ELVIS DUMERVIL

Linebacker / Defensive End, 2006–12

Clearly, Wikipedia had never met Elvis Dumervil as he was bursting into NFL stardom in 2009.

The Internet encyclopedia that is otherwise the world's most popular reference tool knew enough about Dumervil to deem him worthy of profile, but it couldn't believe his given middle name was "Kool." His dad, a US Marine for 13 years, gave Elvis his "Kool" middle name at birth. Wikipedia, though, listed Dumervil's middle name as "Cornelius."

Wikipedia corrected the error once it became aware, but the mistake never would have happened had its author met its subject. For Elvis Dumervil is no Cornelius. Elvis Dumervil is Kool.

"He's such a genuine guy," said Dumervil's former teammate, Champ Bailey. "Honest. Real laid-back. And he's very professional. He's come a long way from where he grew up."

Maria Noel (Dumervil) and Frank Gachelin both migrated from Haiti, settling in Miami's Little Haiti neighborhood. Although they separated when Elvis was three, they still raised 10 kids, with mom staying in a tiny triplex in Little Haiti, and dad moving to the Opa-locka neighborhood of Miami.

For Dumervil to make our top-50 Broncos list despite his bizarre, acrimonious, and unnecessary departure from the team following the 2012 season is testament to the strength of his play during his six active seasons in Denver.

Still, today, there is a tinge of bitterness within Dumervil about the circumstances leading up to a tardy fax exchange that caused his exit. It began when the Broncos asked him to take a pay cut from the $14 million he was supposed to draw for the 2013 season. After weeks of contentious negotiations, there was an oral agreement 40 minutes before the free-agent deadline on a reduced $8 million salary for the 2013 season—not enough time, apparently, for the two sides to fax over signed contracts.

When the fax carrying Dumervil's signature didn't arrive as the deadline ticked down, he was released. Although the Broncos tried to re-sign him, the damage was done, and he signed with Baltimore.

Happy as a Baltimore Raven, where he had 32.5 sacks through his first three seasons, Dumervil was asked in July 2016 about his most vivid memories as a Bronco.

"Nothing positive, to be honest," said Dumervil, who signed up to play for the San Francisco 49ers in 2017. "Losing that playoff game [to Baltimore in the second round to finish the 2012 season], that was awful. And then the follow-up with the contract situation."

Dumervil deserves his place on this top-50 list, though, for several reasons. One, in Denver's long lineage of defensive standouts, he is the only player in franchise history to have led the NFL in sacks during a single season, which he did, with 17.0 in 2009.

Two, despite only playing six seasons in Denver, Dumervil ranks seventh on the team, with 63.5 sacks. His 10.6 sacks per season was better than the six pass rushers ahead of him on the Broncos' all-time sack list. And his 20 multi-sack games are tied for the most in team history with Simon Fletcher, who is the overall franchise leader in sacks, with 97.5.

And three, Dumervil was named to three Pro Bowls in his six seasons. Only 16 Broncos were named to more Pro Bowls—John Elway (9), Champ Bailey (8), Steve Atwater (8), Randy Gradishar (7), Shannon Sharpe (7), Karl Mecklenburg (6), Dennis Smith (6), Louis Wright (5), Tom Nalen (5), Al Wilson (5), Von Miller (5), Ryan Clady (4), John Lynch (4), Riley Odoms (4), Rick Upchurch (4)—or AFL All Star teams—Goose Gonsoulin (5).

"What I am thankful for is that Mike Shanahan drafted me," Dumervil said. "Mike Shanahan gave me a chance to play defensive end in this league. Josh McDaniels came in and gave me a chance to be a linebacker.

"There were always obstacles. There was always a first rounder I had to prove worthy of beating out. Jarvis Moss and Robert Ayers."

Neither Moss nor Ayers could replace Dumervil. Another first-round pass rusher, Von Miller, became Dumervil's pass-rushing sidekick in 2011–12.

Dumervil wasn't as highly regarded coming out of college. Although he earned the Bronko Nagurski Award as the NCAA's defensive player of the year in his senior season at Louisville—when he posted a remarkable 20 sacks and college-record 10 forced fumbles—he wasn't selected until the Broncos' second selection in the fourth round of the 2006 NFL Draft.

Why? He was considered undersized as a pass rusher at 5-foot-11, 248 pounds. (Wide receiver Brandon Marshall was the Broncos' first, fourth-round pick in 2006. With returner/receiver Domenik Hixon becoming the third of the Broncos' selections in that round, Denver arguably had the best single fourth round in NFL Draft history.)

Never mind that Dumervil's relatively short stature included uniquely long arms that helped him gain leverage on lumbering offensive tackles.

"Physically, it's the leverage thing, but I think the biggest thing about Elvis is he plays the game with a little bit of a chip on his shoulder," Mike Nolan, Dumervil's defensive coordinator, said during his league-leading 17.0-sack season in 2009. "He is a little shorter and people bring it to his attention, including me, but he overcomes it. He's very competitive."

It was the 3-4 defensive system implemented by Nolan, first-year head coach Josh McDaniels, and linebackers coach Don "Wink" Martindale in 2009 that transformed Dumervil from a "third down" pass rusher to one who made the Pro Bowl three consecutive seasons, in 2009, 2011, and 2012. (Dumervil suffered a torn pectoral muscle in training camp of 2010 and missed the entire season.)

The new defensive alignment moved Dumervil from a 4-3 defensive end who rushed from a three-point stance, to a 3-4 outside linebacker who took off from the standing position.

"They drafted Robert Ayers to be the 3-4 edge rusher going into my contract year [of 2009]," Dumervil said. "They told me to figure it out and get in there somewhere. I remember [inside linebacker] Andra Davis was an integral part of that season. He was a motivator for me. He sat next to me in the meeting room. Andra Davis was a really cool teammate."

Known for his "bull-rush" technique, Dumervil had a second 17.0-sack season as an outside linebacker for Baltimore in 2014. His 99.0 career sacks through 11 seasons rank 32nd on the NFL's all-time list. Mario Williams, who as the No. 1 overall selection in 2006 and was drafted 125 spots ahead of Dumervil, is tied at No. 34 with Fletcher with 97.5 sacks.

The breakout game in Dumervil's career came in week 2 of the 2009 season, when he had four sacks in a 27–6 home win against the Cleveland Browns. Dumervil beat perennial All Pro left tackle Joe Thomas for one sack and right tackle John St. Clair for the other three.

Despite his sour ending, Dumervil did enjoy Denver during his playing days there.

"The fans there were awesome," Dumervil said. "It was always a pleasure playing in that stadium. It's one of the top environments to play in.

I had great teammates. Loved my teammates. Champ. Brandon Marshall. Von. Chris Harris, Derek Wolfe. Nate Jackson. Robert Ayers was cool, too." Just not as Kool as Elvis.

ELVIS DUMERVIL STATS

YRS	G	S	FF	TCK
7	91	63.5	21	264

43

GENE MINGO

Halfback / Kicker, 1960–64

Gene Mingo had it all figured out.

He had just scored 123 points to lead the American Football League in scoring in its inaugural season of 1960, a feat that said something when another two-way player—quarterback/kicker George Blanda of the scoreboard-lighting Houston Oilers—was the league's biggest star.

Those 123 points by Mingo came in the most resourceful of ways. There were six touchdowns—four rushing, one receiving, and one on a 76-yard punt return in the first AFL game ever played—a league-leading 18 field goals, and 33 extra points.

After the season, historians noted that Mingo was the first black field-goal kicker in NFL–AFL history.

"I love being able to say that I was the first black kicker in the NFL," Mingo said.

Mingo naturally figured he deserved a raise. He had his pitch prepared as he walked into team owner Calvin Kunz's office.

"I made $6,500 that first year," Mingo said in July 2016. "When I went in to try to negotiate my contract after leading the league in scoring, all they did in that office—as Von Miller said, 'They have their tactics.' They throw everything that you did wrong at you. In my day, we didn't have agents to step forth on behalf of the players."

Even with inflation, Mingo's $6,500 in 1960 would be worth only $54,000 today. The Broncos' "tactics" couldn't stop Miller from getting a six-year deal worth an average of $19.083 million a year.

So Mingo took what he could get, which in those days was little more than his job back. In 1962, Mingo again led the AFL in scoring, this time with 137 points on a whopping 27 field goals that again led the league, 32 extra points and 4 rushing touchdowns.

"I'll tell you this: If Gene were playing now and had a placekicking coach, he'd have been one of the best kickers ever," said Lionel Taylor, a star

Broncos receiver in the 1960s. "He had a str-o-o-o-ng leg. But he didn't have special teams coaches like they have now. If Gene had a coach like everybody else has now, I don't know what he would have done. Because he could kick that ball."

Mingo also further demonstrated his versatility by throwing two touchdown passes—both in the same 1961 game, both to Taylor, and both going at least 50 yards. Mingo's 82-yard touchdown run against the Raiders in the following season of 1962 is still the longest scoring dash in Broncos history.

Think about that. Floyd Little. Terrell Davis. Sammy Winder. Clinton Portis. Mike Anderson. No Bronco has a longer touchdown run than Gene Mingo's 82-yard dash in 1962.

Through his first four seasons, Mingo's 375 points trailed only Boston's Gino Cappelletti (448) and Green Bay's Paul Hornung (396) among NFL–AFL scorers. Like Mingo, Cappelletti and Hornung were offensive receivers / runners who also kicked.

Mingo's stay in Denver was cut way too short when midway through the 1964 season, he and another black teammate, Willie West, were seen with two white women the night before a game in Oakland. This would hardly be considered scandalous today, but in those racially charged times, Kunz promptly traded Mingo to the Oakland Raiders.

Have foot, will travel, and Mingo was on his way to becoming an AFL–NFL journeyman. He wound up playing for Miami, Washington, and Pittsburgh before his AFL–NFL career ended after 11 seasons.

It took the perspective of history for Mingo's versatility as a player to become appreciated. Besides scoring six different ways (field goals, extra points, and touchdowns rushing, receiving, passing, and punt returns), Mingo also played some defensive back, covered his own onside kicks, and rushed to fill in at guard and tackle.

"One time Frank Tripucka looked down the line of scrimmage and saw me lining up at guard," Mingo said. "Somebody got hurt and came out and I was about the only one paying attention on the sideline. I weighed all of 200 pounds at the time. Frank said, 'Mingo, what are you doing lining up here?' I was the fool who would run in if I noticed we were about to take a 5-yard penalty [for not having enough men on the line]."

In all, Mingo rushed for 777 yards on 4.2 yards per carry and 8 touchdowns for the Broncos. He had another 47 catches for 399 yards and 3 touchdowns. He completed 6 of 18 passes for 200 yards and 2 touchdowns. There were 112 field goals with a 53-yarder. And there was the 76-yard punt return for a touchdown.

He was a man of firsts. The NFL's first black kicker. The AFL's first punt return for a touchdown that helped the Broncos win the first AFL game. If only Mingo had known he was making history as he was doing it.

"I didn't keep anything when I played," Mingo said. "I was just happy to be a pro football player. And loved doing whatever I did to please the fans. It was my life. It was a kid's dream. When you don't graduate high school or you don't go to college and you accomplish what I was able to accomplish, what more can you ask for?"

Perhaps, a spot in the Pro Football Hall of Fame in Canton? Maybe someday. At least, Mingo in 2014 joined returner/receiver Rick Upchurch as the 24th and 25th players inducted into the Broncos Ring of Fame.

"I remember we were practicing at the [Colorado] School of Mines," Mingo said, referring to the college campus in Golden where the Broncos held training camp in their early years. "And coach Frank Filchock yelled up to us, 'Hey, you guys, quit [messing] around.' And one of my teammates who was with me in the Navy yelled down, 'Hey, Mingo can kick.' The next thing you know, Filchock is yelling to Fred Posey [the team's trainer and equipment manager], 'Get that guy a kicking shoe!' That's how it all started."

Mingo's rise to professional football was too remarkable to start there in Golden, downwind from the Coors Brewing Co. Growing up in Akron, Ohio, there were periods when Mingo didn't attend elementary school. He didn't graduate from high school. He didn't attend college.

His football skills were honed while playing for the US Navy service team. There was a time in this country when service ball could rival the talent on the college football fields. Dick "Night Train" Lane came to the NFL in 1952 by way of the United States Army. Mingo's service team played against the likes of Rosey Grier, Sherman Plunkett, Lee Riley, and Eugene "Big Daddy" Lipscomb.

In his first AFL game—the AFL's first game—Mingo was the game's leading rusher, with 66 yards on just 8 carries in the Broncos' 13–10 win against the Boston Patriots.

It was a Friday night, September 9, 1960, at old Braves Field.

It wasn't televised, but there is a video from the vault that shows Mingo's 76-yard punt return down the right sideline that gave Denver a shocking, 13–3 lead early in the third quarter.

Shocking, because a month earlier, the Broncos had lost to the same Patriots, 43–6, in a preseason game. Back then, starters would play a full preseason game.

The Broncos lost all five preseason games in 1960, their first four by scores of 43–6, 31–14, 42–3, and 48–0—a combined score of 164–23. And that wasn't the worst of it.

"They were laughing at us because we had the vertical stripes [socks], the gold and brown and then the white and brown uniforms," Mingo said. "They just laughed at us."

After his football career, Mingo struggled with personal addiction demons, but he wound up kicking his habits and doing great work as an alcohol and drug counselor.

In October of 2014, Mingo became the fourth "original Bronco" to be elected into the Broncos Ring of Fame, joining Tripucka, Lionel Taylor, and safety Goose Gonsoulin.

"It means a lot to me," Mingo said. "The Broncos gave me a start. They gave me my chance, and I took advantage of it. As they say, I took it and ran with it. I did the best I could."

GENE MINGO STATS

YRS	G	C	Y	TD	REC	Y	TD	FG	PTS
5	59	185	777	8	47	399	3	72	408

44

TYRONE BRAXTON

Cornerback/Safety, 1987–93, 1995–99

It was the darnedest thing.

For most athletes, the end of their playing days arrives when their phone doesn't ring. Some might get a chance to say good-bye in the locker room with an exchange of handshakes. Some of the Broncos greats got sendoff press conferences, including John Elway, Peyton Manning, Champ Bailey, Randy Gradishar, Ed McCaffrey, and Jason Elam, to name a few.

Tyrone Braxton got an official day named in his honor as proclaimed by Denver mayor Wellington Webb.

"I'm so shocked," the guest of honor at "Tyrone Braxton Day" said during the ceremony.

Webb, it seems, had a soft spot for overachievers. There were 12 rounds and 335 players picked in the 1987 NFL Draft. Braxton was player No. 334.

He grew up in Madison, Wisconsin, in a family where two of his brothers wound up in prison from crimes related to drugs. Braxton was too small, at 5-foot-10, 180 pounds, coming out of tiny North Dakota State, to play safety. With a 4.7 time in the 40, he was too slow to play cornerback.

Yet, Braxton not only played 13 seasons in the NFL, 12 with the Broncos, but the city of Denver gave him his own day.

Braxton announced on Wednesday, December 29, 1999, that the final game of the Broncos' 6-9 season on Sunday, January 2, 2000, would be his last. He didn't start that game, as he'd been demoted to nickelback the week before, and the Broncos suffered a dreary 12–6 loss to San Diego at Mile High Stadium to finish 6-10.

But when starting cornerback Tory James came up with an interception, he presented the ball to Braxton on the sideline in an expression of gratitude for all the help the veteran had given the youngster. Broncos fans gave Braxton a standing ovation as he left the field.

And five days later, on January 7, 2000, Mayor Webb announced it was "Tyrone Braxton Day," in a ceremony in front of City Hall that included balloons, posters, flags, and short speeches by teammates, coaches, and owner Pat Bowlen.

"It's kind of weird," Braxton said, as he was accompanied by his wife and two children, 6-year-old daughter Chloe and 11-month-old son Tyrone Jr.

"He being so low in the draft and making it, and me being so low in the polls and getting elected, I kind of draw a parallel," Webb said at the ceremony. "Tyrone Braxton is a survivor."

In the early days of this project there were some drafts where Braxton was not among the 50 Greatest Broncos of All Time. There were various drafts where linebacker Bob Swenson, defensive lineman Bud McFadin, and offensive tackle Eldon Danenhauer were among the top 50. It wasn't easy leaving receiver Vance Johnson, guards Paul Howard and Mark Schlereth, and Ring of Fame kicker Jim Turner off the main list.

It also wasn't easy delineating between Braxton and Mike Harden, another longtime cornerback/safety who was finishing up his stay with the Broncos as "Chicken" was breaking in.

It was not the first time Braxton almost didn't make the cut. Nicknamed "Chicken" by his Broncos teammates because of his skinny legs, Braxton wound up starting at both cornerback and safety for so long, only four defensive players—Tom Jackson, Dennis Smith, Barney Chavous, and Billy Thompson—played more seasons with the Broncos than his 12.

His 34 interceptions are tied with none other than Champ Bailey for fourth on the team's all-time list. And that total doesn't include Braxton's three interceptions in 17 postseason games—numbers that rank second in the team record books in both categories. There was a first-quarter interception Braxton had of Green Bay's Brett Favre in the Broncos' Super Bowl XXXII upset. He then recovered a fumble in the Broncos' rout of Atlanta in Super Bowl XXXIII.

Snubbed annually by Pro Bowl voters, they finally couldn't ignore him in 1996 when Braxton tied for the NFL lead in interceptions, with nine.

"Tyrone was very intelligent," said Chavous, who was a Broncos defensive coach during the Braxton years. "And a personality that fit in with anybody. He was always around the ball. You look at him and would never think he could play football. And all he did was start in two Super Bowls."

He actually started in three Super Bowls, playing in four. It was playing on the Broncos' winning Super Bowl teams in 1997 and 1998 that helped separate Braxton from Harden.

"Chicken. I loved Chicken," said Broncos linebacker Bill Romanowski. "He's one of those guys, you don't realize how good he really was. Made a lot of plays for us. He was a playmaker, an unsung hero. He didn't get a lot of credit, but a great guy in the locker room. Great guy to have as a teammate, and a great player."

Braxton first started beating the odds in his youth. He said during the Super Bowl week leading into the 1989-season title game against San Francisco that at least seven of his high school friends either wound up dead, or in prison, because of drugs or other crimes. One of his brothers served a year in prison for assault and battery and drug possession. Another of Tyrone's brothers was given a 25-year prison term for armed robbery.

Braxton was able to negotiate past the transgressions of his brothers and friends to star in basketball, track, and football at James Madison Memorial High School. He was a two-time all-conference performer for NCAA Division II North Dakota State, where he barely got noticed by the Broncos. But noticed enough.

Braxton didn't have the stature or speed, yet his awareness brought him to the ball. He was in on 905 tackles in his 12 seasons, and 4 of his 34 interceptions were pick sixes.

Including his first one. In his very first NFL career start in the 1989 season opener, Braxton intercepted a pass from Kansas City quarterback Steve DeBerg and returned it 34 yards for a score.

No. 34 had gone 34.

Braxton's first task as a 12th-round draft pick was to make the team. He got a break when star cornerback Louis Wright surprisingly retired just before training camp. Braxton went full out on special teams his first two seasons, then started exhibiting an uncanny knack for the ball at cornerback.

When the Broncos pass defense ranked 27th in the 28-team NFL in 1993, Braxton became the scapegoat and was released. He signed with the Miami Dolphins, but he never started in his 16 games in 1994, and was released again.

The Broncos re-signed him, but only after ignoring the objections of new defensive coordinator Greg Robinson, and only after head coach Mike Shanahan thought Braxton had the instincts to play strong safety. Robinson admitted later that he thought Braxton was too small to play safety. In the second season of Braxton II, he tied the St. Louis Rams' Keith Lyle for the NFL's interception lead, with nine.

"An underrated player that just seemed to be where he needed to be and always made plays," Elam said. "He was a guy who was always smiling. You always saw him in a good mood. A fun guy to be around, guys wanted to be around him. A leader not because he was trying, but because he drew it out of people.

"And to see a guy that's not expected to do that much but to have the career he did and be a huge contributor in the Super Bowl, interceptions. Just a guy I'm so glad I got to play with."

As you can tell, Braxton's popularity blossomed not only from his instinctive play, but also from his infectious personality that included some honest, if not blunt, assessments. For instance, late in his final season of 1999, Braxton was on his way to having no interceptions, no forced fumbles, and no fumble recoveries. A turnover machine for most of his career, Braxton dried up.

He blamed the coaches, saying he wasn't put in position to utilize his ball-hawking instincts. Two weeks later, Braxton was benched, and after a heart-to-heart talk with Coach Shanahan, the player knew the real reason for his diminished play: His heart wasn't in it.

Thus, his decision to retire late in the Broncos' difficult season of 1999.

"I always thought I'd be one of those guys you'd have to drag off the field," Braxton said after his final game. "But I knew it was time. It was just the way I was going about the game. I wasn't hustling out on the field. I wasn't getting fired up. I wasn't getting any butterflies before a game. I remember Dan Reeves used to tell me when I was younger, 'Look, if you can't get butterflies before a game, you know it's time to stop and shut it down.' And I just couldn't get them."

Although "Tyrone Braxton Day" was a glorious sendoff to retirement, Braxton's post-playing days weren't always easy. In 2007 he pled guilty to cocaine and marijuana possession stemming from his arrest on December 2, 2006. He received a two-year deferred sentence, but Braxton turned his embarrassing moment into a positive, becoming a Denver court drug and alcohol caseworker. In many ways, Braxton's recovery justified Mayor Webb's decision to give the popular defensive back his day.

Tyrone Braxton was, and remains, a survivor.

TYRONE BRAXTON STATS

YRS	G	I	Y	TCK
12	165	34	614	889

45

FRANK TRIPUCKA

Quarterback, 1960–63

Peyton Manning was about to move into his retirement press conference at the Denver Broncos headquarters, but before he did, he took a seat across from Joe Ellis.

During the exit interview in the office of the Denver Broncos president and chief executive officer, Ellis informed Manning that there were plans to display the team's three retired numbers inside the stadium for the first time.

As part of that celebration, Ellis told Manning the team would recognize the quarterback for his accomplishments while wearing one of those retired numbers.

The Broncos honored their retired numbers during their game on September 18, 2016, against the Indianapolis Colts. There was number "7" for John Elway, number "44" for Floyd Little, and—the first number ever retired by the organization—number "18" for Frank Tripucka.

Banners of those three numbers were placed to the left of the South Stands scoreboard. Elway and Little were there as their numbers were officially displayed in immortality.

And on the 18th of September, there were 18 members of the Tripucka family representing Frank, who had died three years earlier, and his wife Randy, who would soon turn 89 and could not make the trip.

"It could have been 15 of us, it could have been 25, or whatever," said Kelly Tripucka, the former Notre Dame and NBA star, and second youngest of Frank and Randy's seven children. "We said, 18? Can you believe it? We have no idea how that happened."

Manning was in the stadium, too. Along with Tripucka's number "18" banner, the Broncos included the name of Manning, with the mention that he wore this number during the 2012–15 seasons.

"I thought it was a great idea," T. K. Tripucka, the fifth of Frank Tripucka's seven children, said of including Manning with his father's number

256

"18." "The Broncos organization has always been great to my dad. I thought it was a great idea. The family's thrilled about it."

"It was always retired; Peyton just borrowed it," Kelly said. "We're thrilled Peyton wore the number. We're thrilled he was successful. We're thrilled the Broncos won the Super Bowl, and he should certainly have a mention because he's one of the greatest quarterbacks to ever play the game.

"And the fact he wore my father's number, it kind of brought back memories and gave him some life. No problem whatsoever that he's mentioned with this number."

In fact, Frank Tripucka—the original Broncos quarterback in 1960, and the first in professional history to throw for 3,000 yards in a season—likely would have gone one more step and welcomed the sharing of the retired number "18" in Manning's honor, as well—as the New York Yankees did in retiring number "8" for both Yogi Berra and Bill Dickey.

"If you knew my dad, he didn't live for honors," T. K. Tripucka said. "I always laughed, if someone called him and said, 'Frank, you're going into Canton.' He'd say, 'Oh, okay. Do I have to be there?'"

"When they retired my father's number, he didn't think much of it," said Mark, the third-oldest Tripucka child, who was nine when his dad played in the Broncos' inaugural season of 1960. "He said, 'Thank you.' It was back in 1966. After that was over—50 years goes by, and Peyton calls, and Dad said, 'Sure, you can have the number.'"

So how did Frank Tripucka become one of three Broncos to have his number retired, despite less-than-stellar stats?

In the Broncos' infancy, Bob Howsam, the team's original owner, believed the credibility Tripucka brought to Denver's franchise was immeasurable.

"Mr. Howsam said to Frank, 'What can I do for you?'" Randy Tripucka, Frank's wife, said in 2012. "He said, 'You helped keep this franchise going. You didn't drop out like other people.' Frank said, 'Nothing, I'm fine.' And then one day, Mr. Howsam said to him: 'I'd like to retire your number.' So it was a different situation than it was for Floyd Little, say. So Frank was thrilled with the honor, but he'd be thrilled the other way, also."

Manning was the most sought-after, free-agent player in NFL history when the Broncos signed him in March 2012. Manning had worn the number "18" with the Indy Colts for 14 years, and before his introductory press conference in Denver, he called Frank Tripucka at his New Jersey residence.

During the conversation, Tripucka encouraged Manning to wear the number "18."

"My father knew how great Peyton Manning had been for the league," Kelly said. "His family—I think my mom has a very high regard for Mr. and Mrs. [Archie] Manning and their kids, and how successful they've been. I think it reminded my mom of her kids, even though we have seven of us."

Frank Tripucka died September 12, 2013, five days after Manning threw 7 touchdown passes in the season opener, on his way to an NFL single-season record of 55 touchdown passes.

Three days after Frank died, the Broncos were playing their second game of the 2013 season against the New York Giants in the Meadowlands. The day before the game, Manning visited with the Tripucka clan at the team hotel.

"As a guy who's older than him and was a professional athlete, I think Peyton's tremendous," Kelly said. "He couldn't have been more of a gentleman in how he handled it."

Only two players ever wore the number "18" for the Broncos. No other player will wear it again.

It was a tricky situation for the Broncos, but credit Ellis with a creative solution. Tripucka's number "18" was retired without ceremony in the 1960s.

"Obviously, today with the media, everything is so much more pronounced and blown up," T.K. said. "Back then, they said we'll retire your number, and there's a picture of him in the newspaper next to a jersey on a hanger. That was it."

Compared to some other sports franchises, the Broncos are judicious in retiring numbers. Elway and Little were franchise players; both are in the Pro Football Hall of Fame. They were no-brainers.

Tripucka was also a rare case. He only played three full seasons for the Broncos, and two games into a fourth season of 1963 when he retired.

He threw 51 touchdown passes against 85 interceptions for the Broncos. But what modern football fans may not realize is in the early American Football League days of the 1960s, the thinking was that if a quarterback didn't throw two interceptions a game, he wasn't aggressive enough with his passes.

Also, quarterbacks were not allowed to throw the ball away. To chuck it out of bounds—whether in the pocket or out—was a 15-yard penalty.

A quarterback had to drill it in there—or else. Joe Namath, George Blanda, Jack Kemp, and John Hadl were all AFL star quarterbacks who threw more interceptions than touchdowns in their careers.

It was Broncos general manager Dean Griffing and owners Robert Howsam and Gerald Phipps who wanted to show their appreciation to Tripucka for lifting the franchise from possible embarrassment to one that was usually competitive each week, if not always victorious.

"They didn't understand back in 1960—it wasn't how good he was, the Broncos didn't have anything," Mark said. "He gave them a little bit of respectability."

Frank Tripucka started his career playing for the NFL Detroit Lions in 1949, then the Chicago Cardinals (now the Arizona Cardinals) in the early 1950s, and then the rest of the decade in the Canadian Football League.

Griffing had also worked previously in the CFL as a coach and scout, and he recruited Tripucka to the Broncos—as a coach.

But after a few practices, it was obvious the Broncos—who lost their first four preseason games by scores of 43–6, 31–14, 42–3, and 48–0—were a disaster at quarterback.

"They said, 'What do you want [in salary],'" Kelly said. "He said, 'Double.' They said, 'You've got it.' And he said, 'Damn, I should have said, 'triple.' That was my father."

Tripucka quarterbacked the Broncos in their fifth and final preseason game, and they lost to the Los Angeles Chargers, 36–30. Tripucka then led the Broncos to wins in their first two AFL games. He threw the first touchdown pass in AFL history.

Perhaps, Frank Tripucka's greatest statistical accomplishment was becoming the first quarterback in professional football history to throw for 3,000 yards in a season. He did so in 1960, the Broncos' first season.

Baltimore's Johnny Unitas and Buffalo's Jack Kemp also finished with more than 3,000 passing yards in 1960—but they crossed the milestone in their final games on Sunday, December 18. Tripucka and the Broncos played their final game on Saturday, December 17.

Thus, Tripucka was the first quarterback in history to surpass 3,000 yards.

"Believe me, that he played those three and a half years was amazing, because he was old," Mark Tripucka said. "He didn't really want to come back and play quarterback. The head coach talked him into it, Frank Filchock."

The beauty of Manning wearing Tripucka's number? With many of the old greats, their names go up in the stadium facade and they are soon forgotten, not talked about for years.

When Manning accepted the number "18," it brought Tripucka's legacy back to life.

"No doubt. I can't tell you how many times in the last couple of years, even people I knew would tell me, 'I did not realize your dad played for the Denver Broncos,'" T.K. said. "'I didn't know his number was retired.' I get comments like that all the time."

The retired number ceremony was a proud moment for Tripucka's children—twins Heather and Tracy are the oldest, followed by Mark, Todd, T.K., Kelly, and Chris. They range in age from 66 to 53. The Broncos flew them out for their dad's big day.

Chris had the most difficult challenge attending the ceremony. His son, Shane Tripucka, Frank's grandson, punted for Texas A&M the day before at Auburn. Chris went to that game in Auburn before he hurried to Denver in time for the retired number ceremony on Sunday afternoon.

"My dad would probably think you're making a big deal out of nothing," Kelly said. "I don't want to speak for him—in fact, it was three years ago today [September 12, 2013] that he passed away—but my dad would think you're fussing over him, and he didn't think he was that big of a star. He loved Denver. Absolutely loved everything about it.

"I'm thrilled with how Pat Bowlen and his family treated him and my mother. Included him in everything.

"But it was just a number to him—he holds it in high regard, but this was Peyton Manning, he wanted to borrow it. Okay, no problem. The last thing he told him was, 'Wear the number in good health, and do one favor for me: Go win a Super Bowl.' And look what happened."

FRANK TRIPUCKA STATS

YRS	G	A	C	PCT	Y	TD	I	RTG	W-L
4	44	1,277	662	51.8	7,676	51	85	55.9	13-26-1

46

JOHN LYNCH

Safety, 2004–07

In some ways, John Lynch was to the Denver Broncos defense what Peyton Manning was to their offense.

In some ways? Make that in many ways.

Like Manning, Lynch was a perennial Pro Bowler who played for more than a decade with the team that drafted him—Manning, with the Indianapolis Colts for 13 seasons; Lynch, with the Tampa Bay Buccaneers for 11.

"May be the third-best safety to ever play the game, behind Jack Tatum and Ronnie Lott, in my opinion," said Hall of Fame defensive tackle Warren Sapp, who was Lynch's teammate in Tampa. "There was no play he couldn't make and no play where he wouldn't stick his nose in."

Like Manning, Lynch was let go by his original team essentially because of fears caused by a serious neck injury that required surgery.

Like Manning, Lynch chose the Broncos for the second chapter in his career. Like Manning, Lynch proved his original team wrong by having a highly successful four-year run with the Broncos.

In fact, in one way, Lynch did a little better than Manning. Manning went to three Pro Bowls in his four years with the Broncos. Lynch went four for four.

"John Lynch was fearsome," said Champ Bailey, the former star cornerback whose 10 years in Denver included Lynch's term from 2004–07 in the Broncos' secondary. "You come across that middle, he would lay you out back in the day when you were allowed to. That's scary in itself.

"Then he was a leader. He prepared well. Being in the meeting rooms with him and how much he loved the games. How do I put this? John Lynch off the field, nice, good guy, family man. On the field? A nightmare. Totally different person. The only guy I saw who came close to being that way was Brian Dawkins. Because of the way they were on and off the field."

Lynch was officially inducted into the Broncos Ring of Fame on October 24, 2016, in a ceremony at Sports Authority Field at Mile High, where he joined kicker Jason Elam and pass-rushing outside linebacker Simon Fletcher in the class of 2016.

After 11 seasons and 5 Pro Bowl appearances with the Bucs, Lynch signed with the Broncos as a free agent in 2004.

The rules were different then, as hard-hitting safeties like Lynch could blast away at receivers who dared—at least once, but never twice—to run routes across the middle. Actually, Lynch was fined a robust $75,000 for his famous hit on Indianapolis Colts tight end Dallas Clark, who was left concussed but without a catch on a pass thrown by Manning's backup quarterback Jim Sorgi in the 2004 regular-season finale.

The hit on Clark may have been the one Broncos fans most remember about Lynch, but it wasn't the most significant. Go back and YouTube his blast of Kansas City receiver Dante Hall late in the first half of the 2004 season opener, Lynch's first game with the Broncos.

"I thought that was important for me for a couple of reasons," Lynch said. "Number one, after that hit, people forgot I came off neck surgery that off-season. You can have a doctor tell you you're going to be all right. You can have trainers say you're going to be all right. Until you actually do it, you don't know you're going to be all right. For me that was the moment where I said, 'You're fine. You're as good as you've ever been.'

"And number two, that kind of set the tone for what I wanted to bring to the Broncos: physical play, and to let people know that if you were going to beat the Broncos, you were going to have to earn it. I think that play kind of symbolized that. And when I came off the field, Mike said right then, 'That's why we brought you here.'"

It was the next year that head coach Mike Shanahan, Lynch, and the Broncos enjoyed one of their finest seasons. Not a Super Bowl appearance, but the closest thing to it. For the first time in seven years—the first time in the post–John Elway era—the Broncos won their AFC West Division with a 13-3 record. Lynch posted career bests, with four sacks and four forced fumbles, plus had two interceptions and one more pick against New England's Tom Brady in that memorable second-round playoff game, which the Broncos won, 27–13.

That set the stage for hosting the AFC Championship Game against Pittsburgh at then Invesco Field at Mile High. For whatever reason, the Broncos came out flat that game and lost. The Steelers went on to win Super Bowl XL.

Asked to name his most vivid memory of his time with the Broncos, Lynch didn't hesitate.

"I would think first and foremost, the night we hosted New England and beat them in the Division [playoff] game," he said. "I had a pick at the end of the game to kind of finish it. But that game was why I went to Denver. I remember how raucous the old Mile High Stadium would get. To be honest—and it happens with all the new stadiums—it was kind of a letdown when I got there, because it wasn't like the old one, where the stadium shook.

"And that night we kind of re-created it. We gave Brady his first loss. He had never lost in the playoffs. I thought we were winning the Super Bowl, too, once we won that game that night. The environment. I'll never forget Champ's play in that game. One of the greatest plays I've ever seen."

Bailey had a pick in the end zone and a 100-yard return that was essentially a 14-point swing play that was the difference in the Broncos' 14-point victory.

The Broncos got off to a fast start in 2006, too, going 7-2 and then leading 24–7 in the second half against San Diego in Game 10, before the season unraveled. Lynch played hurt in his final season of 2007, but still made his ninth Pro Bowl. Only Ken Houston made more Pro Bowls among safeties, with 10.

Houston was inducted into the Pro Bowl Football Hall of Fame 30 years ago. Lynch has been close to following him through Canton's doors the past four years, when he was a top-15 modern-era finalist. Lynch got inside the top 10 in the Hall voting the past two years, so there is hope he will be among the five modern-era players elected in 2018 on the eve of Super Bowl 52 in Minneapolis.

Safeties have struggled to measure up to the standards applied by the Hall of Fame voting committee. A pure safety (with no conversion from cornerback) hasn't been elected from the modern-era ballot since Paul Krause in 1998.

But first, Lynch was inducted into the Broncos Ring of Fame, and then the Tampa Bay Bucs Ring of Honor. Some may view Lynch more as a Buc than a Bronco, but he has always considered himself part of both families.

"When he came here he had the ability to be one of the guys," said former Broncos quarterback Jake Plummer. "Be a superstar, but also be one of the guys. Not just the guys that matter, but everyone on our team, how much he cared about us. He was another teammate that cared. A hard hitter. Golly, a guy who just laid the wood. Not fast. Didn't have a crazy skill set, but just a student of the game.

"Guys like him made it tough in practice. They knew our stuff in and out, and then to get stuff over on them in practice, you had to be right on. The ball had to be accurate, on time, no delineation on that. He made me a better player."

By the way, when Manning is eligible for the Broncos Ring of Fame in 2021? He'll become the second four-year Bronco in the new millennium to get elected.

JOHN LYNCH STATS

YRS	G	S	I	FF	TCK
4	60	7	3	9	304

47

SAMMY WINDER

Running Back, 1982–90

Had Woody Hayes first seen Sammy Winder before he spoke, his coined phrase would have been "3.6 yards and a cloud of dust."

Winder was John Elway's first starting running back. Winder started the famous "Drive" with a 5-yard reception from the shadow of the end zone, then picked up the first of seven first downs on The Drive with a 2-yard run to convert a third-and-2. Winder was unquestionably the best less-than-4.0-yards-per-carry running back in Broncos history.

Not once in Winder's nine seasons did he average more than 3.9 yards per carry. The key stat in that sentence? Nine seasons.

"I don't think having the number 4.0 was the goal for backs," Winder said in April 2017. "I do think that's reasonable and that's fair. But I gave them the best I had. Playing with Elway, with the style he had, you had to step up and attack the pass rush, and I think I helped out a lot in that area. In that offense, you had to do both."

Winder averaged 3.9 yards as a part-time playing rookie out of Southern Mississippi in 1982. He averaged 3.9 yards per carry in his first season as a starter in 1983. He averaged 3.9 yards per carry in his only 1,000-yard season of 1984, when he made his first Pro Bowl.

The NFL became so enamored of Winder's rugged, if unspectacular, style of running, he made the Pro Bowl again in 1986 despite averaging just 3.3 yards per carry.

Winder finished his career with 5,427 rushing yards—at the time, the Broncos second all-time rusher behind Floyd Little—on 3.6 yards per carry.

Here's the thing about the Woody Hayes axiom, which is more accurately referred to as "three yards and a cloud of dust": If you average just a little bit more than three yards per play, your offense picks up a first down and keeps moving the chains down the field.

Winder was a chain mover.

"Mississippi Mud," said Rubin Carter, a Broncos nose tackle during the first half of Winder's career. "A special guy. Another guy who was really quiet, didn't say very much. But when he had his hands on the football, you talk about somebody electric. He could make people slide off his body like he did have mud on his body. He would slide through some holes and the next thing you know, he's in the end zone and he's picking one foot up, and then his right leg up, and the left leg up, and he's doing the Mississippi Mud Dance, because he just scored a touchdown. Very electric and exciting young man."

Electric may not be the first word that comes to mind when people think of Winder. Unless they are remembering him breaking down his Mississippi Mud Dance in the end zone after scoring one of his 48 career touchdowns. That 1986 season when he averaged 3.3 yards per carry on his way to his second Pro Bowl? Winder scored 14 touchdowns that season. Nine rushing and five receiving. That's a lot of Mississippi Mud dancing.

"Sammy was a fun runner," said Ken Lanier, the Broncos right tackle during the Sammy years. "He was durable, and he was going to lay it on the line all the time. Not real flashy. But you could count on him. You give him a little crack, he was going to make something out of it."

A Broncos fan could almost guess by his running-back style that Winder grew up on a farm. It was in the unincorporated town of Pocahontas, Mississippi, which is just outside of Jackson.

"I would pull corn, chase cows," Winder said in his ever-folksy manner. "I was a farm boy. I swore if I ever made it big, I'd get out of Pocahontas and never look back."

And?

"I live about a mile from where I grew up," Winder said.

When he retired, he went back to operate his Winder Construction Company, which he ran for 25 years. He lived his dream and now works for a garbage company. The man knows how to make a clean, honest living.

"That was a vision, the type of work I always wanted to do," said Winder, who has a wife and two children. "Even before football. I wanted to be a bulldozer operator. I probably had more visions of that growing up then I had of becoming a professional football player.

"In eighth grade and high school, I never thought I had the talent to play professional football. I just never thought I was that guy. I would have loved to have been that guy, don't get me wrong."

He turned out to be an extremely tough, between-the-tackle, consistent guy. He was also the type of running back whom Broncos head coach Dan Reeves was always looking to replace.

From the start. They called the 1982 draft "The Year of the Running Back." There were seven running backs taken among the top 21 picks in the first round. The Broncos used that No. 21 overall selection on Gerald Willhite, a speed back from San Jose State.

Winder was the 21st running back taken, and not until the fifth round. The running backs drafted ahead of Winder, in order: Darrin Nelson, Gerald Riggs, Marcus Allen, Walter Abercrombie, Barry Redden, Butch Woolfolk, Willhite, Robert Weathers, Joe Morris, Del Rodgers, Stan Edwards, Dwayne Crutchfield, Dennis Gentry (who turned out to be a nice receiver), Van Williams, Reggie Brown, Dave Barrett, Rodney Tate, Earl Ferrell, Mike Meade, and Del Thompson.

Those who had more career rushing yards than Winder: Allen, Riggs, and Morris.

"I was sitting around thinking about that," Winder said prior to his final game in 1990. "I was thinking not only that the Broncos had a number-one pick at running back, I was also thinking about all the other backs who came out that year.

"The fact that I've been durable and been able to hang in there even though I was selected in the later rounds . . . It's very gratifying."

Willhite couldn't beat out Winder. In 1985, Reeves drafted multipurpose running back Steve Sewell in the first round. Winder remained the workhorse, gaining 715 yards that season on, you guessed it, 3.6 yards per carry. The two, first-round picks, Sewell and Willhite, rushed for 275 and 237 yards, respectively.

"My whole career I was facing that pretty much," Winder said. "Even in college, everybody wants the breakaway back. I was never that guy. That's the ideal back to have in your backfield. I don't fault Dan Reeves for that. But every time they seemed to bring in a guy, that guy would get hurt and I was back in the lineup."

During "The Drive" game in Cleveland, Winder had a typical Sammy game: 83 yards on 26 carries. A 3.2-yard-per-carry average. But 3.2 yards on 26 carries gets the job done. At least it did in Reeves's offense.

"The Drive" started with the Broncos down, 20–13, with 5:32 remaining in regulation. Denver had the ball at its own 2-yard line, or, as left guard Keith Bishop said in the huddle, "right where we want 'em."

On the first play, Elway threw a short pass to left flat to Winder for 5 yards. Then it was a pitch to Winder, who picked up—what else?—3 yards.

Now, it's third-and-2. If you needed 2 yards, Winder was the best running back in the NFL. If you wanted 3 yards, Sammy was your guy. If you wanted 6 yards? Find another running back.

Often when Elway is asked to look back at "The Drive," he has said the most underrated play in the 98-yard march was Winder picking up 2 yards on third-and-2 for the first, first down.

"I remember a couple plays from 'The Drive,'" Winder said. "But you've got to remember, I got hit in the head a couple times. I remember Steve Sewell catching a pass over the middle to keep 'The Drive' going."

Yep, for 22 yards, moving the ball from the Broncos' 26 to their 48.

"And I remember Elway throwing the touchdown pass to Mark Jackson to tie the game," Winder said.

Winder had five carries—for 11 yards—during the Broncos' game-winning field-goal drive in overtime.

"The play I think about the most was the next year against the Browns," Winder said.

It was otherwise known as "The Fumble" game. This time, the 1987-season AFC Championship Game was played in Denver. Winder caught a screen pass from Elway and ran it in for a 20-yard catch-and-run touchdown that gave the Broncos a 38–31 lead in the back-and-forth game with about four minutes remaining. The Broncos won 38–33.

"I probably reflect on that play more than any other play I was involved with," Winder said. "It was a high-scoring game, last team that had the ball."

The Browns, who had rallied from 21–3 behind to tie the game, 31–31, before Winder scored, got the ball last. They were about to score the tying touchdown when Earnest Byner had the ball stripped by cornerback Jeremiah Castille at the 1-yard line.

But the enemy of good is great, and Reeves continued to seek an upgrade to Winder. An aging Tony Dorsett was brought in for one year in 1988. He rushed for 703 yards on 3.9 yards per carry. Sammy could have done that. In fact, Winder in a 1B role that season rushed for 543 yards on 3.6 yards per carry.

That pretty much was the end of Winder's best days, as he served as a seldom-used backup to Bobby Humphrey in 1989 and 1990.

To Reeves's credit, he let Winder start the final game of the 1990 season. The Broncos were 4-11 and had nothing to lose. Three days before the final game against the Green Bay Packers, Winder announced at teammate Mark Jackson's restaurant that the game Sunday would be his last.

In that final game, Winder was told just prior to the game by Reeves that he would be starting. Keep in mind, in the first five games of the 1990 season, Winder had 10 carries for minus-10 yards. In a seven-game stretch leading into the final game, Winder got just one carry. For 1 yard.

But in his final against the Packers, Sammy had a day. He gained 80 yards on 15 carries. A robust 5.3 yards per carry. The Broncos won, and afterwards, the Mile High Stadium crowd chanted, "Sam-my! Sam-my!" as Winder left the field.

"I didn't know he was going to let me play as much I did," Winder recalled 27 years later. "Dan came up to me right before kickoff and told me I was starting. I remember I got the ball the first play, and I was coming off the field and Bobby was waving, 'Get back out there, get back out there.' That was great. I really enjoyed that."

SAMMY WINDER STATS

YRS	G	CAR	Y	Y/C	TD	REC	Y	TD
9	127	1,495	5,427	3.6	39	197	1,302	9

48

KEN LANIER

Right Tackle, 1981–92, '94

There was a 12-year stretch where Ken Lanier put Woody Allen to shame.

Allen has been credited with saying a now oft-repeated motivational quote: "Eighty percent of success is showing up."

From the Denver Broncos' 13th game in 1981 through their 16th and final game in 1992, Lanier showed up 100 percent of the time. A team-record 166 consecutive games in all, including 131 starts in a row at right tackle.

"I'm definitely proud of that," Lanier said. "I think I played consistently for a long period of time."

Not that he was necessarily properly rewarded. Lanier was good enough to block for the stationary Craig Morton and scrambling John Elway, game after game, year after year, yet he never made a Pro Bowl.

"A lot of times you didn't know where John was going to end up," Lanier said. "That took some time to get used to. I'd be blocking a guy and he'd back off and start running a different direction, and you'd be like, 'What's going on?' Next thing you know, John's on the run."

Lanier lined up against the likes of Howie Long, Art Still, Derrick Thomas, and Lee Williams, twice a year. He opened holes for Sammy Winder, Bobby Humphrey, and Gaston Green. Yet, the 28-player Broncos Ring of Fame through 2016 included just two offensive linemen: left tackle Gary Zimmerman and center Tom Nalen.

"Lanier is a holder, a strangler, a takedown artist," *Sports Illustrated*'s Paul Zimmerman wrote after a Broncos–Los Angeles Raiders game in 1984. "Long, his foe in Denver's regular alignment, bit the dirt many times in Lanier's grasp, but Jerry Markbreit's officiating crew doesn't like to call offensive holding penalties."

Good for Jerry Markbreit.

Funny thing is, Paul Zimmerman had it wrong. Lanier's strength was not his hold. The key to Lanier's durability?

"I had great lower-body strength," said Lanier, who was 6-foot-3, 270 pounds. "My upper-body strength was so-so. A lot of times against the pass rush, I would get off balance, but I would still be able to block them with one leg."

In a twisted sense, it was music that led Lanier to the NFL by way of Florida State. Lanier grew up in Columbus, Ohio, but familiarity did not work in favor of Ohio State or its legendary coach, Woody Hayes.

"Growing up, I wasn't crazy about football," Lanier said. "We played in the yard, we played out in the streets. We had fun with it. But my aspirations were to compete in the Olympics. I wanted to be a shot-putter in the Olympics. That was my goal."

Still, after high school, he had the chance to play football at Ohio State.

"I did go to one recruiting trip there, but I realized at a young age that the personality of Woody Hayes and my personality, it wasn't going to be a good fit," Lanier said. "I grew up in Columbus, Ohio, but I didn't plan on staying in Columbus. I wanted to leave the state."

Which brings us to how music brought Lanier to Florida State. Lanier's father, James Lanier, was a highly respected high school music teacher in Columbus, Ohio.

"If you did something wrong at school, they didn't have cell phones back then, but for some reason [my dad] always knew about it when he got home," Lanier said.

Dad played the clarinet and saxophone when he wasn't teaching. Lanier played the trombone in his Marion Franklin High School band. His mom, Alice, was a homemaker to Ken and brother Andre.

"Both parents raised us and taught us commitment and how to be respectful," Lanier said. "And we were definitely going to go to college. What really stuck out to me with our upbringing was that no matter what you started, be the best at what you're going to be."

One of Mr. Lanier's music students, Kent Schoolfield, became a receivers coach for Bobby Bowden's Seminoles.

"He kind of had the inside track," Lanier said. "He convinced me to play football, and at the last minute I changed my mind and I said, 'Yeah, I'll go ahead and play.'"

Lanier first attended Florida State as a shot-putter and defensive tackle. It was one week into his freshman season that he was converted to the offensive side after a consultation with Seminoles offensive line coach Bob Harbison.

"You know how it is, everybody wants to hear their name called making a tackle," Lanier said. "But Coach Harbison told me, 'Ken, you're a defensive player, and I don't know when, or if, you're going to get on the field playing here. But if you were to play offensive tackle,' he said, 'I guarantee you'll start the next game.' So, I said, 'Okay.'"

Lanier started Florida State's second game of his freshman season, and started 46 games in a row, through its Orange Bowl loss to Oklahoma in his senior year of 1979. It was an Iron Man streak Lanier bettered by 3.6 times in the NFL.

"I was definitely a better offensive tackle," he said.

It was Lanier's junior year at Florida State that he started to realize the Olympics weren't going to happen for him. Football took too much time away from the shot-put pit.

"I had a split scholarship where I could do track and football," he said. "It was a football scholarship with an understanding of track. I didn't do spring practice. During the spring, I did track. In the fall, I played football."

Lanier graduated with a degree in industrial arts, but pushed that aside after he was part of Dan Reeves's first Broncos draft class in 1981. Lanier was taken in the fifth round. Dennis Smith was taken in the first round, Steve Busick in the seventh.

As a rookie in 1981, Lanier was inactive half the season, but he got his first start in place of an injured Claudie Minor on November 8.

"It was a good first game because it was against the Cleveland Browns, and I knew the game would be televised in Ohio," he said. "I wanted to show everybody I could play, and I had a big game that game. From then on, they knew I could play."

The Broncos beat the Browns, 23–20, in overtime. Denver quarterback Craig Morton completed 21 of 33 for 291 yards and a touchdown. Dave Logan had a big day for the Browns, catching a 23-yard touchdown from Brian Sipe. Logan, a former Wheat Ridge High School and University of Colorado star, has long been the Broncos play-by-play radio announcer.

Lanier got the game ball after his start. He later was on the field blocking for Elway in "The Drive" at Cleveland in the 1986-season AFC Championship Game.

"It was a lot of fun playing with John," Lanier said. "It was excitement. You always knew you were in the game as far as him making things happen. 'The Drive' was one of those things where we knew we had to get it done. It wasn't, 'Oh no, it's third and long.' It wasn't, 'Oh no, it was fourth down.' We knew what we had to do, and we just kept plugging and plugging away."

Lanier was caught up in the start of free agency in 1993, and signed a one-year contract with the Los Angeles Raiders.

"Everything we complained about with Al Davis—you know, a helicopter would go by and we'd say, 'That's Al Davis, spying on us,'" Lanier said. "Then we got to the Raiders, and it was, 'That's Pat Bowlen up there!'"

Lanier then came back in the second half of 1994 to add depth to the Broncos' injury-ravaged offensive line.

"I went back to retire a Bronco, basically," he said. "I knew that was it. Fourteen years was long enough."

Since retiring as a player, Lanier has stayed in the Denver area and worked for a couple of businesses. In early 2017 he was managing a self-storage facility.

He has two sons, Dwayne and Kelyn, and one daughter, McKenzie. He and his wife Arlene have been married 15 years.

KEN LANIER STATS

YRS	G
13	177

49

— # LYLE ALZADO —

Defensive Lineman, 1971–78

Lyle Alzado wanted so badly to be great, he crossed the line of fair play to get there.

Alzado was an admitted fraud. A liar and a cheat. Those wild, raging outbursts that popularized him with fans and broadcasters were, as it turns out, artificially enhanced.

Looking back, Alzado exhibited all the symptoms of a steroid user—in particular, the violent mood swings—before the sports world had caught on to the disease.

The steroids epidemic in sports largely remained behind bathroom-stall doors until the late 1980s. Alzado was a phony football star of the 1970s to mid-'80s.

"Very sad," said Rubin Carter, the Broncos nose tackle who played alongside Alzado, upon hearing how steroids had led to Alzado's demise. "Because I didn't think he needed that."

Carter is a gentleman. Truth is, Lyle Alzado most likely would not have made it in the NFL, never mind played 15 seasons with a certain kind of celebrity and acclaim, if not for his continual use of performance-enhancing drugs.

Without artificial aid, he would have been too small. This isn't my opinion; this is Alzado's own admission in a first-person *Sports Illustrated* interview, conducted 10 months before he died, at age 43, due to complications from brain cancer.

"I lied," Alzado wrote for his opener. He then described, in shocking detail, how far from the truth he had wandered since he started using steroids in 1969—two years before he was selected by the Broncos in the fourth round of the 1971 draft.

"It wasn't until I got to college when I realized that, even though I'd been high school All American, that wasn't enough to make it as a football player," Alzado wrote. "I didn't have the size. I had the speed, but not the size."

Alzado deserves credit for publicly confessing his transgressions, and because he did, I have forgiven him enough to place him among the 50 Greatest Broncos of All Time.

"He was a great ballplayer," said quarterback and teammate Craig Morton. "At the time there was nothing really illegal about it. I think he looked at it as doing something he thought would improve his play. So I'm glad you included him, because he was a great player."

Granted, Alzado didn't confess until well after his NFL playing career was finished. (I am ignoring his failed comeback attempt with the Oakland Raiders in 1990 at the age of 41, five years after he had played his final game.) And he didn't confess until after he'd learned a brain tumor had brought him to death's door.

But I don't think Alzado was the only standout NFL player who was artificially enhanced by steroids. I also believe the sport of football through its combative nature perpetuates the use of stimulants, substances, and enhancers.

Baseball holds on to its romantic past to the point where artificial enhancements are considered sacrilegious. Football fans expect their warriors to play at all costs, to the point where pain-numbing agents are considered a badge of honor.

Performance-enhancing drugs are considered taboo in the NFL today. But the ethical line is far more blurred in football.

Doped up or not, there were times when Alzado was a terrific football player, and he was always a fan favorite.

"Lyle was a very physical ballplayer," said Barney Chavous, who played the defensive end opposite Alzado in defensive coordinator Joe Collier's 3-4 front. "Lyle could get to the ball. Lyle was fast. That was one of his best assets. He had good speed, and he could get to the ball."

There may have been a few Broncos from the Orange Crush defense who were suspicious of Alzado's steroid use, but not many. Steroids were largely unknown in the sports world in the 1970s, with the possible exception of championship bodybuilders and weight lifters.

And no one could have possibly known the extent of Alzado's steroid use. Alzado penned an autobiography, *Mile High: The Story of Lyle Alzado and the Amazing Denver Broncos*, with the help of acclaimed NFL writer Paul Zimmerman. The book, which chronicled Alzado's life through the Broncos' Orange Crush season of 1977, did not once broach the subject of steroids or his blatant use.

"We didn't know what steroids were," Morton said. "The only thing was his mood swings, but we always thought it was just Lyle. People do that. Lyle, his body—oh my gosh, how in the world could he be so taut? His skin looked like it was going to burst. He was so muscled."

A symptom Morton knows how to read now. But at the time, everyone just thought Alzado was a physical freak.

"When I retired in '82, steroids were not part of the game, or even talked about," Morton said. "I could have been oblivious to a lot of things, but I think I can speak along with the majority of the team—we didn't have any idea what steroids were, or who was using them, or why they were using them."

If there was an irritant among his teammates, it was Alzado's self-promoting style.

"I had no problem with Lyle," Carter said. "Lyle and I got along really good. I think Lyle thought I was kind of crazy, like he was. He had this air about him, the way he carried himself. He loved attention. He loved people, he loved being around people."

Indeed, Alzado was a man of contradictions. He had a violent temper but he was also hypersensitive. He would rip off an offensive lineman's helmet and heave it in a mad rage, but he was also the recipient of the Byron "Whizzer" White NFL Man of the Year Award for his dedicated work in the community, particularly with underprivileged children.

He had his way of hogging attention, but he also said something to Morton that made the veteran quarterback's career when he joined the Broncos in 1977.

"When I walked in the locker room, Lyle looked up at me and said, 'Now we'll win the championship,'" Morton recalled nearly four decades later.

If I read Alzado's story correctly, he'd have been the first to give the shirt off his back, only to later rip that shirt to shreds.

"But when it was time to go, and it was game day, Lyle Alzado turned his motor on," Carter said. "I mean, that engine was full speed. I learned a lot from him in his acceleration coming off the edge and the way he used his hands to ward off blockers. I didn't pick up on the verbal part of his game, the intimidating part. He was very good at that, but as far as the intensity level, that's what I learned from Lyle Alzado."

In 1977, the year of the famed Orange Crush? Alzado was voted by United Press International and the Kansas City 101 Club as the AFC's Defensive Player of the Year. He was first-team All Pro in 1977, when he tied Chavous for the team lead with 8 sacks, and second-team All Pro in 1978, when he had a team-most 9 sacks.

"Alzado was so tall," said Broncos tight end Riley Odoms, who matched up against Alzado in practice. "Oh my God. And so active. His arms were so long, you had to get in on him quick before he could get his arms on you."

In Alzado's book, Zimmerman talked to Stan Jones, the Hall of Fame defensive end and offensive guard for the Chicago Bears. (Jones passed away in 2010, at the age of 78.)

"Lyle has great endurance," Jones said in the book. "He goes, I guess, as hard as anybody who ever played the game."

And now we know why.

"In the history of defensive ends, Lyle would rate in the upper echelon, and against the run he might even be in the upper tenth percentile," Jones said. "He's a better end than Deacon Jones against the run, and he might even be as good as Gino Marchetti against the run, too."

It wasn't so much Alzado's defensive skills that made him a fan favorite as his maniacal intensity.

"He was a wild man," said Broncos safety Billy Thompson. "He was a guy—we had to stop him from fighting. We would tell him, You're going to kill us, man. I know the guy low-blowed you or whatever, but you have to think about the team. If you get a personal foul, you're going to cost us 15 yards. We had to keep him under control."

Knowing what we know now, Alzado often demonstrated classic cases of 'roid rage. Only such a term wasn't part of the sports vernacular in the 1970s.

"He was crazy," said Broncos cornerback Louis Wright. "His mentality was out of control. Which is good for a defensive lineman. He just took a challenge personally, that he was going to beat that guy in front of him, and he often did. He made some plays. He'd be fired up. He was fiery in a way that he'd get the whole defense fired up. He didn't leave anything on the field. He had a motor that was nonstop."

Alzado didn't just dabble in steroids. He was an addict for 20-plus years. His habit began with 50 milligrams of Dianabol a day. Then he moved on to the stronger stuff, like Bolasterone and Quinolone. He never cycled off the recommended length. He would mix the 'roids and increase the doses. Later came human growth hormone.

"Lyle, he wanted to be great," said Rich "Tombstone" Jackson. "He would hang around and he would work out in the gym afterwards. We had a small group of guys who would work out; they knew the importance of being physically prepared and ready. He worked out hard. I think his attitude of being great is what, like a lot of guys, led to him feeling like he needed some enhancements."

Jackson was coming off his third-consecutive All Pro season in 1971 when Alzado was a Broncos rookie. Stan Jones had called Jackson "the best defensive end in the history of the game against the run."

Alzado worshiped Jackson. Jackson suffered a season-ending knee injury halfway through the 1971 season, and Alzado was appalled when during the following 1972 training camp, Broncos coach John Ralston had Jackson take every practice rep, even though it was clear the knee had not fully recovered.

Ralston's treatment of Jackson was one reason why Alzado helped lead the "Dirty Dozen" Broncos players to oust the coach following the 1976 season. (It helped lead to Red Miller and the Broncos' magical Orange Crush season of '77, so give Alzado some credit.)

"I reached out to him after I found out the problem he had with [steroids], and he never did return my call," Jackson said. "I often think about that. I feel bad to even think that maybe I had something to do with it. I remember he came in the gym one day. We put 600 pounds on the bar and he said, 'You can't do that.' And I dead-lifted 600 pounds all the way up here, and I just dropped it and walked off."

Jackson shouldn't carry any guilt, because as Alzado later admitted, the steroids started during his days at Yankton (South Dakota) College. Alzado was a full-blown user by the time he met Jackson—and he still couldn't keep up with Tombstone.

For this project, I had some respected Broncos followers argue that Alzado should not have made the top 50. Others said he had to be included because to a majority of the casual Broncos followers, Alzado carried more appeal than 40 of the top 50 players.

Ultimately, I was left to reconcile Alzado's 64.5 sacks, placing him at No. 6 on the Broncos' all-time list, along with Stan Jones's testimony regarding his prowess against the run, versus the defensive lineman's heavy steroid use.

The compromise I reached was No. 49. Not No. 50, which, perversely carries some esteem. A project like this, I envisioned people asking, "Who is number 1? Number 2? So, who is number 50?"

No. 49, in my view, was the least glamorous of the 50 spots. Alzado lands at No. 49. It beats No. 51, which fell to the group of honorable mentions.

"I always said if you were going to war, you wanted to have a guy like Lyle with you," said Broncos middle linebacker Randy Gradishar. "On game day, there weren't too many guys better than he was."

"He was a promoter," said Broncos receiver Haven Moses.

"Lyle was a player now," said Steve Foley, who played cornerback on Alzado's right side of the defense. "He was fierce. He was a fighter man."

All of this was true of Lyle Alzado. So was this:

"It wasn't worth it," he said, in what turned out to be his farewell letter, published by *Sports Illustrated*. "I know there's no written, documented proof that steroids and human growth hormone caused this cancer. But it's one of the reasons you have to look at. You have to."

LYLE ALZADO STATS

YRS	G	S	TCK
8	99	64.5	593

50

OTIS ARMSTRONG

Running Back, 1973–80

He was drafted in the first round with the idea of becoming heir apparent to The Franchise. That's all.

"That is true, except Floyd had other ideas," Otis Armstrong said with a small laugh at the memory.

When it comes to following legends, Armstrong learned there is no such thing as getting used to it. He left Farragut Career Academy High School on the West Side of Chicago for Purdue in 1969. The year before, the Boilermakers running back was Leroy Keyes. Other than USC's O. J. Simpson, there was no bigger college-star running back than Leroy Keyes.

In fact, in 1968, Simpson and Keyes finished 1-2 in the Heisman Trophy balloting.

Armstrong made his own name at Purdue, rushing for 3,315 yards and adding another 389 yards receiving in just 31 games. In those days, college teams only played 10 or 11 games a season, and freshmen couldn't play.

Armstrong was sensationally fast—so much so that he was a first-team All American along with Oklahoma running back Greg Pruitt. Again, this was a time when the All American team meant more than whether or not a college player was considered first-round caliber.

Armstrong was ready for the NFL in 1973 when the Broncos made him the first running back selected, No. 9 overall, in the draft. Only Floyd Little wasn't ready to surrender his mantle as The Franchise, a nickname he was given when he became the Broncos' first first-round draft pick to sign with the American Football League franchise in 1967.

Armstrong played in every game his rookie year of 1973, but only had 90 yards on 26 carries. Little finished ninth in the NFL, with 979 yards rushing in the 14-game season, and tied Simpson with 12 rushing touchdowns—the same year Simpson rushed for 2,003 yards.

Armstrong, it seems, was always following a legend.

"Isn't that the truth?" he said from his home in the Denver suburb of Centennial in February 2017. "Everywhere I'd go, I was moving somebody out who everybody loved. I wanted everybody to get a chance to see me for who I was. It was hard when everybody was saying 'Leroy Keyes was my favorite guy!' [or] 'I loved Floyd Little!'"

"It wasn't easy for Otis," said Rick Upchurch, a rookie in Little's final season of 1975. "Floyd was a fan favorite, and he helped keep this team here. That was like trying to follow Muhammad Ali into the ring.

"But, Otis always wanted to be the man. He would say, 'Put the ball in my hands, because I want to do some damage to these bums.' He used to call the other team 'bums.' He was very inspiring. A hard worker."

In his second season of 1974, Armstrong became *the man*. He led the NFL in rushing with 1,407 yards on 5.3 yards per carry. The key was his finish. He had 792 yards through his first 10 games, then ran wild in his final four games. He picked up 146 yards against the Oakland Raiders, 144 against Detroit, 183 against Houston, and 142 against San Diego. That's an incredible 615 yards on 6.03 yards per carry in those final four games.

It was the best rushing season in Broncos history, and held up as a single-season record for 23 years, until Terrell Davis rushed for 1,750 yards in the Broncos' first Super Bowl–title season of 1997.

"That was a big surprise, because I was just happy to be playing," Armstrong said. "All of the sudden my name was in the paper. I had a good line, I really did. We had Paul Howard. They got me started."

Armstrong grew up on Chicago's West Side, across the street from Franklin Park.

"Played there every day growing up," Armstrong said. "We played basketball, football, every day we played something."

He had five older brothers and two sisters. John Armstrong, the dad, was a mechanic, and Rosie Lea Armstrong was a stay-at-home mom.

"My brothers played before me, so that's why football became my cup of tea," Armstrong said. "The neighborhood where I grew up, it was nice back then. Things deteriorated a little bit, but the people are strong. They get through it."

At Purdue, Keyes had just left when Armstrong showed up on the West Lafayette, Indiana, campus for his freshman season of 1969, but he did get to practice with quarterback Mike Phipps, who became the second Boilermaker in two years to finish second in the Heisman balloting. (Oklahoma running back Steve Owens won the top college player award.)

Armstrong's Heisman experience was strange. He rushed for more than 1,000 yards as a sophomore in 1970 (1,009 in 10 games), and as a senior in 1972 (1,361 in 11 games), yet the only time he finished in the top 10 in the Heisman voting was as a junior, when he had 945 yards.

Truth is, following Little in Denver wasn't a problem. Armstrong considered Little his mentor.

"I did everything he did," Armstrong said. "I tried to copy Floyd as much as I could. It worked out really well for me."

After Armstrong's sensational season in 1974, he tore his hamstring four games into 1975.

"That's how Floyd got his glory at the end," Armstrong said.

Little came off the bench and had such an inspiring finish, he got carried off the field after his final home game at Mile High Stadium.

The greatest draft class in Broncos history? Their 1973 draft has to be in the top five. There was Armstrong in the first round, Barney Chavous in the second round, Paul Howard in the third, and Tom Jackson in the fourth.

That 1973 season was also when the Broncos started winning. The team had suffered 13 consecutive non-winning seasons until it turned in 1973. The Broncos went 7-5-2 in '73, 7-6-1 in '74, 9-5 in '76, and 12-2, with two more playoff wins, to reach the Super Bowl in 1977.

Armstrong had a second, 1,000-yard rushing season in 1976, but he said the team's trip to the Super Bowl was the highlight of his career.

"I missed the last four games that year with a sprained ankle, but I came back for the playoffs," Armstrong said. "I scored a big touchdown against the Steelers."

It was a 10-yard scoring run that put the Broncos up, 14–7. He also had a 29-yard run in that game and the Broncos won, 34–21, to advance to the AFC Championship Game.

"We were kind of surprised we beat the Steelers, but it happened," Armstrong said. "We were pretty good at home."

At 5-foot-10, 196 pounds, Armstrong struggled to stay healthy as the NFL went from 14 to 16 games in 1978, and the Broncos went to a running-back rotation that also featured Jon Keyworth, Rob Lytle, and Lonnie Perrin.

"Otis was my running mate," Upchurch said. "Otis was everything I wanted to be. I was a running back coming out of college, but I saw this guy and . . . he was my roommate, and the punishment he would take, I said, 'Nah, that's all right. You stay at running back, I'll stay out here at receiver.'"

Armstrong's final blow came on his 1,023rd and final carry of his eight-year Broncos career. Houston defensive star Elvin Bethea drove him into the Mile High Stadium turf, leaving Armstrong with a neck injury. Doctors discovered a narrow passage in Armstrong's upper spine and recommended he never play football again.

He retired as the Broncos' second-leading all-time rusher.

When he was finished, Armstrong and Keyworth went into business together, first as beer distributors, then for vitamins.

Armstrong was 66 years old at the time of his writing, and though he was inducted into the College Football Hall of Fame in 2012—Little showed up for his enshrinement ceremony in South Bend, Indiana—he is hoping to become a member of the Broncos Ring of Fame.

"I had a nice following when I played," he said. "I think I deserve a mention."

He is among the 50 Greatest Players in Broncos History.

YRS	G	CAR	Y	Y/C	TD	REC	Y	TD
8	96	1,023	4,453	4.4	25	131	1,302	7

OTIS ARMSTRONG STATS

HONORABLE MENTIONS

GREG KRAGEN, DEFENSIVE TACKLE, 1985-93

Kragen got serious top-50 consideration. A starter on three Broncos teams that won the AFC Championship and got blown out three times in the Super Bowl. An undersized nose tackle at 263 pounds, but also a first-team, all-AFC nose tackle as selected by the Pro Football Writers in 1989. UPI gave him the same honor in 1991. Karl Mecklenburg would have put Kragen in the Broncos' top 50. "Why I mentioned Greg is, he took on so many blockers for me," Mecklenburg said. "He would grab two guys and take on double teams—he only weighed, like, 260 pounds, and they'd bend him up like a pretzel and I'd be free to the ball and he'd keep on ticking. Unbelievably dedicated player and tough player. A guy I owe a lot of my success to."

JIM TURNER, KICKER, 1971-79

This hurts. It pained me to not include Turner among the 50 Greatest Broncos—starting with the fact that he's one of only two of the 28 Broncos Ring of Fame players who didn't make the top 50. It also hurt because I have a personal attachment to Turner. I was once the biggest fan of Joe Namath's New York Jets, and Turner was the unsung hero of Super Bowl III, as his three field goals were the difference in a 16–7 monumental upset of the Baltimore Colts.

And to this day, Turner is second in Broncos history with 742 points—6 coming on a memorable touchdown reception off a fake field goal at Oakland that was a signature play in the Broncos' famed Orange Crush season of 1977.

When the American Football League named its all-time first and second teams for the 1960–69 period, Turner made the second team—although it should be noted that all of his AFL years were with the Jets.

In the end, Turner didn't make the top 50 because after Jason Elam—whose 1,786 points are more than 1,000 beyond Turner's second-place total—and Gene Mingo—who twice led the AFL in scoring, but also played halfback and returned punts—it was difficult to squeeze in a third kicker. There were just too many great players in Broncos history to put three kickers in the top 50.

Besides, the Broncos had too many other very good kickers come along after Turner. Rich Karlis booted some of the most memorable field goals in franchise history, and hit on 71.0 percent of his attempts to Turner's 65.1.

Matt Prater, whose 64-yard field goal in a December 2013 game broke a 43-year NFL record, converted 82.9 percent of his field goals in a seven-year period. And David Treadwell connected on 78.0 percent of his field goals in his four-year term.

So, huge apologies to Jim Turner. In his 16 seasons, 9 with the Broncos, he never missed a game. He retired as the NFL's second-leading scorer, with 1,439 points (behind only George Blanda's 2,002).

VANCE JOHNSON, WIDE RECEIVER, 1985-93, 1995

Vance Johnson was John Elway's leading receiver in the late 1980s, when the Broncos kept winning AFC championships, but also kept getting crushed in Super Bowls. Johnson caught 35 touchdown passes from Elway; only tight end Shannon Sharpe had more, with 41.

Johnson's best season was 1989, when he tied for ninth in the NFL, with 76 catches that were good for 1,095 yards and 7 touchdowns.

Retired as Broncos' second-leading receiver in catches (415), third in yards (5,695), and fourth in touchdowns (37), Johnson still ranks within the top eight in each category.

CHARLEY JOHNSON, QUARTERBACK, 1972-75

Regrettably, Charley Johnson is the second Ring of Famer who didn't make the top 50. I can see why he was inducted into the Ring of Fame. The Broncos never had a winning record until Johnson led them to a 7-5-2 record in 1973 to break the skid at 13 seasons. His teammates voted him their MVP that year.

But working against Johnson for this top-50 project was the fact that I'm old enough to consider him more St. Louis Cardinal than Bronco. He spent his first nine seasons with the Cardinals, including his best years of

1963–64. He then played two more with the Houston Oilers before he was traded to the Broncos for a third-round draft pick.

He was 33 when the Broncos got him, and he wound up only playing two seasons when he was the full-time quarterback, plus two more when injuries had him splitting time with Steve Ramsey.

Johnson was the second-best Broncos quarterback in franchise history when he retired (after Frank Tripucka), but since then, the team has employed the likes of Craig Morton, John Elway, Brian Griese, Jake Plummer, Jay Cutler, and Peyton Manning.

BRANDON MARSHALL, WIDE RECEIVER, 2006-09

A potential Pro Football Hall of Famer, former fourth-round draft pick Marshall had 102 receptions in his second season of 2007, 104 catches in 2008, and 101 in 2009, even though he was suspended from playing in the Broncos' final game by head coach Josh McDaniels.

In one 2009 game at Indianapolis, Marshall had 21 receptions, an NFL record that still stands.

Marshall's period with the Broncos was stormy both on and off the field, causing the team to trade him to Miami after the 2009 season. He later admitted to immaturity, but wound up having two more 100-catch seasons with the Chicago Bears and one more with the New York Jets. Through 11 seasons, Marshall ranked 18th all-time with 941 catches, 23rd with 82 receiving touchdowns, and 24th with 12,061 yards.

CLINTON PORTIS, RUNNING BACK, 2002-03

They don't make Fantasy League running backs like Clinton Portis anymore, especially the way he played in his first two NFL seasons. Selected in the second round of the 2002 draft out of the University of Miami, Portis rushed for 1,508 yards and 15 touchdowns as a Broncos rookie, and added 364 more yards and 2 touchdowns receiving.

In his second season of 2003, Portis ripped off 1,591 yards rushing and 14 touchdowns, and another 314 yards receiving. Yet, Portis would not have a third season with the Broncos. He wanted a new contract and he got it—by getting traded to Washington in exchange for cornerback Champ Bailey and a second-round draft pick that turned out to be Oklahoma State running back Tatum Bell.

Portis would have four more seasons of at least 1,200 yards rushing in Washington, but he was never quite as effective there—averaging 4.1 yards per carry—as he was while averaging 5.5 yards per carry in his two seasons in Denver.

Bailey played 10 seasons in Denver and made eight Pro Bowls. He will certainly be elected into the Pro Football Hall of Fame, the only question being whether he makes it in his first year of eligibility. Bell was primarily a 1B back to Mike Anderson in Denver, but he did have one 1,000-yard rushing season.

It remains one of the most blockbuster star-player-for-star-player trades in NFL history, and was the second biggest in Broncos history to the John Elway swap with Baltimore in 1983.

MARK SCHLERETH, LEFT GUARD, 1995–2000

Schlereth is known for his remarkably swift recoveries from knee surgeries. He played 12 NFL seasons—six as a right guard with the Washington Redskins, and six as a left guard with the Broncos. Schlereth had 20 knee surgeries during his career—15 on his left—yet he missed just six games through his first five seasons with the Broncos.

A 250-pound guard who helped spring six 1,000-yard rushing seasons for Terrell Davis (1995–98), Olandis Gary (1999), and Mike Anderson (2000).

Hated to leave him off the top-50 list. Schlereth has enjoyed a successful post-NFL career as an ESPN commentator, green chili distributor, Denver sports-radio talk-show host, husband, and father of three, including actress Alexandria and former major-league pitcher Daniel.

AQIB TALIB, CORNERBACK, 2014–PRESENT

Talib wasn't eligible for the top 50, as he had only played three seasons for the Broncos when this project was published. He did earn three Pro Bowl berths in those three seasons, and he was a first-team All Pro in 2016. A rambunctious and emotional player, Talib had 33 interceptions and 9 pick sixes since he entered the NFL in 2008—tops in the league in each category. He had 10 of those interceptions, and 5 of those pick sixes, in his first three seasons with the Broncos. Even with only three full seasons with the Broncos entering 2017, Talib would have to be considered the third-best cover corner in team history, behind Champ Bailey and Louis Wright.

BOB SCARPITTO,
FLANKER/HALFBACK/PUNTER, 1962–67

You will have a difficult time finding a better all-around performance in a single season than Bob Scarpitto's in 1966. Playing for a horrible offensive team that ranked last in the AFL, with 14.0 points per game, Scarpitto led the AFL in punting that year with a 45.2-yard average, plus had 21 catches for 335 yards and 4 touchdowns, and had 110 yards rushing on just 4 carries, including a 63-yard touchdown run.

Named to the AFL's all-time second team as a punter, Scarpitto also led the AFL in punting in 1967, when he averaged 44.9 yards on an astounding 105 punts in a 14-game season—7.5 punts per game.

Scarpitto had seasons of 35, 35, and 32 receptions for the Broncos. In 1962, he had 35 catches for 667 yards—an incredible 19.1 average—with 6 touchdowns. Hated to exclude him from the top 50.

TOM GRAHAM, LINEBACKER, 1972–74 /
DANIEL GRAHAM, TIGHT END, 2007–10

The Pro Football Hall of Fame has documented 224 sets of fathers and sons who played in the NFL, but only one—Tom Graham and his son Daniel—each played for the Broncos.

For this, the Grahams deserve special commendation in this book. They were pretty good players, too.

Tom Graham was a middle linebacker whom the Broncos took in the fourth round out of Oregon in 1972. In his first two NFL seasons, Graham led the Broncos in tackles, with 73 (plus three sacks and two interceptions) in 1972, and 95 in 1973.

In 1974, Graham gave way to a first-round draft pick named Randy Gradishar, a middle linebacker from Ohio State. Graham was traded at midseason to Kansas City before becoming a three-year starter for the San Diego Chargers. Ever present in the Bronco community after his playing days, Tom Graham passed away May 30, 2017 after a battle with brain cancer.

Daniel Graham played at Thomas Jefferson High School in Denver, then was a terrific player at the University of Colorado, winning the John Mackey Award as the nation's top tight end during his senior year in 2001.

Daniel was the first-round draft choice of the defending-champion New England Patriots in 2002. Daniel had his best seasons with the Patriots before the Broncos made him the highest-paid tight end in NFL history, in 2007.

Known as a lethal blocker in the NFL, Daniel Graham had 24, 32, and 28 catches in his first three seasons with the Broncos.

ELDON DANENHAUER, RIGHT TACKLE, 1960–65

Danenhauer got strong top-50 consideration on the strength of his two AFL All Star berths in 1962 and '65. He was considered monstrous in his day, at 6-foot-5, 245 pounds. His older brother Bill Danenhauer was a Broncos defensive end in 1960.

Eldon's career was cut short when he broke his arm pushing a stalled car up an icy hill in January 1966. During training camp that year, he broke his arm again and decided to retire.

MARLIN BRISCOE, QUARTERBACK, 1968

I always remember Marlin Briscoe as a fine receiver for the Buffalo Bills. I didn't realize till later that Briscoe was first a quarterback for the Broncos. Briscoe may have been a Bronco—and a quarterback—for just one year, but he also became the first-ever African-American NFL-AFL starting quarterback in that one year.

Briscoe wasn't the most accurate passer—he completed 93 of 224, for a 41.5 completion percentage—but he threw for impact, as those 93 completions were good for 1,589 yards and 14 touchdowns. He also rushed for 308 yards on 7.5 yards per carry and three touchdowns. Briscoe was Russell Wilson long before professional football welcomed African Americans as quarterbacks.

Briscoe's most memorable game as a quarterback was in late November against Buffalo, when he completed just 12 of 29 passes, but for 335 yards and 4 touchdowns, in a 34–32 win.

In that game, the Broncos were leading 31–29 when star running back Floyd Little fumbled with 42 seconds left at his own 10. But Buffalo didn't run off any clock, deciding to quickly kick a go-ahead field goal.

With 25 seconds remaining, Briscoe, nicknamed "The Magician," threw a deep completion to the atoning Little for a 59-yard gain. A face-mask penalty put the ball at the 5, setting up Bobby Howfield for a 12-yard field goal to win it.

When he learned that Broncos head coach Lou Saban was not going to start him at quarterback for the following season of 1969, Briscoe asked to be moved, and he was dealt to Buffalo, where he wound up as a 1,000-yard receiver. Briscoe later had four touchdown catches for the undefeated 1972 Miami Dolphins.

ALFRED WILLIAMS, DEFENSIVE END, 1996–99

The best team that never was: the 1996 Broncos. They were cursed by dominance, as they started 12-1 to clinch the AFC's No. 1 playoff seed by December 1. Williams had 13.0 sacks in the Broncos' first 12 games, then rested with the remainder of the starters down the stretch.

He had one more sack in the Broncos' devastating second-round play-off loss to Jacksonville.

The next year, Williams suffered a torn left triceps in a preseason game against Miami, and then tore his right triceps in a regular-season game against San Diego, but still finished with 8.5 sacks, plus 2.0 more in the postseason when the Broncos finished off their first Super Bowl championship.

That's 24.5 sacks in his first two seasons with the Broncos.

Surgeries to repair those two torn triceps forced Williams to miss the first six games of 1998. He returned to play in third-down packages in his final 10 games, registering another 3.0 sacks.

Healthy at the start of 1999, Williams had 4.0 sacks in seven games, but then blew out his Achilles, which essentially ended his career.

It was an interesting career that only became more fascinating. Williams is part of this book not only for his two stellar seasons with the Broncos, but also because he has hit the Holy Trinity of Colorado and Denver football.

He was a Butkus Award winner as the nation's top linebacker for the University of Colorado 1990 national championship team. He then became a first-round draft pick of the Cincinnati Bengals.

After registering 10.0 sacks in his second season of 1992, Williams underwent two heart surgeries before he could resume his career. He had 9.5 sacks for the Bengals in 1994, played one year for the 11-5 San Francisco 49ers, then wound up having his best individual season for the Broncos in 1996.

After his playing days, Williams became a top football commentator on local and national television, before becoming the number-one sports-radio personality in the Denver market, on The Fan.

JERRY STURM, CENTER, 1961–66

As honest as he was tough, Sturm was named to the AFL All Star team in 1964 as a center, and in 1966, as a left guard. He also played offensive tackle and fullback with the Broncos. That's right; in 1961, Sturm had 8 carries for 31 yards, and added 2 receptions.

He played in the Canadian Football League for Calgary in 1959–60, before joining the Broncos. Another quality player who was dispatched by new coach Lou Saban before the 1967 season.

While playing for the Houston Oilers in 1971, Sturm was approached by a former Broncos player who offered a $10,000 bribe if the center would mess up snaps on kicks and to the quarterback in a December 1971 game against the Pittsburgh Steelers. Sturm turned in the incident to Houston head coach Ed Hughes, who went to the NFL, who went to the FBI.

"He is an honorable man," said Sturm's wife Deb.

Since 1970 Sturm has owned and operated The South restaurant, a popular Mexican-American eatery in Englewood. He is currently in the NFL's 88 Plan, which provides assistance for former NFL players who have been diagnosed with dementia. As of November 2016, Sturm's wife said he is happy and still going to his restaurant every day.

PAUL HOWARD, RIGHT GUARD, 1973–86

Counting the 1976 season, which he spent on injured reserve because of a back injury suffered in the preseason, Howard spent 14 seasons with the Broncos, tied with Dennis Smith and Tom Jackson for the third-longest term. His 187 games played for the Broncos are fifth on the all-time list. His 146 starts rank 12th. One of the most underappreciated players in Broncos history, Howard never received a Pro Bowl nod.

A third-round draft pick out of Brigham Young, Howard didn't get his first start until halfway through his second season, and he stayed at right guard so long as he was healthy. He would have started in the Broncos' first two Super Bowls (1977, 1986 seasons), but he tore up his left knee during the Broncos' 1986-season division-round playoff win against New England. Following surgery, Howard tried to return and play one more season in 1987, at the age of 37, but it didn't work out.

BUD MCFADIN, DEFENSIVE TACKLE, 1960–63

Go ahead and say it, senior citizens of Broncos fandom: It's an outrage that Bud McFadin didn't make the top 50. It wasn't just that McFadin earned three AFL All Star selections. It was the manner in which he played.

"The person you need to ask about Bud McFadin is Jim Otto," said Broncos Ring of Famer Gene Mingo, referring to the Oakland Raiders Hall of Fame center. "I have never seen a player in my eyesight afraid of another player. Bud McFadin was one guy Jim Otto did not want to go up against. Bud McFadin's forearm was powerful. He used to knock the center back into the quarterback so often. He was a tough dude."

Indeed, McFadin was coming off back-to-back Pro Bowl seasons in 1955–56 with the Los Angeles Rams when he was accidentally shot in the stomach by a disgruntled employee of a side business he owned. McFadin was out of football for three seasons, until Broncos coach Frank Filchock lured him back.

"I was scared of McFadin," said another Broncos Ring of Famer, Lionel Taylor. "Bud was something else. He was from the old school. He would flip you. Bud was dangerous; I didn't play around with Bud."

WILLIE BROWN, CORNERBACK, 1963–66

Nobody puts a stamp on the unfortunate side of the Lou Saban era more than Willie Brown. Like so many quality players Saban inherited when he became the Broncos head coach in 1967, he wanted nothing to do with them. Brown wasn't just quality; he turned out to be one of the best cornerbacks in NFL history. He had nine interceptions for the Broncos in his second season of 1964, when he was selected to the All-AFL first team. After the 1966 season, Saban came in and traded Brown and quarterback Mickey Slaughter to Al Davis's Oakland Raiders in exchange for Rex Mirich, who bounced between offensive and defensive tackle, and a third-round draft pick. (When Slaughter promptly retired, the Broncos did not get the third-round draft pick.) Brown played 12 years with the Raiders, recorded 54 regular-season interceptions, and had a 75-yard pick six in Super Bowl XI against Minnesota's Fran Tarkenton. Brown was later elected into the Pro Football Hall of Fame.

MIKE ANDERSON, RUNNING BACK, 2000–05

Mike Anderson was one of the unlikeliest major league athletes in the history of sports. He didn't play sports in high school, instead playing the drums in the school marching band. He then spent four years in the US Marines. While playing for his home base contact football team, his coach Ron Prater pitched him to some coaches at nearby Mt. San Jacinto Junior College.

After two years there and two years at Utah, Anderson was 11 days shy of his 27th birthday when, in his first NFL game, he rushed for 131 yards on 31 carries against the Atlanta Falcons. In his second game, Anderson rushed for 187 yards on 32 carries. Later that season he set an NFL rookie record, with 251 yards rushing and 4 touchdowns against the Saints. He finished with 1,487 rushing yards, 15 touchdowns, and the NFL Offensive Rookie of the Year Award.

He never had another season that came close to that one, although he did have 1,014 yards rushing and 12 touchdowns in helping the 2005 Broncos finish 13-3 and reach the AFC Championship Game.

BOB SWENSON, LINEBACKER, 1975–83

Broncos president Joe Ellis and former special teams coordinator Joe DeCamillis won't be happy. They both insisted I place Swenson among the top 50. I did try, but ultimately there were too many great linebackers who have played for the Broncos over the years. Swenson played part-time as a rookie, and became a part-time starter in the second half of 1976 as defensive coordinator Joe Collier began experimenting with the 3-4 alignment.

In 1977, Collier went all in with the 3-4 alignment, and Swenson started at left outside linebacker with Joe Rizzo inside him, then Randy Gradishar and Tom Jackson.

Swenson was a four-year starter for the Broncos, making the Pro Bowl in 1981, when he had 145 tackles, 3 sacks, 3 interceptions (and 53 return yards), and 3 fumble recoveries. He missed the 1980 season with a broken arm suffered in the preseason that required surgery. A contract dispute cost him most of the 1982, season and after starting the first two games in 1983, torn ligaments in his right knee effectively ended his career. So while Swenson was on his way to becoming one of the Broncos' 50 Greatest Players, two season-ending injuries and a contract dispute relegated him to the still-distinguished recognition of honorable mention.

Fun fact: In the Broncos' 1983 media guide, Swenson described himself as "the self-proclaimed greatest Monopoly player in the world."

MIKE HARDEN, CORNERBACK/SAFETY, 1980–88

Mike Harden was under top-50 consideration, but was ultimately bumped by a guy he helped mentor, Tyrone Braxton. Like all of the Broncos' best defensive backs who played for Joe Collier in the 1970s and '80s, Harden played both cornerback and safety. His 33 interceptions rank sixth on the team's all-time list (Braxton is fifth, with 34). Harden should have made the Pro Bowl in 1986, when two of his picks were returned for touchdowns, and he finished second in the NFL with 179 return yards.

BILLY BRYAN, CENTER, 1977–88

Billy Bryan—the human transition from Morton to Elway. Only 10 players played more seasons for the Broncos than Bryan's 12. And only Bryan started when Morton was taking his snaps in 1978, and in 1986, when Elway delivered "The Drive."

Bryan started 151 games—all but one game when he was healthy, from his second season of 1978 until his final year in 1988. Had he not played at a time when Hall of Fame centers Mike Webster and Dwight Stephenson were hogging Pro Bowl berths, Bryan would have been more decorated.

D. J. WILLIAMS, LINEBACKER, 2004–12

I have mentioned players who I hated to leave off the top-50 list. Williams was a guy I didn't want to mention anywhere, because he too often was surly with the media. But personal feelings should not cloud judgment, and the truth is, Williams's performance could not be denied. He didn't make the top 50 because he never made a Pro Bowl, and he had just two interceptions in his nine seasons with the Broncos, eight as a starter. But he was always a solid player, starting from Game 1 of his rookie year in 2004, averaging more than 14 starts a season in his first eight years with the team.

Williams registered 106 tackles in 2007 and 100 in 2009. He played weak-side linebacker in the 4-3, inside backer in the 3-4, and occasionally strong-side linebacker. He was somewhat burdened by expectations. Williams played for national powerhouse De La Salle High School in the Bay Area. At his high school banquet, the guest speaker was former Raiders coach John Madden, who said of Williams: "[He] was the only player I have ever seen who could go straight from high school to the pro level." Williams went to the University of Miami instead, and was the Broncos' first-round pick, No. 15 overall, in the 2004 draft.

MATT LEPSIS, OFFENSIVE TACKLE, 1998–2007

A four-year tight end at the University of Colorado, Lepsis became a starting tackle in his second season of 1999, and developed into one of the NFL's best left tackles. He retired following the 2007 season rather than play on for $9 million in salary because he didn't think his playing was up to it following knee surgery.

JIM RYAN, LINEBACKER, 1979–88

Ryan missed just two games in his 10-year career. He was a starter at outside linebacker during his final seven seasons with the team, and gets extra credit for the four years he served as an assistant coach to Mike Shanahan, from 2005–08.

RICK DENNISON, LINEBACKER / SPECIAL TEAMS, 1982–90

As a player alone, Dennison may not have been mentioned, although he was a three-and-a-half-year starter at inside linebacker, and a superb special teams player. But as a player and an assistant coach, Dennison was darn near Mr. Bronco. He had a combined 26 seasons as a player (9 years) and coach (17). Elway had 23 seasons—16 years as a player, and 7 as general manager—through the 2017 season.

DAVE STUDDARD, OFFENSIVE TACKLE, 1979–88

Waived by the Baltimore Colts prior to the season opener of his rookie year, Studdard caught on with the Broncos and started 16 games at right tackle. In his first nine seasons, he missed just 1 game, starting 129 of 134 games at right tackle, right guard, and left tackle. He was John Elway's blind-side protector through the first five seasons of Elway's career, a run that included "The Drive" and Super Bowl appearances against the New York Giants and Washington Redskins.

Studdard blew out his ACL in Super Bowl XXII and was slow to return the following season. He did start the final four games at left tackle in 1988, then called it a career. His son, Kasey, who was four years old in Dave's final season of 1988, went on to play a couple of years with the Houston Texans.

KEITH BURNS, DEFENSIVE TACKLE / SPECIAL TEAMS, 1994–98, 2000–03, 2005–06

Burns was the best special teams player in Broncos history, outside of kickers. He wound up playing 166 games in 11 seasons over three separate stints with the team. He had 24 special teams tackles in both 2000 and 2003. He also had a team-record 231 special teams tackles in 11 seasons with the Broncos. In four seasons, he was elected by his teammates as the Broncos' special teams captain.

CLARENCE KAY, TIGHT END, 1984–92

Having high-jumped 6 feet, 8 inches in high school, the 6-foot-2, 237-pound Kay became one of the NFL's best blocking tight ends in his era, averaging 14 starts and 15 games in his nine years with the Broncos. He also averaged 21 catches and 237 yards, with 13 total touchdowns. He had the ability to play a couple more seasons, but off-field trouble expedited the end to his career.

TOM ROUEN, PUNTER, 1993–2002

Perhaps the best punter in Broncos history, as he's the only one who lasted 10 seasons. He holds the team record with 641 career punts—nearly 70 more than next-best Billy Van Heusen. Rouen was the Broncos' Super Bowl punter in 1997–98, then led the NFL with a 46.5-yard average in 1999.

He gets extra-credit points for having attended Heritage High School in Littleton and the University of Colorado during the Buffs' co-national championship season. Near the end of his stay with the Broncos, Rouen married six-time Olympic gold medalist swimmer Amy Van Dyken.

DWAYNE CARSWELL, TIGHT END / OFFENSIVE TACKLE, 1994–2005

Carswell was such a terrific blocking tight end throughout his career that he was switched to offensive tackle in his final two training camps. Not a bad receiving tight end, either. When Shannon Sharpe left for free agency and

Baltimore for two years, Carswell had 49 catches in 2000 and 34 in 2001. Carswell played seven games as a backup offensive tackle in 2005, when he was involved in a multicar accident that left him with a ruptured spleen and diaphragm and fractured ribs, injuries that ended his 12-year career.

GARY KUBIAK, QUARTERBACK, 1983–91

Kubiak gets mentioned not because he was John Elway's backup for nine years, but because he was a backup quarterback who went on to help coach the Broncos to all three of their Super Bowl titles—as offensive coordinator in 1997–98, and head coach in 2015. As a quarterback, Kubiak was 3-2 in his five career starts, and he threw for 1,920 yards and 14 touchdowns while posting a 70.6 rating. He was better at coaching NFL quarterbacks. He posted a 24-11 record in his two seasons as head coach, including a 3-0 run in the 2015 postseason. He retired for health reasons after the 2016 season.

TIM TEBOW, QUARTERBACK, 2010–11

Tebow's magical, eight-win run in 2011, including six in a row, spawned a national movement. Remember "Tebowing"? For two months, he was the biggest star the NFL had ever seen since Broadway Joe Namath in the late 1960s.

Here was a typical Tebow-led Broncos victory that year: He would pass poorly for three and a half quarters, get hot in the final drive or so, and then pull out the victory. Some of the victories, particularly against the Miami Dolphins and Chicago Bears, included the type of unusual sequence of events where you'd swear there was divine intervention involved.

Tebow also played well for large parts of games. In a first-round, AFC playoff upset win against Pittsburgh on January 8, 2012, in which he threw for 316 yards, including an 80-yard touchdown to Demaryius Thomas on the first play of overtime that is arguably the most exciting single play in Broncos history.

Tebow was discarded following the 2011 season, though, as general manager John Elway signed free agent Peyton Manning. Tebow was traded to the New York Jets, a transaction that effectively doomed his football career.

JOHN MOBLEY, LINEBACKER, 1996–2003

A Division II All American from Kutztown University, Mobley was a first-round draft pick who started all 16 games as a rookie, then was a first-team All Pro in his second season of 1997—a season topped off with a fourth-down pass breakup with 32 seconds remaining to give the Broncos their first-ever Super Bowl championship. It was a play so big, safety Steve Atwater said it was the most memorable of *his* career. Mobley was credited with 854 tackles and 10.5 sacks in his eight seasons, when he suffered a spinal cord contusion in his neck on October 26, 2003, effectively ending his career.

BRIAN GRIESE, QUARTERBACK, 1998–2002

Griese, the heir apparent to Elway, later admitted he wished he'd been a little more mature when thrust into the harsh Broncos spotlight in the four years he was the team's starting quarterback. Griese was never bad, but because he didn't have Elway's skill set, which could win games in the fourth quarter, he was never a fan favorite.

Griese did have a terrific, if injury-plagued, season in 2000, when he posted a 7-3 record as a starter, and threw 19 touchdown passes against just 4 interceptions for an NFL-best 102.9 passer rating.

JON KEYWORTH, FULLBACK, 1974–80

A multi-purpose threat who in 1975 rushed for 725 yards and had another 314 yards receiving on 42 catches. A fullback with hands, he was always part of a running back rotation in Denver, yet was ranked No. 3 on the team's all-time rushing list (behind Floyd Little and Otis Armstrong) when he retired after seven seasons. One of the more popular players during the Orange Crush years, he recorded a song during the Broncos' 1977 season, "Make Those Miracles Happen," which was a huge local hit. He also played for the Colorado Buffaloes, where after rushing for 667 yards as a freshman, he played eight positions in his next three years.

MARK JACKSON, RECEIVER, 1986–92

Jackson's catch finished "The Drive." The No. 3 receiver in his rookie year, he still had 38 catches for 726 yards. A consistent performer, he averaged 39 catches and 678 yards in his seven Bronco seasons. He's still active in the Denver community today. Piece of trivia: Jackson had zero catches with

5:32 remaining in the 1986-season AFC Championship Game at Cleveland. He then had the two biggest receptions in "The Drive": A 20-yard catch off third-and-18 that set up first down at the Browns' 28, and the knee-sliding, 5-yard catch in the end zone on Elway's fastball that finished off the 98-yard "Drive" and tied the game, 20–20, with 39 seconds remaining in regulation. Those were Jackson's only catches of the game.

RICH KARLIS, KICKER, 1982–88

Karlis made so many clutch kicks, people thought he was a Bronco for well more than seven years. No kick was bigger than his 33-yard field goal in overtime that capped the famous "Drive" game and lifted the Broncos past Cleveland in the AFC Championship into the Super Bowl. A rare, bare-footed kicker, Karlis surpassed 100 points in four of his last five seasons in Denver, and was the Broncos' second-leading scorer when he lost his job to David Treadwell to start the 1989 season. Karlis was always active in the Denver community during his playing days, and remains so today.

RAY CROCKETT, CORNERBACK, 1994–2000

A ball-hawking corner, Crockett had 17 interceptions, 2 he returned for touchdowns, in his seven Broncos seasons. In the 1997-season AFC Championship Game at Pittsburgh, Crockett had a sack and an interception, and he recovered a fumble by his punt returner, Darrien Gordon. He started every game at left cornerback in the Broncos' Super Bowl seasons of 1997 and '98.

MATT PRATER, KICKER, 2007–13

Prater was on his way to replacing Jason Elam as the best kicker in Broncos history, but off-field issues led general manager John Elway to replace him. Prater was remarkably clutch in 2011, when he helped Tebow become a hero by making a 52-yard field goal in overtime at Miami; by making three late field goals, including one in overtime, to beat San Diego; and by making a 59-yard field goal at the end of regulation and a 51-yard field goal in overtime to beat Chicago.

Prater's .829 field-goal percentage is the best in Broncos history. More impressively, he was 21 of 27 in field goals of at least 50 yards—including a 64-yarder against Jacksonville in December 2013 that broke a 43-year-old NFL record.

GLOSSARY

A: pass attempts

AVG: average

C: pass completions

CAR: carries

EXPA–EXPM: extra points attempted–extra points made

FF: forced fumbles

FG: field goals

FGA: field goals attempted

FGM: field goals made

FR: fumble recoveries

G: games played

I: interceptions

PCT: percentage

PR: punt returns

PTS: points

REC: receptions

RTG: quarterback rating

S: sacks

TCK: tackles

TD: touchdowns

W-L: wins-losses

Y: yards

Y/C: yards per catch

Y/R: yards per return

Yrs: years played

ABOUT THE AUTHOR

Mike Klis is a longtime Colorado sports reporter who covered the Broncos from 2005 to 2015 as the team's beat writer for the *Denver Post*, and is now the Broncos Insider for 9News KUSA-TV in Denver. This is Klis's seventh book. He has won awards, including the Associated Press Sports Editors (APSE) first place, breaking news category, for his work on the Elvis Dumervil Fax Fiasco that is featured in this book.